ANTHROPOLOGICAL PAPERS OF
THE UNIVERSITY OF ARIZONA
NUMBER 62

Prehistoric Sandals from Northeastern Arizona

The Earl H. Morris and Ann Axtell Morris Research

Kelley Ann Hays-Gilpin
Ann Cordy Deegan
Elizabeth Ann Morris

THE UNIVERSITY OF ARIZONA PRESS
TUCSON
1998

About the Authors

KELLEY ANN HAYS-GILPIN is Assistant Professor of Anthropology at Northern Arizona University and a Research Associate at the Museum of Northern Arizona. She completed a B.A. in Anthropology at the University of Michigan in 1982 and received her M.A. (1985) and Ph.D. (1992) degrees in Anthropology at the University of Arizona. Her professional work focuses on understanding production, distribution, and stylistic variation of Colorado Plateau ceramics; additional research explores gender, ritual expressions, and cross-media studies of style and iconography.

ANN CORDY DEEGAN is Curator of Collections at the Smoky Hill Museum in Salina, Kansas. She received her M.S. degree in Textiles from the University of California at Davis (1977) and her Ph.D. degree in Textiles at the University of Maryland, College Park (1983). Her research is directed toward prehistoric Southwestern sandals and textiles, including their construction and the technology used to create them.

ELIZABETH ANN MORRIS is Professor Emerita at Colorado State University and Research Associate at the Arizona State Museum. She received her A.B. from Antioch College. She earned her M.A. degree (1957) and Ph.D. degree (1959) in Anthropology at the University of Arizona. Her professional career and continuing interests are in Southwestern prehistory, the archaeology of the mountains and Plains in northern Colorado, and human adaptation to arid lands in general with emphases on material culture, regional adaptations, and cultural ecology.

Cover: Basketmaker III twined sandals from the Prayer Rock District, Arizona (*top views*). Drawing by Ronald Redsteer (see Figs. 4.7, 4.5, 4.11).

THE UNIVERSITY OF ARIZONA PRESS

Copyright © 1998

The Arizona Board of Regents
All Rights Reserved

This book was set in 10.7/12 CG Times.
∞ This book is printed on acid-free, archival-quality paper.
Manufactured in the United States of America

02 01   3 2

Library of Congress Cataloging-in-Publication Data

Hays-Gilpin, Kelley, 1960–
    Prehistoric sandals from northeastern Arizona : the Earl H. Morris and Ann Axtell Morris research / Kelley Ann Hays-Gilpin, Ann Cordy Deegan, Elizabeth Ann Morris.
        p. cm. -- (Anthropological papers of the University of Arizona ; no. 62)
    Includes bibliographic references (p.) and index.
    ISBN 0–8165–1801–7 (pbk.)
    1. Indians of North America--Arizona--Costume. 2. Indians of North America--Arizona--Antiquities. 3. Sandals, Prehistoric--Arizona. 4. Morris, Earl Halstead, 1889–1956. 5. Morris, Ann Axtell, 1900–1945. 6. Arizona--Antiquities. I. Deegan, Ann Cordy, 1952- . II. Morris, Elizabeth Ann, 1932- . III. Title. IV. Series.
    E78.A7H39 1998
    685'.31'008997--dc21   97-33785
                                                CIP

Publication of this book is made possible in part by the proceeds of a permanent endowment created with the assistance of a Challenge Grant from the National Endowment for the Humanities, a federal agency.

To Earl and Ann Morris
and their research team

Earl and Ann Morris in northern New Mexico about
1934 (photo courtesy of Elizabeth Ann Morris).

*Then some day we expect to have ready for the press a detailed description of
cross-woven sandals that will show not only the sequence and variations of the
processes by which they were produced, but which will also, through copious
illustration, reveal to the degree that the remarkable patterns deserve, the rich
beauty which the Anasazi wrought into the ephemeral bits of fabric that were to
afford their feet brief protection against mud and stones and thorns.*

Earl H. Morris, 1944a

Contents

FIGURES

TABLES

Foreword

Richard B. Woodbury and
Nathalie F. S. Woodbury

When we stopped in Boulder in the summer of 1952 to pay our respects to Earl Morris, we found him presiding over several trestle tables covered with pieces of fiber. On closer inspection these appeared as foot-forms—literally, footprints from the past. These, and the many still boxed on the shelves around the room, were the sandals which walk in the pages of this book. On closer inspection, with Morris' guidance we could distinguish the intricate patterns, with no pair precisely like another, and notice the degree of wear which left some not much more than bunches of fiber to the undiscerning eye.

When we saw these sandals, they had been out of the ground for twenty years or so and had been sorted, recorded, and analyzed by Earl Morris and his wife Ann Axtell Morris and their assistants, work that Morris continued following Ann Morris' death in 1945. However, in citing his research in progress for the International Directory of Anthropologists Morris does not mention work on the sandals until the 1950 edition, when he includes "Anasazi cloth sandals."

Today, it is gratifying to see these sandals again, in a report that brings to completion the work begun so many years ago. But a long gap between the start and the finish of archaeological work is not unique. Emil Haury published material on the Hemenway Southwestern Archaeological Expedition some sixty years after Frank Cushing's fieldwork ended. It was forty-five years after Frederick Hodge's excavations at the Zuni town of Hawikuh that a monograph appeared in print, by Watson Smith and ourselves. Some forty years after the end of the Awatovi Expedition's work in northeastern Arizona James C. Gifford and Watson Smith wrote about the gray corrugated pottery from Awatovi, and still two more studies of Awatovi materials are currently in progress.

At long last sandals are receiving the attention they so much deserve. Those collected by Byron Cummings, starting in 1908, and in the Glen Canyon work directed by Jesse Jennings in the 1950s have recently appeared in *Treading in the Past: Sandals of the Anasazi* by Kathy Kankainen (University of Utah Press, 1995). Are there more collections of sandals in the storage areas of museums, languishing decade after decade, unstudied and forgotten?

The present volume, in addition to its meticulous descriptions and thoughtful analyses, explores many of the fascinating questions raised by examination of these sandals. Why was so much care expended on something destined to be scuffed, scarred, and soon worn to fragments during its utilitarian use? Did these individually distinctive sandals serve as personal identifications, as clues to the wearer's village, kinship, or social affiliation? Definitive answers cannot be given for such questions but asking them reminds us that "material culture" always has much non-material significance. The authors go from straightforward description to examination of the many things we can learn or suspect from analysis of sandals, but they are careful not to mistake suggestions and speculations for certainty. We hope others will be inspired to continue exploring the meanings that these sandals may have.

This book is also impressive as a successful three-way collaboration among scholars, each with individual interests and experience. They include Earl Morris' archaeologist daughter, Elizabeth Ann, who was instrumental in bringing the sandal collection to the Arizona State Museum. The three authors discovered their shared interests in the 1990s and began working together to expand and complete the illustrations, descriptions, and manuscripts that were already available. Together they bring an expertise that could hardly be expected of any single author, blending art, archaeology and technology, and ethnography. This successful collaboration reflects their deep concern with these remarkable "over-decorated" objects of everyday use that offer clues to much more than ancient technical skills. Although this study has been more than half a century on the way, it is now wonderfully welcome as an important contribution to the archaeology of the southwestern United States and to the technical skills and aesthetic sensibilities of its early inhabitants.

Preface

Elizabeth Ann Morris

The beauty and complexity of Basketmaker sandals have impressed their viewers ever since the first examples of this ancient Indian craftsmanship came to light in the dry caves of the American Southwest in the early decades of this century. In this volume, the authors address that beauty and complexity from three different orientations: historical, technological, and anthropological.

The Anasazi sandals described here were excavated from caves in the Prayer Rock District of northeastern Arizona by Earl Halstead Morris in 1931. Working for the Carnegie Institution of Washington and assisted by his wife, Ann Axtell Morris, and several art students at the University of Colorado in Boulder, he spent the next 25 years overseeing the analysis, description, and illustration of these intricately twined specimens. Other manuscripts intruded on his time, and Ann Morris died in 1945. Earl Morris' gradually deteriorating health and his eventual death in 1956 prevented this manuscript's completion. The sandals, an extensive portfolio of annotated illustrations, and a draft of the first chapter of the planned text by Ann Morris were deposited in the Arizona State Museum, Tucson in 1956 at the suggestion of then Director Emil W. Haury. I included a brief summary of the sandals in a description of the Prayer Rock caves and their contents in my doctoral dissertation, published in 1980 in this series of *Anthropological Papers* (No. 35).

It was in the 1990s when we three authors discovered that our research interests overlapped in these marvelously executed textile sandals. We determined that the efforts already expended deserved to be made available to a larger audience, with as much additional information as we could provide. The more than 50 years that separate the context of the original excavations from the context expected by modern archaeologists does not detract from the uniqueness of the sandals themselves and the precision-oriented descriptions by the early analysts. It is likely that under today's conditions of excavation, a comparable collection could not be unearthed. Additionally, any sandals found today would not be subjected to the dissection and rigorous analysis used by the original technicians.

The purpose of this book is to present the Morrises' work, including their essentially correct chronology and technical insights, with updated standard terminology, contextual clarifications, expansion in the areas of technological and stylistic analyses, and an admittedly speculative interpretation of functions and meanings of sandals in Basketmaker life. In a brief opening essay, Hays-Gilpin places sandals in the broad perspective of dress, its cultural significance and its symbolism in various cultures throughout the world (Prologue), and she focuses attention on the artistic complexity of the soles of Basketmaker sandals that remained so largely hidden from view. I recount in Chapter 1 the historical context of the discovery and early analysis by my parents of this remarkably well-preserved collection of sandals.

Two manuscripts by the Morrises, written many decades ago, appear in Chapter 2. The first is a draft of Ann Axtell Morris' introduction to the volume she hoped to write describing sandals from Canyon del Muerto, northeastern Arizona, and from Grand Gulch, southeastern Utah. The article following is a preliminary report of Earl Morris' research on sandals from the Prayer Rock District, not far from Canyon del Muerto. As explained by Deegan in her comments on these manuscripts and her following annotations, contemporary archaeologists use a standard textile terminology derived from the work of Irene Emery (1980). The archaeological context of the original excavations and subsequent analyses are elaborated on by Hays-Gilpin in Chapter 3, with particular attention to the temporal placement of the sites and the sandals they contained. She discusses the original developmental typology formulated by Earl Morris in his analysis of sandals from the Prayer Rock District.

A detailed account of the Anasazi textile construction techniques used in these sandals is in Chapters 4 and 5 by Deegan. She provides a system of numbered zones to help explain concisely and consistently where each construction technique or design field appears on each sandal. Her analyses intend on the one hand to provide archaeologists with the means to identify whole and fragmentary sandals and place them in temporal and regional contexts and, on the other, to demonstrate numerous long-lost construction techniques to contemporary fiber artists, who, we hope, will find much to emulate in the art of their ancient predecessors.

Analysis of the decorations (Chapter 6) and several hypothesized significances of Basketmaker creative art work (Epilogue) are presented by Kelley Hays-Gilpin. She demonstrates how intricate patterns were devised by repeating small geometric elements using a limited number of motions, such as rotation and reflection. She then compares sandal decoration with designs in other media, such as pottery. Symmetry analysis is based on Earl Morris' tentative classifications, which were probably inspired by his colleague, Anna O. Shepard. In presenting the decorative patterns drawn by Morris' research team, we have clarified and updated his symmetry system, based on Dorothy Washburn's recent work, but because of its complexity we have not adopted her precise mathematical terminology.

The numerous illustrations, mostly created during Earl Morris' decades of analysis, constitute a historic contribution to this presentation. Instead of redrafting unfinished drawings, the detailed laboratory worksheets and in-progress pencil and ink drawings have been sharpened, cleaned, and transformed into publishable figures by means of computer graphics technology that has only recently become available and affordable. In this way, we have preserved the informal character of the original drawings. Sandal and design illustrations are from the Earl H. Morris Papers in the Archives of the Arizona State Museum, Tucson, unless otherwise indicated.

During the 1990s, the years during which the three of us came together in recognition of the beauty and uniqueness of this ancient footwear, colleagues suggested several additional directions for research. Because of time and space limitations, we decided not to include them all, but they are indicated as directions for future research by Hays-Gilpin in the Epilogue, and we are grateful for the interest and stimulating ideas expressed by so many of our associates.

We remain as fascinated as the Morrises were by the mystery of Basketmaker twined sandals: why did these ancient craftspeople invest so much labor and artistic expression in perishable objects they wore, and wore out, on their feet? We wonder what the Morrises' conclusions would have been, had they finished this study as they had planned. We offer ours in the Epilogue, with no way of knowing whether Earl and Ann Morris, or the sandal makers, would have approved, but we are pleased to be able to bring these aspects of their historic work and prehistoric craft at long last to the public.

This book presents the current knowledge compiled by many dedicated individuals, mostly working separately at different times during the last six decades. If we add the ancient Indian artisans and wearers to this group, nearly two thousand years of creativity may be claimed. We hope these pages will lead to further creativity in reconstructing lifeways of the past and inventing more beauty in the future.

Acknowledgments

Many people and institutions assisted with ideas and support during the lengthy period of gestation of this volume. Ronald Redsteer of the Research Imaging Laboratory, Northern Arizona University, prepared most of the illustrations from Arizona State Museum archival materials and authors' sketches; his work was supported in part by grants from the Arizona Humanities Council, the Arizona Archaeological and Historical Society, and Northern Arizona University. The Navajo Nation Archaeology Department provided the scanners and computers necessary to produce some of the other figures included here. Funds for publication were generously provided by Nathalie F. S. Woodbury and the Elizabeth Ann Morris Research Fund.

Various portions of Kelley Hays-Gilpin's research were supported by the University of Arizona Graduate College and Department of Anthropology, and she received a resident scholarship from the Museum of Northern Arizona. Ann Deegan's research was supported by a grant from the Women and Gender Research Institute at Utah State University, Logan, Utah.

We would like to express our special appreciation to Alan Ferg, Archivist; G. Michael Jacobs, Collections Manager; Lynn S. Teague, Curator of Archaeology; Raymond H. Thompson, then Director; and the archives and library assistants of the Arizona State Museum, Tucson. Dr. Nieves Zedeño ably translated the Abstract into Spanish. Carol Gifford, Editor (Department of Anthropology, University of Arizona), turned a constantly changing manuscript into the real book that the Morris family had always planned to publish.

We thank Jeanette Mobley-Tanaka, acting assistant curator of Anthropology, University of Colorado Museum, Boulder, for assistance with archival letters and files. Opal Zchiesche, M.D., examined the handwriting of several of the manuscripts cited here. Laurie Webster conducted library research for us and made useful comments on the manuscript. Phil Geib of the Navajo Nation Archaeology Department provided information on sandals of the Archaic period.

The contributions of Dorothy Washburn (Division of Liberal Arts, The Maryland Institute) to Chapter 6 were extensive and insightful. She helped Kelley Hays-Gilpin clarify Earl Morris' use of symmetry analysis and bring our terminology up to date. Any errors must be attributed to Hays-Gilpin and not to Washburn.

Lynn Teague's textile expertise and editorial assistance also proved invaluable. We are grateful to her and to two anonymous reviewers whose thoughtful advice has made this a better book than it otherwise would have been.

Prologue: The Anthropology of Dress

Kelley Ann Hays-Gilpin

Anthropologists, clothing psychologists, and textile historians find items of clothing and adornment a rich source of knowledge about human beings worldwide, because all humans deliberately alter their appearance to communicate various kinds of information about themselves. The term "dress" subsumes items like clothing and jewelry that are put on and taken off and includes modifications to hair and the body itself, such as tattooing and scarification. Aside from utilitarian functions such as protection from cold, dress may also be highly aesthetic. Ideas of beauty are expressed for the pleasure of both wearer and viewer, group ideals of beauty emerge and individuals challenge them, and ideals change. Although we can never know what particular features of dress prehistoric peoples considered beautiful, we can be sure their aesthetic ideals were an important aspect of their creation of items such as the Basketmaker sandals. The sandals depicted in this book must have been as aesthetically pleasing to their makers and wearers as they are to us today.

Anthropologists and clothing psychologists realize that aesthetics are culturally and historically constructed and are highly specific to a time and place. They tend, therefore, to study aspects of dress that can be compared across cultures, across other social groups such as socioeconomic classes, or through time. Alfred Kroeber published one of the first anthropological studies of dress in 1919, demonstrating that change in European women's fashions proceeded in regular, wavelike patterns through the centuries, including peaks of high variability separated by periods of stability and uniformity (see also Richardson and Kroeber 1940). The goal of clothing psychology and the anthropology of dress is to understand *social meanings* (Kaiser 1990, Schneider 1987). Dress is a particularly good medium for studying how people express and even negotiate changes in social identities such as gender, age, and class categories. Dress serves physical and social-psychological needs for the individual; it simultaneously identifies the individual with social roles and statuses and differentiates individuals from each other. Dress is both social and personal.

Expression of difference in any medium involves manipulation of oppositions and contrasts. Because social categories rarely stay the same for very long, especially under conditions of competition among classes, ethnic groups, between men and women, young and old, the means of identifying such categories is always changing. Claudia Brush Kidwell, Curator of the Costume Division of the Smithsonian Institution, writes:

> The language of clothing is not static. The only constant seems to be that distinctions will always be made between men and women, though the significant gender symbols change. When the language of clothes from one time period is learned, this knowledge does not necessarily help one understand the vocabulary of another time or place. To translate the meaning of clothes with any degree of accuracy requires a thorough knowledge of the specific way in which it was used (Kidwell 1989: 126).

To illustrate a variety of ways in which clothing communicates information about social identities and even influences behavior and ideas, I turn to some examples using the common vocabulary of European and American clothing. In nineteenth- and early twentieth-century America and Europe, the opposition between masculine and feminine was clearly expressed by the contrast between trousers and skirts. This was not so everywhere, and was not always so in Europe. In China, flowing robes were not historically associated with femininity, but with the high status of scholars and administrators. Trousers were not associated with masculinity, but with the low status of manual labor. Peasant men and women wore trousers, and elites of both genders wore robes. Nor have European men always worn trousers. Their masculine association there probably came about when the attire of soldiers of particular times and places was adopted by men of other occupations but not by women (Steele 1989a: 14). Western women can now wear trousers in most circumstances without being viewed as threats to morality and the social order, but this change came about only after a century of struggle with several advances and retreats. Nineteenth-century feminists' attempts to free women from the confines of long, heavy skirts by introducing the "bloomer" costume failed miserably (Foote 1989; Roach 1979). The acceptance of trousers for women was partly due to women's entry into factory work and other occupations where skirts were impractical and unsafe (Steele 1989b) and to women's use of trousers as a symbol of independence, freedom of movement, and higher status. This acceptance was not a shift toward unisex clothing like the uniforms Maoist Chinese men and women wore to mask former class distinctions and gender difference.

The Scottish kilt is not considered a "skirt" but rather a powerful symbol of ethnic identity, bearing family-specific patterns and denoting high social and economic status. Oddly enough, the kilt in its present form does not date back to the Iron Age days of the proud, independent warring clans that it now evokes, but emerged in the last few centuries in what some might say were waves of nostalgia for such a past and increased concern with ethnicity in a rapidly changing modern world that threatens to erase such identities (Chapman 1995). In fact, ethnic dress is rarely static through time anywhere (Eicher and Sumberg 1995: 301).

Language, shared history and origins, religion, and nationality are the "building blocks of ethnicity." Dress, together with language, and "culturally denoted physical features" communicate ethnic identity (Nash 1989, cited in Eicher 1995: 4–5). Ethnicity is flexible. An individual's identity can change or be changed. One of the most powerful ways to change one's identity is to change clothes. Karen women of Thailand wear skirts and blouses that differentiate them from ethnic Thai neighbors, for example. Karen dress is part of a complex of material symbols that "express resistance to change and threat and assert commitment to a particular world view" (Hamilton and Hamilton 1989: 20). A woman's dress determines in part how other Karen treat her. "For a Karen woman to remove her symbol of Karenness, that is, to adopt Thai dress, is a moral outrage that can result in ostracism" (Hamilton and Hamilton 1989: 21). The Hamiltons, a textile scholar and an anthropologist, witnessed the ostracizing of a

Karen woman who tried to leave her community and become at once Thai and Karen.

This example demonstrates that dress is not a set of passive objects, used simply to convey information. Dress is also active; it has effects. An individual's behavior in putting on certain items of clothing affects how others treat him or her. Therefore, dressing is a behavior that shapes further behaviors.

Many cultures mark age grades with changes in dress. Members of one's own culture then treat an individual as a child, adolescent, or adult based on dress. As one grows up, changes in clothing signal the changes in behavior and responsibilities that others expect one to display. Until early in this century, very young Americans wore long, white dresses regardless of sex until they graduated to unisex "rompers," and, finally, gender-differentiated clothing such as dresses for girls and shorts, then knickers, for boys (Paoletti and Kregloh 1989). An adolescent boy's transition from knickers to trousers marked his status as an adult, and the exact age at which this event took place depended not just on his parents' assessment of his emotional and physical development, but on social class. Bush and London (1960) argued that the progression from knickers to trousers disappeared, giving way to a great deal of variability in the dress of adolescent males, as the "stability of common perceptions and expectations" of adolescent males decreased. The variety allowed in dress for little girls was even greater, but some outfits were "coded" as more or less feminine, more or less appropriate for physical activity, and even shaped expectations of personality traits such as "niceness" versus "meanness" (Kaiser 1989).

Textiles, and clothing worn by members of various cultures, are important symbols not only in marking age transitions but in other life events such as weddings and funerals. Weddings not only mark adulthood for two individuals in many cultures, but they join two families in new social relationships. Exchange of textiles and jewelry is a frequent requirement. A Hopi bride grinds corn for weeks to bring food to her groom's family, and his father and uncles must weave an entire outfit, dress, blankets, and sash, for the bride. Kodi women of Indonesia dye and weave elaborate ikat cloth. At weddings, the groom's family gives livestock and gold to the bride's family. Her family gives cloth and pigs in return. The patterns in the cloth represent bulls' eyes and horses' tails, because in the wedding procession the buffalo gifts come first and the horses come last (Hoskins 1989: 161). Food, guinea pigs, and cloth were exchanged at peasant weddings in the Inka empire (Murra 1989: 280).

Funerals are also times when social relationships change, this time by the loss of a member of the system. Beliefs that one's social identities persist in a land of the dead are frequent, although different in detail, in many parts of the world. The Inka believed the dead should be dressed well to enter the next world, and apparently this belief goes back thousands of years. Not only at Inka funerals observed by the Spanish, but in ancient graves throughout the Andes the dead were dressed in new clothes and buried with an extra set of clothes, sandals, bags, and headdresses (Murra 1989: 280). The Kuba of Zaire dress corpses in elaborate raffia textiles. They say that if the dead were dressed in modern Western or pan-African style clothing instead of traditional raffia clothing, their ancestors would not recognize them and would not make them welcome in the land of the dead (Darish 1989: 135). In addition, many relatives contribute textiles to the grave. This process reinforces traditional culture and beliefs among the living and actively supports and re-creates identities and relationships among those who take part in the ritual.

In societies with class stratification, that is with marked, mostly inherited differences between rich and poor, powerful and powerless people, clothing is one of the most important ways to signal class identity. Many societies enforced "sumptuary laws" dictating who could wear what kinds of cloth, what style of dress, what kinds of jewelry. The Inka restricted use of fine cloth to the elite class to the point that "unauthorized wear of a vicuna cloth is reported to have been a capital offense" (Murra 1989: 291). In Japan, Tokugawa leaders regulated food, housing, and dress according to income. A farmer's income even determined exactly what kind of fibers he could use to make sandal thongs (Roach and Eicher 1979: 13).

Although display of status and power through dress is almost universal, sometimes less is more. Prior to the start of the fur trade in the Great Lakes, Potawatomi leaders apparently demonstrated their high status by giving away all that they had to their subjects, including most of their clothing (Miller 1979: 321). The leader's "poor and scanty raiment" symbolized his generosity, his ability and inclination to be generous, and, therefore, his power and virtue. Significantly, the Potawatomi were not what anthropologists call a "complex society" but were relatively egalitarian. An individual's generosity, leadership skills, and spiritual knowledge formed the basis of leadership rather than wealth and inheritance. This situation began to change with the fur trade, however. French, and later American, traders bestowed gifts such as cloth, ribbons, medals, beads, and buttons on ambitious young Potawatomi men, who no longer gave their wealth away but wore it to display their influential connections.

One of the most powerful cases of the manipulation of dress to negotiate change in class (and ethnicity as well) was Mahatma Gandhi's *Khadi* movement. When Gandhi first brought his family to South Africa in 1896, he thought Englishness and Indianness should be compatible, and one ethnicity should not be viewed as superior to the other. After being thrown off a train for wearing a turban, he returned in impeccable English dress and was allowed to ride first class. He then argued that Indians should dress like Europeans "in order to look civilized" and won the right for all Indians dressed as Englishmen to purchase first or second class tickets (Bean 1989: 357). Dark skin was not so easy to change, however, and Indians still faced discrimination throughout the British Empire. Gandhi continued to experiment with attire and think about the meanings of dress. Finally, he united "the semiotics of cloth" and economics, promoting hand-spinning and native Indian cotton cloth production as an important means to economic independence and a dignified independence of Indian identity. Gandhi himself dressed as a poor man, in loincloth and shawl. This image resonated with the traditional Indian image of the ascetic and saint, a high-status identity. Europeans recognized in his dress something of their traditional image of Christ on the Cross (Bean 1989: 368).

In an article that was instrumental in showing archaeologists how important clothing and other artifacts can be in actively communicating information about social identities, Martin Wobst used Yugoslavian folk costume to show that most of the time highly visible items like hats and embroidered shirts and blouses communicate social identities such as ethnicity. Low visibility items, like underwear, are less likely to bear decoration recognized as socially significant (Wobst 1977).

Compared to hairstyle, headgear, upper body adornment, and the trouser-skirt system, footwear has low visibility. Where then, does footwear fit in the anthropology and psychology of dress? Shoes have been more or less important in various eras and cultures. Sandals appear as early as 3000 B.C. in what is now Syria and 1450 B.C. in Egypt. In the American Southwest, the Archaic examples described in Chapter 4 are even more ancient.

Sandals and shoes are sometimes incidental, a matter of personal choice, economic means, and the kind of terrain one must traverse. Footgear influences the way people walk and move, and gait is a highly visible and potentially distinctive characteristic. A successful female impersonator must wear high heels to affect the mincing step of the movie star he parodies. The female soldier must march with the same steps as her male counterpart, and her boots will be virtually identical to his. Scottish and Irish dance steps are easily distinguished, but neither can be imitated without the soft or hard shoe, respectively, required to achieve the right steps; likewise, a ballerina could not be recognized as executing the classic lines and movements of ballet were she divested of her toe shoes (Keali'inohomoku 1979). Venetian "chopines" of the seventeenth and eighteenth centuries, Chinese footbinding, and today's high heels effectively hobble women, limiting their mobility and range of possible activities at the same time that they signal high social status and femininity (Tobert 1993). Sandals, on the other hand, protect the sole of the foot, thereby increasing the variety of terrains one can access comfortably. They do not seem to noticeably change one's gait from a standard barefoot stride.

In some times and some places, shoes are highly informative symbols. To understand past symbolic meanings, we must know about the context of use, and written texts help greatly. Roman peasants went barefoot, soldiers wore sandals with nail patterns (and hence footprints) unique to each regiment, and elites wore sandals trimmed in gold and silver. Pale-colored sandals marked the highest statuses, because the process of steeping the leather in alum was slow and costly. Egyptian elites showed contempt for an enemy by painting an image of him on their sandal soles. The use of shoes as love tokens probably has a long history among European peasants. Young men gave shoes to a girl to symbolize a desire to share all worldly goods. By the eighteenth century, elite couples were exchanging porcelain models of shoes. The sexual imagery in the story of Cinderella's glass slipper (in the original story, it was made of fur) becomes even more obvious when one becomes aware of the ancient role of shoes in wedding and fertility rites throughout Europe (McDowell 1989).

Orthodox Hindu women attend to complex symbolism of face and hair ornaments, the way they drape the sari, and the sari's colors and fabrics, but little attention is given to footgear. The type of shoes worn has little importance except that high-heeled sandals are considered "too Western" (Joshi 1992). Nonetheless, the symbolism of the foot and wearing or not wearing shoes is very strong in Indian culture. In Indian cosmography, the head is the locus of power and superior forms of knowledge. The feet and the shoes on them are the opposite, inferior and dirty not just from walking around but "as the repository of base substances from the wearer's body" (Cohn 1989: 346-347). One must remove shoes in the presence of a superior and sit so that one never displays the sole of the foot. The English made much of this native custom, refusing to take off their shoes as a sign of respect even when entering Indian temples. Yet the English required Indians to remove their shoes in the presence of Europeans, thereby acknowledging their foreign rulers as superior. Indians who adopted Christianity were allowed to wear shoes at all times (but were probably made to remove their hats, the Western sign of deference). The Bagada, a refugee tribe in India, refused to wear shoes at any time "for fear of offending the deity they walked upon" (Hockins 1979: 146).

Although the rich cultural and symbolic aspects of footwear in Europe, the Middle East, and Asia can clearly be gleaned from the existing literature, as McDowell (1989) and others have done, concepts from these areas do not translate to the Americas. Euroamerican anthropologists cannot read the symbolic code of ancient American sandals, nor can modern day Native Americans of the Southwest, whose ancestors stopped making sandals and switched to leather moccasins probably in the period from A.D. 1300 to 1540. Ethnographers in the Americas were interested in the distribution of footwear types, moccasins versus sandals, for example, as cultural traits that might help trace migrations and other kinds of relationships between groups (Mason 1896; Wissler 1950), but they wrote little about the uses and meanings of footwear. Each Plains tribe apparently had a distinctive way of decorating moccasins, and even shaped them so that footprints were identifiable by tribe, but in the Southwest, moccasins worn by members of different tribes and villages were apparently much the same. Basketmaker sandals remain, in a way, an island in our understanding. To learn more about them, and most important, to learn about the people who made and wore them, we have to rely entirely on the evidence presented by the artifacts themselves, their archaeological context, and analogies derived from cross-cultural studies. Perhaps we may also be allowed to exercise our imaginations as sources of ideas and possibilities.

The efforts of Southwestern archaeologists to learn about social dynamics through artifacts have traditionally focused on painted pottery styles (Longacre 1970; Plog 1980). Occasional studies using textured plain ware pottery (Brunson 1985) and other media have appeared. Yet clothing, not pottery, is the most likely medium for signaling social identities (ethnic, gender, age, and occupation, for example) because of its high visibility and clear association with individuals. The perishable nature of clothing and other body adornments and modifications limits our ability to study the social dynamics of the ancient Southwest. Art depicting clothed individuals in any detail or quantity is limited largely to Basketmaker II period rock art, dating about 500 B.C. to A.D. 400 (Cole 1990: 109–130; Robins 1997; Schaafsma 1980: 109–121), to Mimbres painted pottery of the eleventh and twelfth centuries A.D. (Brody 1977; Davis 1995; LeBlanc 1983; Moulard 1984), and to kiva murals of the late Pueblo IV period from A.D. 1400 to about 1540 (Adams 1991; Crotty 1995; Hibben 1975; Smith 1952). Numerous textiles are preserved only in recent sites such as Spanish conquest-era parts of the Zuni village of Hawikuh (Howell 1995; Webster 1997) or in dry cave sites. The people of the Archaic, Basketmaker, and Pueblo III periods (see Table 2.3) favored such rockshelters, but other time periods present gaps in the textile record.

Kate Peck Kent's (1983a) summary and analysis of prehistoric textiles of the Southwest demonstrates that although textiles are rare, more than enough have been recovered to show a range of variation across space and through time (see also Magers 1986). Textile structures and elaborateness of decoration vary even in the same time period, revealing that dress was a potentially complicated matter in ancient times as it is today.

Textiles are even important in religious practice, historically and in the Pueblos today. Ethnologist Elsie Clews Parsons (1936: 136, 555) notes that a miniature suit of clothes is presented to the Sun at Acoma Pueblo at solstice time. Many of the Hopi prayer offerings called *pahos* must not only be prepared with correctly colored paints and feathers, but they must be "dressed" in miniature blankets or wrapped in cotton thread that represents a blanket. Kent (1983a: 253–254) illustrates what may be prehistoric examples of pahos. Even though Pueblo people today dress like any other Americans, elaborate traditional textiles are still made and used for ritual occasions. Southwest textiles, then, are a living tradition with a long, unbroken history that includes many changes in form and, undoubtedly, in meaning.

The Prayer Rock District sites excavated in the 1930s by Earl H. Morris were rich in baskets (Morris and Burgh 1941) and textiles that date to the A.D. 400s and 600s in the Basketmaker III period. In the previous Basketmaker II period, about 500 B.C. to A.D. 400, rock art

depictions of humans often included beads, headgear, belts, bandoleers, and fringed aprons. After A.D. 400, however, rock art depictions tended to be smaller, monochromatic human figures devoid of adornment. Dress is not displayed in any detail in such self-portraits, so we have to rely on perishable remains. Those recovered include shoulder blankets made of strips of rabbit fur in a twined yucca yarn framework; belts, the finest made of soft, silky, brown and white dog hair; string aprons with human-hair waistbands for women; and shell jewelry. The most labor intensive and highly decorated clothing items are the twined sandals (Fig. P.1).

Clothing, like language, is a system of signs (McCracken 1988). Yet we do not understand information communicated by clothing and by language in the same way. Appearance is interpreted using codes that lie somewhere between linguistic codes and nonverbal systems of meaning, including aesthetics (Kaiser 1990: 238–239). Basketmaker sandals, then, are not just footgear, but signs. As signs, their shapes, textures, and colored designs are potentially just as complicated and informative as designs on pottery, in baskets, and in rock art. Visually distinct from earlier and later sandals in the same region, Basketmaker sandals signal that their makers and wearers were different from previous and subsequent generations. Similarities in shape, colors, and textures indicate a group identity, but decorative differences speak of individual identities. Sandals could have communicated specific meanings to those well versed in the codes of Basketmaker clothing and other artifacts.

Basketmaker sandals viewed as signs present a dual dilemma. The first is characteristic of most kinds of clothing: they simultaneously identify the wearer with a group that shares a way of making sandals and differentiate the wearer through decorative patterns unique to each sandal (or possibly, to each pair of sandals). Secondly, sandals are not as highly visible as most sign systems. They are relatively small compared to blankets, belts, aprons, and headgear, for example. They are mostly covered by the wearer's foot when in use and are worn as far from eye level and the wearer's face as possible, the latter presumably his or her most socially interesting feature. Their accessibility to the perceiver is low, yet the labor input by the maker is extraordinarily high. With this paradox in mind, we turn to the fascinating story of Basketmaker twined sandals and the archaeologists who studied them, that we may return later to somewhat more informed speculation on their meanings.

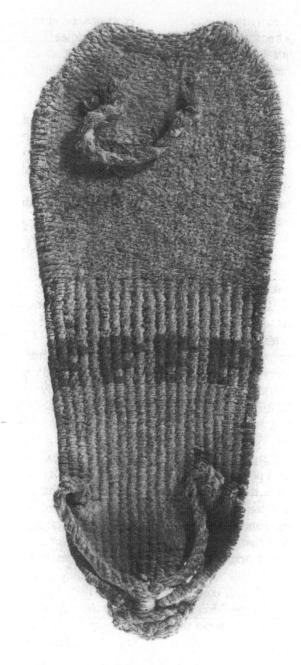

Figure P.1. Child's sandal with scalloped toe
and puckered heel, from Broken Flute Cave,
Arizona; full size. (Photo by Ken Matesich,
Arizona State Museum Neg. 99788.)

*Why the Anasazi saw fit to expend the best of their mechanical ability
and their full craving for beauty on footgear that would but little
outwear the time it took to produce it, we shall never know. But in so
doing they left the richest heritage of early North American art as
expressed in perishable media, that has survived to the present.*

(Earl H. Morris to A. V. Kidder, June 12, 1944)

CHAPTER ONE

The Morris Research

Elizabeth Ann Morris

During the years that it took for me to grow tall enough to see over the edge of the laboratory tables in my father's home, I became increasingly aware of the neatly laid out rows of sandals that covered their surfaces. It was apparent that the persons working on them, artists and archaeologists, as well as the occasional visitor, regarded them with awe. But it was some years before I understood why and came to view them with great respect of my own.

Not only were they incredibly beautiful and complex in their construction, they were also very old. Ancestors of modern Pueblo Indians, such as the Hopi, Zuni, Acoma, Jemez, and the Rio Grande pueblo tribes, had created this footwear in the fifth, sixth, and seventh centuries A.D. They had used yucca fiber, from a plant abundant in their desert environment (Fig. 1.1). The tough leaves provided ancient artisans with fibers to make sandals and other textiles. The strong, straight elements combed from their leaves were spun into sturdy yarns of various diameters (Figs. 1.2, 2.1). Sometimes they were softened by soaking and pounding. On occasion, their natural golden color was altered with mineral dyes to shades of red, yellow, dark brown, and black. The resulting strands were then crafted into beautifully twined bags, articles of clothing, and the sandals that are described in these pages. Not only were some decorated with the bright colors men-

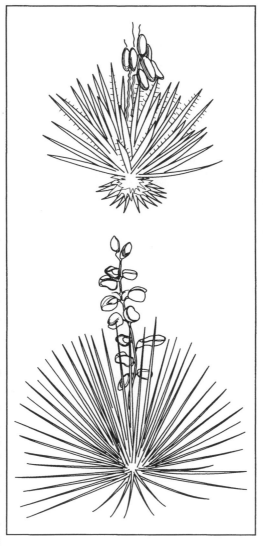

Figure 1.1. Yucca plants: broadleaf (*top*) and narrowleaf. Drawing by Ronald Redsteer.

tioned above, but the warps and wefts were manipulated to form intricate textured designs as well.

Even more intriguing, apparently each design was unique. Such articles as a "pair" of sandals, even when found on the feet of a single interred individual, did not often duplicate each other. In one notable example, the dyed and textured designs on right and left sandals were mirror images of each other!

The dry caves of the American Southwest have preserved hundreds of examples of these sandals buried in their soft, sandy floors. Accompanying them are other remains of human existence such as items of clothing, hunting and farming tools, bags and baskets, flutes, religious relics (Fig. 1.3), their houses and storage chambers, and occasionally, the people themselves when death overtook young and old alike in its often unexpected way.

Such materials as wood, leather, fiber, and feathers that are usually destroyed by the passage of time may be recovered in almost new condition in these caves. One of the most awe-inspiring realities of archaeological research is that the resilient remains of early ceramics, fragments of chipped stone, and occasionally a broken piece of jewelry that we find in the thousands of sites known throughout the Four Corners area were once accompanied by such things as beautiful textiles, carefully carved and polished tools of wood, and shell jewelry

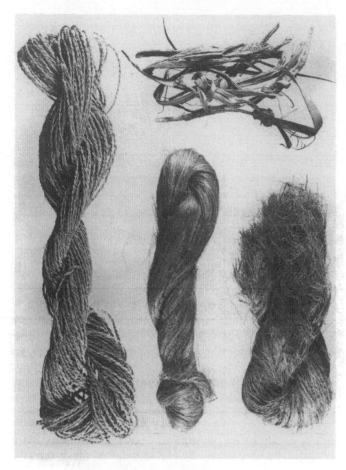

Figure 1.2. Yucca fibers and yarn. (Photo by Elizabeth Ann Morris, Arizona State Museum Neg. 6056.)

from Texas, the Gulf of California, and the Pacific coast. The local landscape offered crystals, oddly shaped stones, and brightly colored feathers and soft downy ones that were tied in small bundles. These items were kept in animal skin bags found in the pit houses and storage cists of the dry shelters. Language, folklore, sacred ceremonies, and other behavioral aspects of Basketmaker life may only be guessed at by extending Puebloan ethnography back into the shadowy recesses of time.

The durable pottery vessels used for cooking and storage were of the earliest kinds known for the northern Southwest. The chipped stone tool assemblage of arrowheads, knives, scrapers, drills, and other artifacts included atlatl dart points, indicating that these ancient sandal wearers witnessed the transition from the thousands-of-years-old hunting tradition using spear throwers (atlatls) and darts to the lighter, more accurate, and more efficient bows and arrows. Bow and arrow tech-

nology was introduced from as yet unknown directions, but at least in these caves its arrival is well dated.

Besides being endowed with a diversity of artifacts made out of perishable materials, the Prayer Rock caves of northeastern Arizona contained many pit houses with remains of large timbers that had served as walls and as roof supports. Tree-ring dating, or dendrochronology, is the most precise method of archaeological dating in the world. The pine and fir trees used in these Basketmaker dwellings are among the most useful species for this dating method. Their annual growth rings indicated precise construction dates in the fifth through the seventh centuries of the Christian era.

Even in graduate school at the University of Arizona in the 1950s, where my dissertation consisted of a comprehensive description of all of the remains from the Prayer Rock caves (E. A. Morris 1959a, 1980), I was not properly aware of the unique diversity of the sandals and other fibrous materials in the collection. It was afterwards, in different archaeological contexts in the United States and abroad, and then in northeastern Colorado where even pottery and architecture rarely accompany the largely lithic remains, that the richness of the Prayer Rock collection deeply impressed me. More recently still, it has become clear to me that, incomplete though this analysis is, the intricate textile techniques and objects represent unique and beautiful craftsmanship by ancient Indians who started with living plants, harvested choice materials, spun their yarn, and fabricated it into complex and magnificently decorated examples of footwear and other rare items.

Most of the sandals are heavily worn, with actual holes in the heel and ball areas of the foot. They were typically found in trash deposits within the rock shelters with other broken and worn out items. Rarely, a whole new pair had been placed on a deceased person or within a burial. Even then, right and left designs did not always match. One wonders, indeed, if they were made by the same craftspeople. It is at least possible that different relatives each contributed a different item to the deceased for the trip to the afterworld. In the same realm of speculation we can wonder if the craftspeople were men or women. The ethnographic record describes male weavers in, for instance, the Hopi tribe and female weavers in other tribes. Cross-culturally, loom weaving is often done by men, and off-loom techniques such as braiding and twining, and weaving that is done with backstrap looms, are almost always done by women.

The Prayer Rock caves that provided the sandals on which this research is based are located near the Cove

Figure 1.3. Basketmaker material culture of the A.D. 600s included stone bowls, skin bags, wooden boxes, medicine bundles, gourds, unfired clay and pottery containers, and baskets. Not to scale. (Drawing by Elizabeth Ann Morris, 1959a.)

and Red Rock Valley communities on the Navajo Indian reservation in the extreme northeastern corner of Arizona (Fig. 1.4). They are naturally formed rock shelters in the towering red sandstone cliffs that are abundant in the area. In geological terms, they are located on the unconformity between the Wingate and Navajo sandstone formations. Many more details are provided in other publications (Hays 1992; E. A. Morris 1958, 1959a, 1959b, 1975, 1980).

Earl Halstead Morris excavated in the caves during the late 1920s and the early 1930s for the American Museum of Natural History in New York City and for the Carnegie Institution of Washington (Dedication page). He became interested in the Basketmaker period of Puebloan prehistory early in his career. In 1923 and 1924 he investigated Tseahatso (Big Cave) and Mummy Cave in Canyon del Muerto. Deep deposits of cultural material in these sites indicated continuous use, or frequent reuse, throughout the Basketmaker II and III and later Pueblo periods, especially Pueblo III. Later residents dug pits and placed structures in earlier layers of trash, and reused stone and timbers. No precise chronological sequence could be worked out in these complicated and disturbed deposits. In 1928, Morris learned of many small cave sites on the east slope of the Lukachukai Mountains, in what he later named the Prayer Rock District. He wondered if they would yield more useful remains from the Basketmaker III period:

> The caves offer rather an attractive appeal for thorough study and explorations. In them there is an opportunity to delimit the complete range of the material culture, especially of the period Basketmaker III. This is possible, because for all practical purposes the caves were not occupied during Pueblo times. Hence there has been no disturbance of the floors, and no consequent mixing together of artifacts of different ages which is so common in sites which continued to be inhabited by the later aborigines, like those in del Muerto and de Chelly (E. H. Morris 1931a: 4).

In the summer of 1930, Morris led Charles Bernheimer to this Red Rock Valley area to look for Basketmaker remains. For several weeks, they worked primarily in Atahonez and Obelisk canyons, deep ravines that drain into the Red Rock Valley. They also traveled across the Lukachukai Mountains, northwest to the Tsegiochong drainage, and west to the Hospitibito.

Of the sites they investigated, the most important to us today, for their tree-ring dates and wealth of artifacts and sandals, are Obelisk Cave and "Owl Head Cave,"

now known as Broken Flute Cave (Figs. 1.5, 1.6; other sites that yielded sandals are listed in Tables 2.1 and 3.1). Collections from this expedition are housed in the American Museum of Natural History and the United States National Museum of Natural History, Smithsonian Institution (Bernheimer 1930).

Earl Morris returned in 1931 to pursue his Basketmaker research under the auspices of the Carnegie Institution of Washington. From mid-July to October first, he reopened many of the sites investigated by the Bernheimer Expedition, but changed their names because he was dissatisfied with Bernheimer's fanciful appellations. Bernheimer's Owl Head Cave became Broken Flute Cave, for example. At that time, Morris named the district Prayer Rock, after an imposing stone monolith rising near the mouth of Atahonez Canyon.

The large and diverse collection of material culture was returned to his home laboratory in Boulder, Colorado. Cataloguing was followed by selection of particular groups of artifacts for immediate analysis. The sandals were one of these. Because of their large number, excellent state of preservation, and elaborate decorations, Ann Morris was attracted to the design elements to be studied. Her artistic work recording rock art in Canyon de Chelly and copying murals at the Temple of the Warriors at Chichen Itza, Yucatan, fostered an interest in symmetry and style as well as in recording the designs themselves. Family and health concerns made demands on her time in the 1930s, and Earl became involved with the Basketmaker II sites that he was digging near Durango, Colorado. There the unusual architecture, the rich material culture, and the unprecedentedly early dates drew his attention away from the Prayer Rock studies.

The advent of World War II reduced the personnel and revenues available for Carnegie Institution archaeological research. Then in 1945 Ann Morris died after a prolonged illness. Artists from the fine arts program at the University of Colorado-Boulder had begun analyzing and drawing the sandals in the mid-1940s, under the direction of Earl Morris. They were Marian Cook, Jean Zeigler, and Kisa Noguchi. They painstakingly examined the specimens and deciphered the faded designs and the intricate manipulations of warp and weft elements. A vast archive of sketches and drawings was created, together with voluminous notes and questions about details. Many of their illustrations are in this volume. The others reside in the archives of the Arizona State Museum, Tucson.

After Earl Morris died in 1956, the Prayer Rock collections, notes, and other records were transferred to

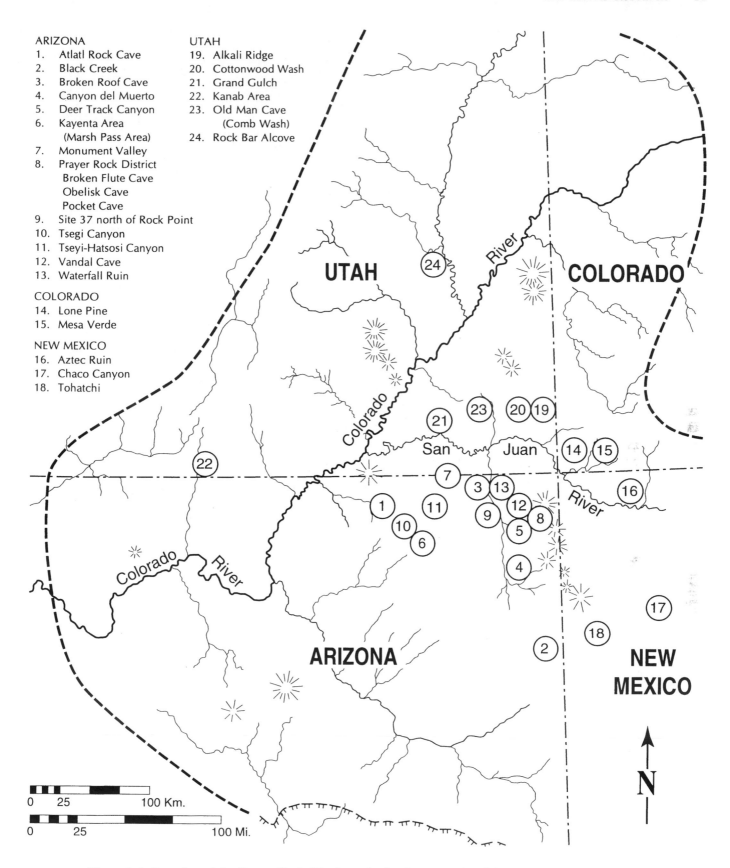

ARIZONA
1. Atlatl Rock Cave
2. Black Creek
3. Broken Roof Cave
4. Canyon del Muerto
5. Deer Track Canyon
6. Kayenta Area
   (Marsh Pass Area)
7. Monument Valley
8. Prayer Rock District
   Broken Flute Cave
   Obelisk Cave
   Pocket Cave
9. Site 37 north of Rock Point
10. Tsegi Canyon
11. Tseyi-Hatsosi Canyon
12. Vandal Cave
13. Waterfall Ruin

COLORADO
14. Lone Pine
15. Mesa Verde

NEW MEXICO
16. Aztec Ruin
17. Chaco Canyon
18. Tohatchi

UTAH
19. Alkali Ridge
20. Cottonwood Wash
21. Grand Gulch
22. Kanab Area
23. Old Man Cave
    (Comb Wash)
24. Rock Bar Alcove

Figure 1.4. Location of the Prayer Rock District and other important localities on the Colorado Plateau.

Figure 1.5. Broken Flute Cave. (Photo by Earl
H. Morris, Arizona State Museum Neg. 6024.)

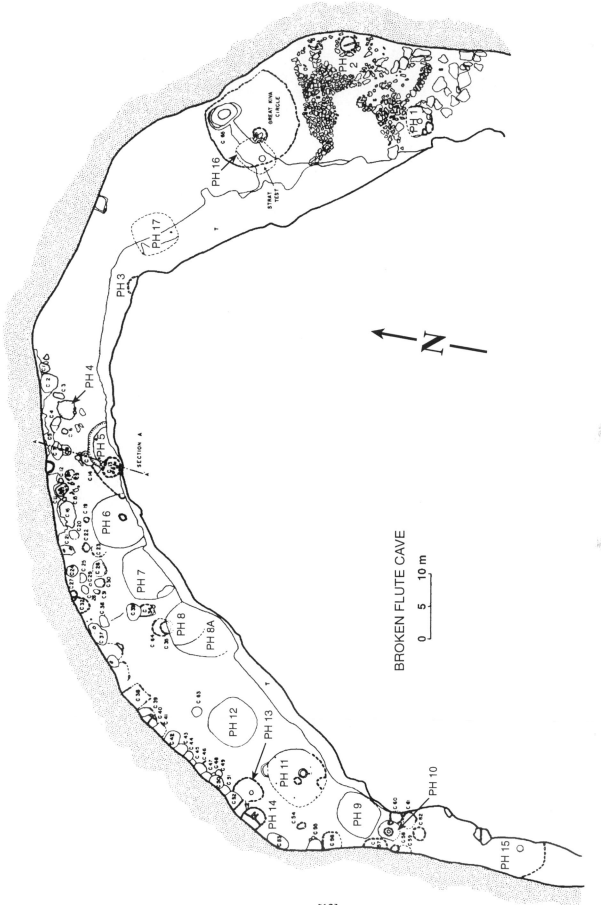

Figure 1.6. Plan of Broken Flute Cave. Reprinted from Elizabeth Ann Morris 1980, Figure 5, by permission of the University of Arizona Press.

the Arizona State Museum. I described most of them as part of my doctoral dissertation (E. A. Morris 1959a). Comparisons of sandal decoration with other media, such as ceramics, were undertaken by Kelley Ann Hays-Gilpin in her doctoral dissertation (Hays 1992). Now, technological analyses updated by Ann Cordy Deegan are presented in this book (see also Deegan 1992, 1995, 1996).

Earl Morris and Ann Axtell Morris wrote the two manuscripts included in this volume (Chapter 2). They are incomplete drafts intended to introduce the intensive description that they planned to write. At that time, research on ancient textiles was just beginning, and no widely accepted, standard terminology for describing textile techniques and structures had been devised. That came later, with *The Primary Structures of Fabrics* by Irene Emery, first printed in 1966. Annotations to the Morrises' manuscripts have been prepared by Deegan clarifying certain points of terminology and describing the Emery descriptive system. The Morrises' writings are included here to reflect the dynamic inspiration and intensity with which they pursued the initial finding of the specimens throughout decades when field research was much more difficult to undertake for logistic and other historic reasons and when analyses preceded modern chemical and data processing.

The sandals themselves, as well as the notes and illustrations concerning them, are in the collections of the Arizona State Museum. In temperature and humidity controlled storerooms, they are protected from further ravages of time. The authors were impressed, as they looked through the collections, that the research done by the Carnegie Institution employees would be virtually impossible to repeat or even sample under modern standards of protective curation. Dissecting a textile artifact to determine the construction details or dampening dyed panels to clarify the designs and colors used would be considered damaging to these rare and fragile specimens under current curatorial standards.

This book contains two of the three surviving commentaries, written more than fifty years ago, by the finder and original analysts, Earl H. Morris and Ann Axtell Morris, and we present modern perspectives on these beautiful items of footwear. The basic descriptions and illustrations have been taken from the archives of notes and drawings. Reconciliations in terminology and alterations to some of the conclusions have been added when necessary. (A longer, highly technical unpublished manuscript on Canyon del Muerto and Grand Gulch sandals, probably written by Ann Morris, is not reproduced here; it is in the Earl Morris Papers in the Archives of the Arizona State Museum, Tucson.)

It is likely that this collection will never be duplicated and that this kind of analysis is too destructive and time-consuming to ever be undertaken again. We are fortunate that the original study was made in the first half of the twentieth century. We feel privileged to be able to assist in presenting the results to interested readers and to textile artists, some of whom we hope will rediscover long-forgotten techniques and designs.

CHAPTER TWO

The Morris Manuscripts

Ann Cordy Deegan

Research on Basketmaker sandals by Earl and Ann Morris extended from their recovery of these ancient specimens, beginning in 1916, until their deaths several decades later. Two summarizing documents written by them remain to give us a hint of their intense interest in the sandals as informative archaeological remains and as objects of incredible craftsmanship.

The Ann Axtell Morris unpublished manuscript that begins on page 19 bears no date, but appears to have been written prior to 1930. It mentions sandals from Grand Gulch and Canyon del Muerto that were collected before 1930, but does not mention sandals from the Prayer Rock District excavated in 1930 and 1931. Ann Morris summarizes the analyses of three assemblages of fibrous footwear: sandals collected "by the Wetherills and McLloyd and Graham" from Grand Gulch, Utah; sandals found by Earl Morris and A. V. Kidder in nonstratified debris in Canyon del Muerto; and sandals excavated from stratified sites in Canyon del Muerto some time in the 1920s but after 1923.

A brief article by Earl H. Morris entitled "Anasazi Sandals" was published in the *News-letter* of the Clearing House for Southwestern Museums in 1944. In it he mentions two other sandal collections, but the focus of his comments is on the "three hundred sandals" from the Prayer Rock District that he excavated early in the 1930s. Morris planned to examine sandals from Broken Roof Cave on the "lower Chinlee Wash" in Arizona and from Aztec Ruin in New Mexico that he collected between 1916 and 1918 and to combine these data with material from the Prayer Rock study. That final report was never completed. He published some of his findings on the Aztec Ruin sandals in 1919. Locations of the various collections and archives are listed in Table 2.1.

TEXTILE TERMINOLOGY

From the 1920s through the 1940s, the interval when both of the Morrises' manuscripts were written, textile terminology was in flux. Many researchers developed their own vocabulary because of the lack of an available standardized textile lexicon. In 1966 Irene Emery published her impressive work on textile terminology, *The Primary Structures of Fabrics: An Illustrated Classification*. This work brought together the earlier terms, sorted them as to their clarity, and discussed which terminology was the most favorable for use. One valuable portion of this book is the discussion of problematic terms, including which ones should be avoided and why. Since its publication, Emery's text has been used by archaeologists, fiber artists, textile historians, and other groups as the preeminent standard textile terminology source. Emery's terminology is used in this book for our analyses and in the annotations to the two Morris manuscripts to update and clarify their discussions. In some specific cases, I have augmented the sandal terminology (see also Deegan 1993) to focus on preferred terms for detailed sandal description.

Basic textile terms are defined in Table 2.2 and illustrated in Figure 2.1 to assist readers in understanding both the manuscripts presented here and our analyses in other sections of this volume. Chapter 5 contains numerous illustrations of textile constructions; some of these construction techniques have not been used since the A.D. 1300s. Terms for these "lost" techniques are provided in Chapter 5 and have been named as close to the Emery terminology as possible.

THE ANN AXTELL MORRIS MANUSCRIPT

Comments

The Ann Morris manuscript is the verbatim text of an unsigned, handwritten document discovered in the Earl Morris archives now housed at the Arizona State Museum (Earl Morris Papers, File A–146: 22–42). The handwriting is not that of Earl Morris, however, but is probably that of Ann Axtell Morris, who had begun a study of prehistoric twined sandals sometime in the 1920s. The handwriting matches that of a longer, more technical manuscript describing sandals from Canyon del Muerto, also found in the Museum archives. Neither of these two manuscripts refers to the investigations by Earl Morris in the Prayer Rock District, probably indi-

Table 2.1. Locations of Sandal Collections and Archives

Sandal Source	Where Cited	Current Location
Prayer Rock District, Arizona (Collected by Earl Morris in 1931)	Basis for discussions in this volume	*Morris Lab Diagrams*: Arizona State Museum Archives, University of Arizona, Tucson *Sandals*: Arizona State Museum, University of Arizona, Tucson
Grand Gulch, Utah (Collected by the Wetherills and McLloyd and Graham)	Ann Axtell Morris manuscript (Chapter 2)	*Sandals*: American Museum of Natural History, New York City
Canyon del Muerto, Arizona (Collected by Earl Morris and A. V. Kidder from nonstratified debris)	Ann Axtell Morris manuscript (Chapter 2)	*Sandals*: American Museum of Natural History, New York City
Canyon del Muerto, Arizona (Collected by Earl Morris in the 1920s from stratified sites)	Ann Axtell Morris manuscript (Chapter 2)	*Morris Lab Diagrams*: Arizona State Museum Archives, University of Arizona, Tucson *Sandals*: University of Colorado Museum, Boulder, Colorado
Aztec Ruin, New Mexico (Collected by Earl Morris between 1916 and 1918)	Earl Morris 1944 article (Chapter 2) Earl Morris 1919	*Morris Lab Diagrams*: Arizona State Museum Archives, University of Arizona, Tucson *Sandals*: Arizona State Museum, University of Arizona, Tucson
Broken Roof Cave, Arizona (Collected by Monroe Amsden in 1923)	Earl Morris 1944 article (Chapter 2)	*Morris Lab Diagrams*: Arizona State Museum Archives, University of Arizona, Tucson *Sandals*: Robert S. Peabody Museum of Archaeology, Phillips Academy, Andover, Massachusetts

Table 2.2. Textile Terminology

Textile Term	Definition
Textile craftsperson or artisan	Someone who creates some or all of a textile product, whether a spinner (making yarn), dyer, weaver, twiner, knitter, or others.
Weaver	A person who creates woven fabric. This term is often misused as a person who makes any type of fabric whether woven, braided, twined, or of other construction. In this book the term weaver only refers to someone who makes woven fabric.
Fabric or Textile	In this book, a fabric is made of fibers and includes any type of fabric construction, including woven, twined, and braided fabric structures. The old definition for textile is woven fabric. This current definition is broader.
Fabric Construction	How a fabric is made (such as woven, twined, braided, knitted).
Fiber	Material with enough flex, strength, and high length-to-width ratio to be used as elements in fabric structures (such as yucca leaves or cotton fibers).
Elements	These can be yarns (fibers twisted together), leaves (crushed, split, whole), or other materials that are used to create textiles.
Yarn	Yarn is the umbrella term for a variety of elements made from fibers.
Single Yarn	A type of yarn made from fibers drawn to a set diameter and usually twisted to hold the fibers together (see Fig. 2.1a).

→

Table 2.2. Textile Terminology (*Continued*)

Textile Term	Definition
Plied Yarn	A type of yarn made from twisting together two or more single yarns (see Fig. 2.1a).
Cord	A type of yarn made from twisting together two or more plied yarns, also called re-plied yarn by Emery (1980: 10). Unfortunately, cord is often used to mean any type of yarn, as are the terms string and thread (see Fig. 2.1a).
Warp	In twined and plain weave sandals, yarn running toe to heel.
Weft	In twined and plain weave sandals, yarn running side to side.
Spinning	The process of drawing fibers to a specific diameter and then twisting to hold these fibers together (produces a single yarn).
Plying	Twisting two or more single yarns for various purposes: to increase yarn diameter, to increase yarn strength, to form a decorative yarn, or all three (see Plied Yarn).
Weaving	Interlacing of two sets of elements, warps and wefts, at right angles to each other. The wefts meet the fabric (sandal) side edges at right angles.
Plain Weave	Over–1, under–1 interlacing of warps and wefts in weaving (see Fig. 2.1*b*).
Loom	A tool that allows warp yarns to be lifted in sets to create the interlacing patterns required in weaving. The lifted warp yarns form an opening called a shed through which the weft yarn is inserted.
Twining	A type of fabric construction method using two sets of yarns where one set of yarns is twisted, commonly in pairs, around another set of yarns. In contrast to weaving, twining involves twisting of yarns around other yarns, not interlacing.
Simple Weft Twining	Paired weft yarns twist around and enclose one warp yarn at a time as they progress across a set of warps. Each twisting action is made directly above that of the previous row, creating columns running toe to heel on the sandal surface (see Fig. 2.1*c*).
2/2 Twill Twining	Paired weft yarns twist around two warp yarns. Each twist action is offset from the previous row by one yarn to create a noncolumnar, smooth surface on the sandal (see Fig. 5.6*a*3).
Open Weft Twining	When each twined row of weft is spaced so that warps are visible between the weft rows, it is called "open" twining. Archaic sandals that have these open spaces are called open twined sandals (see Figs. 4.1, 4.2). Emery (1980: 196) uses the term spaced for this open twining.
Complex Twining	Many other variations of twining are used in these sandals. Some involve combined twining and wrapping of yarns. See Figure 5.6 for examples.
Braiding or Plaiting	Interlacing of one set of elements (warps) in a variety of interlacing patterns, including over–1, under–1 (1/1 interlacing) or over–2, under–2 (2/2 interlacing). Interlacing occurs as the elements move diagonally down the fabric. Elements meet the sandal side edges at a diagonal, not at a right angle as in weaving. The preferred term for this technique from Emery (1980: 62, 68–69) is oblique interlacing, but the term braiding is an optional term used here because of its recognition factor. The term plaiting has become murky in its definition, causing it to be considered an imprecise term. Emery (1980: 60–61) does not recommend using it for this technique. See Figure 2.1*d* for an illustration of the braiding technique.
Soumak Wrapping	A weft wrapping fabric construction technique where one weft yarn repeatedly goes over two warps and then wraps back around one warp as it progresses across the sandal. This technique was combined, in the Prayer Rock District sandals, with an additional laid-in weft to form a raised ridge on some sandal soles (see Fig. 5.9*b*1a).
Zones	Both the Ann Axtell Morris manuscript and the 1944 Earl Morris article use the term "zone" in reference to colored, geometric patterned, cross-wise bands on the sandals (see pp. 22–24, 27). These bands differ in their construction techniques. Other bands of differing constructions are also found on the sandals, including raised sole patterned areas; therefore, I use the term zone when referring to a specific construction area on these sandals and zone terminology appears in Deegan 1992, 1995, and 1997.

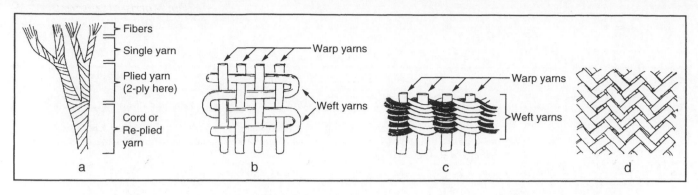

Figure 2.1. Yarn and fabric constructions: *a*, yarn structures; *b*, plain weave; *c*, simple weft twining in two colors; *d*, 2/2 braiding. In sandals, warp yarns run toe to heel and weft yarns run side to side.

cating that they date prior to 1930. Reference is made to collections from Grand Gulch, which the Morrises examined in 1923, and to Earl Morris' Canyon del Muerto material, collected between 1923 and 1927.

In 1931 Samuel Guernsey wrote that Mrs. Earl Morris was working on Canyon del Muerto sandals at that time. It is highly probable, then, that between 1923 and 1930 this first manuscript was penned by Ann Morris on her own, or in collaboration with her husband. A few clerical errors in the manuscript have been corrected. Table 2.3 by Kelley Hays-Gilpin provides a summary of the prehistoric cultural sequence and correlates the terms used for temporal classifications in these two documents. Later, in 1944, Earl Morris wrote summaries of their sandal research, including the Canyon del Muerto and Aztec work and his subsequent study of the Prayer Rock District collections, for the Carnegie Institution's *Yearbook* (Earl Morris 1944c; the Carnegie did not publish his entire submission) and for the *News-Letter* of the Clearing House for Southwestern Museums. The Clearing House article begins on page 26. The Carnegie Institution draft report has not been included here because it is substantially the same as the Clearing House article.

Table 2.3. The Prehistoric Puebloan (Anasazi) Cultural Sequence of the Northern U.S. Southwest (*Kelley Ann Hays-Gilpin*)

Morris Classification (Ann Morris ms)	Pecos Classification (Earl Morris 1944a News-Letter article)	Date Ranges	Characteristics
Cliff Dweller	Pueblo III	A.D. 1100 to 1300	Multistoried masonry pueblos, sometimes in caves as at Mesa Verde; polychrome pottery in some areas; whole-leaf braided sandals, twined shaped toe sandals
Early Pueblo	Pueblo II	A.D. 900 to 1100	Small unit pueblos with kivas, large pueblos with multiple kivas and great kivas in some areas; little use of caves so few sandals known, mostly whole-leaf braided sandals
Prepueblo	Pueblo I	A.D. 700 to 900	Pit houses with above-ground slab structures, simple great kivas; large villages in some areas such as Chaco Canyon; black-on-white pottery; little use of caves so few sandals known, mostly whole-leaf braided sandals
Post Basket Maker	Basketmaker III	A.D. 400 to 700	Cultivated maize, squash, and beans; larger, deeper pit houses, simple great kivas, some surface storage rooms; bow and arrow; pottery, but few decorated vessels; twined sandals, many elaborately decorated
Basket Maker	Basketmaker II	500 B.C. to A.D. 400	Cultivated maize and squash; small pit houses and storage cists, sometimes in caves; atlatls and darts for hunting; some decorated baskets; no pottery; twined sandals
	Archaic	6500 to 500 B.C.	Wild foods; temporary camps; low population density; baskets for gathering food; atlatls and darts for hunting; no pottery; open twined sandals

Text
[Ann Axtell Morris]

The Southwestern part of the United States with its sequent and long established chain of cultures has proved rich ground for study based on chronological types of pottery obtained therefrom. The questions raised by these pottery types have only of late years been recognized, and to date have only been conclusively settled in a few details. Chiefly through the work of Dr. A. V. Kidder, Mr. S. G. Guernsey, Mr. Frank Roberts, and Mr. Earl H. Morris, comparative lines of chronologic demarcation have been laid across the area comprised in the San Juan drainage system separating the unbroken sequence of cultures into consistent and pronouncedly differentiated units. To sum up briefly: As far as is now known, the Basket Makers—a non-pottery making agricultural, dolichocephalic people were the first occupants of the region. (Traces of a possible earlier type have been recently found in Lovelock Cave, Nevada by Mr. Harrington. The remains at this spot indicate a non-agricultural culture.) [Footnote in original manuscript; see Loud and Harrington 1929, Cressman 1942.] *This period was brought to a close by the introduction of the art of ceramics heralding the dawn of the Post Basket Maker period in crude unfired basket moulded vessels of clay. Distinct improvement along this line, and the rapid infiltration of a new brachycephalic stock were indicative of many changes which took place in the life of these peoples. This interval, one of supreme excellence ceramically and artistically appears to have persisted for a long space of time but finally gave way to the less easily defined Prepueblo Period* [see Table 2.3].

By this time all trace of dolichocephaly had disappeared and although an improved architecture ensues, the old rigid clarity of design and artistry in artifacts shows a marked decrease. The early pueblo periods with the first coursed masonry marks again an improvement culminating in the great Chaco and Mesa Verde periods before the final decadence and disappearance of these prehistoric peoples.

As said before, the pottery of this succession of cultures has proved the best check for their chronological study. However, within the last few years the discovery and study of material occurring in the dry sheltered caves of this region has promised an invaluable addition. However, casual inspection revealed almost insurmountable difficulties in this. In the course of centuries the almost unbroken occupations of these cave shelters resulted in the soil and debris being turned and returned in the process of continuous building operation and periodic internments of the dead. House was built upon house and the most recently deceased was ceded the respect and burial room of momentary opportunism. These conditions produced a melee of material practically impossible to classify with the ease which undisturbed stratigraphy would have produced.

The enormous number of sandals among the recovered specimens and their obvious differences of structure and design gave rise to the conviction that there must be a relative sequence of types among them as clearly defined as that of pottery. Therefore, following my first field season in 1923 I took occasion to examine and carefully study the specimens possessed by the American Museum of Natural History.[1] *This consisted of a collection from Grand Gulch, Utah, collected by the Wetherills and McLloyd and Graham and denominated without further notes "Basketmaker." In addition the Museum possessed a large assortment collected by Mr. Earl Morris in Canyon del Muerto, Arizona, which had come from unstratified and disturbed trash mounds. A minute study of these seems to reveal clear lines of evolutionary sequence, although this was derived solely from internal evidence. Knowing the dangers and fully aware of precedent folly from classification of this sort, it was used solely as a working basis. Two subsequent seasons in the same canyon were more satisfactory since many well shod mummies were exhumed with which were other distinctive artifacts, in addition to sandals found on room floors in association with known types of pottery. With great satisfaction I found the classification thus established to be entirely correct in its continuity, although the late Post Basket Maker period stretched out to such engulfing years as to almost completely swallow all the sandals previously allotted to the Prepueblo period. With the exception of this minor misfortune, the series of more than 500 was subjected to proof at point after point and has emerged tried and satisfactory to be a coadjunct to ceramics in the designation of period.*

The following technical discussion must necessarily be so brief as to suffice but for an outline of a subject involved in such incredible intricacy. For the sandal comprehended by the simple definition—"footgear consisting of a sole only and fastened to the foot by means of thongs" took on complications of development and intricate designs as to give it a foremost place among world textiles. A short description of the sequent types may serve as partial proof of this statement.

The typical sandal as assigned previously to the Basket Maker had already achieved such sophistication of technique as to preclude the hypotheses that such an object could leap full fashioned from the hands of [a] very primitive weaver.[2] Therefore certain crude specimens found in association with these, must necessarily stand as forerunners of the type. These earliest sandals composed of cedar bark, split yucca leaves, human hair and yucca fiber are more or less platter shaped and are constructed without a loom.[3] Two or three heavy strands were laid as warps parallel to the long axis of the foot, over and under[4] which were passed equally coarse weft hanks. The protruding ends at heel and toe were twisted and knotted fairly fast in a hit and miss method. The results needless to say are as ugly as they must have been short lived.

The developed type belonging to the Basket Maker period was reached by various recognized stages from these early beginnings and achieved marked stylization. The materials of composition from this time on to the practical disappearance of the textile sandal remain fairly constant. Twisted yucca fiber cords[5] provided the warps and some finer fibrous material of silver tawny color, possibly Indian hemp or apocynum, were twisted into cords for the weft crossings. The sandal becomes practically rectangular, presents a compact smooth facing to the foot occasionally bearing a colored design made by the over–under or the twined weave,[6] a ridged sole to provide for slippery rocks and, most curiously, a large bolster toe stuffed to a diameter of as much as one inch and adorned gratuitously with a heavy, flapping, buckskin fringe.[7] This element was of no conceivable human use and must have proven a distinct impediment to rapid walking. On the contrary, the transversely ribbed sole of undoubted non-skid utility proves a triumph of the art of textile manipulation. By the various means of secondary warps, introduced wefts, etc. an apparent similitude was obtained, while in one specimen, the main warp, two twined wefts, an active introduced warp and a triple super-imposed secondary weft all find place in a single crossing. The writer admits of due respect to the weaver who could control this weave without the use of three hands. No knots were utilized, jointures being accomplished by overlapping the weft strands. This was wise as the strength of the weave[8] depended upon its smooth unbroken solidity. A few of the specimens bore colored decoration similar to that found upon twine woven bags of the period, i.e. two narrow lines of bars offset from one another and colored black and red upon the natural ground. This sort of decoration, however, is rare. Additional definitive points often occurring lie in a braided three ply selvage appearing upon the sole, and a narrow thread of red following the edges of the reverse face. None of these sandals were stretched upon a loom for indeed the technique involved requires warps free for manipulation on their own count, nor is there any sign of their suspension.[9] This mechanical is as yet unsettled.

One specimen bears trace of the method prevailed through the time of greatest productivity—the Post Basketmaker period and the early Prepueblo period. The following method illustrated the procedure in the early Post Basket Maker period.[10] The number of warps desired for the width of the sandal were laid side by side. These were cut to somewhat more than the length of the proposed sandal. At a distance of ½" from their ends a weft was passed through the loose warps in the Over–Under weave.[11] This was repeated proceeding towards the heel until a small strip of one inch wide was completed. At this point the woven portion was doubled over a suspended loop of cord. This result was possibly obtained by first wetting the creases, pounding it with a smooth stone to overcome the unyielding qualities of the closely woven[12] material. After being suspended, the short ½" warps then hung parallel to the long or the side nearest to the weaver. The next few weft crossings included both of these warps as a single one thereby knitting[13] them firmly together. Each crossing endeavored to exert as much pressure as possible upon that preceeding. This produced a drag upon the central part of the unrigid suspending loops, tending to incurve the center of the toe. Although slight at first, this scallop becomes more and more pronounced with time.[14] When completed the sandal was cut down by clipping the suspending cord at either side of the toe. These fragments are often found inside the small hollow cylinder.

Likewise with the passage of time, the amount of warp doubled over the loop gradually increased until a doubled portion from 7 to 9 inches long was produced, or a good 3/4 or 5/6 of the entire length of the sandal.[15] This extension of the toe weave is coincident with the deepest form of toe notch.[16]

There is no adaptation to a right or left foot until Cliff Dweller times, although a certain widening under the ball of the foot and narrowing at the heel is consistently observed.

In addition to the change of mechanical adjustment and style of toes, two additional factors undergo radical revolution during the Post Basket Maker period. One of these involves the sole corrugations[17] and the other, color ornamentation.

Detailed analysis of the former would bulk far out of proportion to the intention of this paper. Suffice it to say that during the elapse of the Post Basket Maker period 29 different manipulations of warp and weft were utilized for the production of the completed sandal, and of these, the majority occur in the earliest part of that period before custom had determined upon these stitches[18] best adapted to need.

The precautions against slipping are as carefully observed as in Basket Maker days, but after a certain amount of fumbling trial a system of small isolated bars and knots[19] was evolved, material which lent itself most readily to the formation of raised patterns upon the sole[20]—an effect comparable in some degree to the carved and intaglic effect of cut gems. Parallel line divisions running lengthwise down the foot and diamond or half-diamond patterns characterized the first specimens adapting this technique. Practice and time carried this trait to textile perfection at no time excelled for beauty upon the face of the globe. Exquisite minuteness was observed and an intricacy of pattern maintained which by a method of inverted and reversed repetition challenges to a degree the powers of the analyzer. At the same time upon the smooth upper sole the weaver[21] was carrying out the pattern of a colored design infinitely more complicated than the simple offset bars of the Basket Makers. Two narrow color zones occupying about 2" approximately 2" from the extreme edge of the toe, each of which usually bore a repetition of pattern worked out in different colors and reversal and inversion of pattern.[22] The colors utilized are red, black, yellow, dark brown and the natural tan of the yucca fiber. The system of patterning, constructed as it always was of reversed and inverted design or both, would seem to involve a design sense of a highly specialized sort. This is the more remarkable as we have no reason for believing that any guide pattern was traced out previous to the actual work.

Later development of the Post Basketmaker sandal enlarged the area to be treated with colored designs to four zones.[23] The second two were applied to that surface described above as the toe weave[24] which tipped by an extremely deep notch[25] at the one end extended for from 3 to 7 inches towards the heel. These two zones similarly to the others repeated a pattern with the usual variations of color, inversion and reversal. However, each group of zones although contiguous bore no design relationship to each other. Indeed this would have been impossible as the basic weaves[26] underlying the 2 colored portions were utterly different, providing the smooth surface resultant from an offset twill[27] at the toe end and well defined ribs of a more complicated manufacture for those zones lying under the instep.

This latest development of the Post Basket Maker sandal stressed the color effect to the detriment of the knotted sole patterns which became coarser and less intricate as time went on. As a complement to the very beautiful color effects obtained on these sandals a plain undecorated winter shoe is found.[28] The technique of construction is the same with the exception of the method of fastening them upon the foot. A series of side loops fastened along the sides of the shoe and laced together over the top form a more secure tie than the usual heel and toe loop joined by a single string over the instep. In addition the top thus provided was found to provide adequate binding for a lining of shredded cedar bark.

The surprising occurrence of a fourth type of sandal in the Post Basket Maker group gives rise to interesting speculation. These have been found solely upon burials and owing to the similarity of certain detailed features of construction, obsolete in Post Basket Maker times, are thought to be a ceremonial survival of Basket Maker methods and were accorded to the dead alone.[29] Be that as it may, the sandals in this group represent the most beautiful specimens that have been found. They are covered with multicolored design from tip to toe and are constructed with an astonishing delicacy of technique.

The next step in chronology[30] leads us to that shadowy, indeterminate period of the Prepueblo and early Pueblo—terms not exactly coincident nor as yet capable of clearly defined separation. The short series of sandals undoubtedly representing this time does not as yet throw further light on the matter.

A definite change in the construction of the footgear occurs at this point. The old string-hung loom[31] is abandoned for no apparent reason as the results do not seem to justify in their crudity. The method of weaving proceeds somewhat as follows.[32] One half as many warps as are required for the width of the sandal are laid out straight upon a flat surface. A few weft crossings in the Over–Under weave[33] were run across the middle of these. Then the warps were bent in the middle and so laid that their lengths lay parallel to each other, the outside one forming the arc of a curved toe, the inner warps following this concentrically until the final warp is reached which is merely bent back to run beside itself. Wefts filled in this curve end by being inserted in a V–shaped form until a horizontal is again reached, after which the weaving proceeds much the same as previously. Tiny, short weft pieces were inserted as "fillers" at the outer edges of the arc to obviate the necessity of too many cords having to meet at the center. But even so, a slight bunchy protuberance was the usual result, which was sure to rub through before very many wearings. This disadvantage combined with the further obvious one of the difficulty of handling the loose lying warps gives rise to wonder that those prehistoric people should abandon the more adequate and beautiful form. However, textile technique was showing a marked decline. Colored decoration was practically obsolete, and the knotted and barred sole patterns so degenerate as to nearly lose their function as design.

The passing into the Cliff Dweller epoch was marked at once by a further decline on the one hand and in a few cases a resuscitation of the finely woven fabric sandal on the other. The round toe persists with the addition of an added doubled warp which is applied against one side a few inches from the extreme tip of the toe and results in the "toe jog" which serves as a shaped surface under the protruding little toe.[34] *Further shaping is found in a distortion of the toe arc to conform more accurately to the foot shape. This leads to a differentiation between the right and left foot for the first time.*

The few fabric[35] *sandals of this time follow the old traditions in material, technique, etc. A few colored specimens have been found and a few with the sole knots resuming their old function of decoration. They are almost invariably of excellent workmanship.*

But as a whole the sandal products of the Cliff Dweller period are woven and plaited[36] *of split yucca leaves, more after the fashion of matting than of textile work. Some are shaped exactly as are those textile sandals above described, others are merely rectangular in form.*[37] *As the technique involved in this work has been presented at length by Drs. Kidder and Guernsey in the B.A.E. Report No.* [65] *a repetition will be unnecessary.*[38]

To summarize briefly: we possess an unbroken series of footgear specimens relating to the culture phases of the San Juan Area of the Southwest. These are now proving to be nearly as practical a check upon the chronology of this region as the pottery has previously been. The earliest of Basket Maker sandals possess the following definitive characteristics—a square bolster toe, usually equipped with fringe, a sole carrying ridges or corrugations obtained by many adaptations of the secondary warp and weft, few specimens bearing colored design and that of the simplest sort. [39]

The Post Basket Maker era is divisible into 3 time units, as represented by the footgear, through all 3 of which however run the highly colored beautifully executed burial sandal bearing distinct ceremonial relationship to certain stylistic details of Basket Maker times. The early Post Basket Maker sandal was constructed upon a string hung loom, had a slightly scalloped toe, bore no color and produced sole ridges and corrugations by an infinity of methods with very crude results.[40]

The Middle period modified this treatment of the sole, established a standard for the construction of knots and bars, by which patterns beautiful and intricate enriched the sandal. Two color zones were introduced running under the instep, each repeating the basic pattern of the other in varied colors and arrangement.[41]

The final Post Basket Maker period added two further color zones on the ever increasing smooth "toe weave" surface, which in their turn repeated and arranged the designs of each other although bearing no relation to the first 2 zones.[42] *The sole patterns suffer a decline and toe scallop becomes a deep narrow notch.*

The Prepueblo period sees a change in technique. The string hung loom is replaced by loose warps which are so arranged as to follow and arc around the foot, producing a round toe.[43] *Coloration and knot pattern suffer a distinct decadence.*

With the Cliff Dweller the series of textile works experiences sporadic revival in a few samples of exceptional beauty.[44] *However the usual Cliff Dweller sandal is plaited, mat like, from split yucca leaves, in some cases excellently shaped to the foot and bearing the distinctive "toe jog," but in others degenerating into a mere crude plat of no beauty and little practical use.*[45]

Arizona State Museum, Earl Morris Papers File A–146: 22–42
Probably written between 1923 and 1930

Annotations to the Ann Morris Manuscript
[Ann Cordy Deegan]

1. Table 2.1 lists sources and geographic origins of the sandals mentioned in the Morrises' manuscripts and in the rest of this volume and indicates where they are currently located.

2. Here "weaver" is used to indicate a textile craftsperson, whether weaving, twining, or creating other textile fabrications.

3. Refers to a plain weave sandal (see Fig. 4.16).

4. In this sentence "over and under" refers to plain weave (see Fig. 5.6c1a).

5. In the Ann Axtell Morris text, the term "cord" means yarn. The modern textile term "cord" is actually a complicated yarn made of other plied yarns.

6. The "over–under" weave is plain weave. "Twined weave" refers to twined construction, not weaving.

7. This is the Basketmaker II square toe–square heel twined sandal type (see Chapter 4, pp 40–42 and Figs. 4.3, 4.4).

8. "Weave" here refers to fabric construction in general, not just to weaving.

9. Some of the Basketmaker II square toe–square heel twined sandals may have been suspended by their warps or may have involved stretched warps in their construction (see Deegan 1996).

10. This construction is shared by scalloped toe–square heel and scalloped toe-puckered heel twined sandal types (see Chapter 5).

11. Here the use of "over–under weave" actually is 2/2 twill twining (see Figure 5.6a3).

12. "Woven" here means twining, not weaving.

13. "Knitting" as used in this phrase does not relate to the textile technique of knitting.

14. At the present time, no definitive chronological dating has been assigned to the various depths of toe scalloping.

15. This refers to the scalloped toe–puckered heel twined sandal type.

16. Toe notch means a scalloped toe.

17. Sole corrugations refer to the sole relief patterning.

18. Here "stitches" does not actually refer to stitchery, such as embroidery. Raised soles were created through complex twining and looping interspersed with plain weave, simple twining, or both.

19. "Bars and knots" refer to twining and wrapping used to make relief patterns (see Chapter 5).

20. See Figure 5.10 for an illustration of raised patterning.

21. Here "weaver" means textile craftsperson, not just a weaver.

22. This is visible in scalloped toe–puckered heel twined sandals with a Zone 2 (see Fig. 5.16).

23. These four zones are actually the two bands of the colored Extended Zone 1a and the two bands that comprise Zone 2 (see Fig. 5.20).

24. The toe weave is Zone 1.

25. The deep notch is actually a deeply scalloped toe.

26. The use of the term "weaves" here refers to twining.

27. An "offset twill" is 2/2 twill twining.

28. See Chapter 4, p. 50, for more data on the "winter" sandal.

29. "Burial" sandals are actually a type of scalloped toe–square heel twined sandal. These sandals do not all come from burials (see Chapter 4, p. 44).

30. Archaeologists have recently determined that the round toe–puckered heel twined sandal described here coexists with the scalloped toe–puckered heel twined sandal rather than follows it chronologically as indicated in the Ann Morris text (see Chapter 3).

31. Use of a loom (see Loom in Table 2.2) for constructing these scalloped-toe sandals has not been proven. A suspension cord, supporting the warps at the toe end, was probably used to provide tension, perhaps with the use of backstrap tension around the waist.

32. This section describes construction of the toe of the round toe–puckered heel twined sandal (see Chapter 5, pp. 69–71 and Fig. 5.28).

33. This use of the term "over–under weave" refers to 2/2 twill twining.

34. This is the shaped toe–cupped heel twined sandal type with a toe jog (see Chapter 4, pp. 47–48 and Fig. 4.14).

35. The term "fabric sandals" means use of spun yarns and, here, to twined construction as well.

36. Plaited means braided where only one set of elements, such as leaves, are interlaced diagonally down the length of the sandal from toe to heel (see Table 2.2).

37. See Chapter 4, pp. 49–50, for more information on braided (plaited) sandal types (Figs. 4.17, 4.18).

38. This reference is to *Archaeological Explorations in Northeastern Arizona*, by Alfred V. Kidder and Samuel J. Guernsey, 1919, Bureau of American Ethnology Bulletin 65, Smithsonian Institution.

Their work included a brief summary of braided sandals; more recent research is expanding on braided sandal techniques.

39. Refers to the Basketmaker II square toe–square heel twined sandal type (see Chapter 4, pp. 41–42).

40. Refers to the Baskemaker III (A.D. 400s) scalloped toe–square heel twined sandal type (see Chapter 4, pp. 42–44 and Chapter 5). As is discussed in Chapter 5, some of the Prayer Rock District scalloped toe–square heel twined sandals did have colored geometric patterns. Perhaps the scalloped toe–square heel twined sandals from Grand Gulch and Canyon del Muerto, which were analyzed for the Ann Morris manuscript, did not have colored patterns.

41. Refers to the Basketmaker III (A.D. 600s) scalloped toe–puckered heel twined sandal type with a Zone 2 (see Chapter 5).

42. Refers to the Basketmaker III (A.D. 600s) scalloped toe–puckered heel twined sandal type using an Extended Zone 1a (see Chapter 5).

43. Refers to the Basketmaker III (A.D. 600s) round toe–puckered heel twined sandal type (see Chapter 4, pp. 45–47, and Chapter 5).

44. Refers to the Pueblo shaped toe–cupped heel twined sandal type (see Chapter 4, pp. 47–48).

45. Refers to the Pueblo braided sandal types (see Chapter 4, pp. 49–50).

THE EARL H. MORRIS 1944 *NEWS-LETTER* ARTICLE

In her early text, printed above, Ann Axtell Morris used the temporal terms "Post Basket Maker" and "Pre-pueblo." In this article, published in 1944 in an obscure newsletter not generally accessible to today's readers, Earl Morris used the terms for these time intervals that Southwestern archaeologists had agreed on at the 1927 Pecos Conference: Basketmaker III and Pueblo I, respectively. He also discussed the Prayer Rock sandal collection, which by this time had become the focus of the sandal study.

Anasazi Sandals
[Earl H. Morris, Boulder, Colorado]

Basic facts in regard to the footgear of the Basketmaker-Pueblo peoples of the northern Southwest probably are familiar to most everyone. Sandals these peoples wore so universally that the moccasins which on rare occasions turn up during excavation, for purposes of generality may be disregarded. The sandals were made, not of animal hide, but of vegetable substances.[1] Dependent upon the technique of manufacture they fall into two general classes: Plaited,[2] made from strips of leaf, usually yucca, whole, split or crushed; and Cross-woven,[3] with longitudinal warps and transverse wefts, in which the component units grade from thick bundles of partially separated fibre to slender well-twisted cords.[4]

Plaited sandals have not been reported from Basketmaker II sites and it is not known just when they began to be made. However, since other kinds of plaited objects have been found in Basketmaker III deposits, it seems likely that the technique of plaiting would have been applied to footgear before the end of that period. At any rate, with the passing of the centuries, plaited sandals became more and more the dominant type, until, by the end of early, or Chaco, Pueblo III, they had completely supplanted the better-woven[5] variety. Skillfully made and pleasing to the eye though many of them are, the very limitations of technique made the plaited sandals drab and commonplace beside the cross-woven ones.

Sandals from the oldest known Basketmaker sites all are cross-woven. Many are coarse, thick and crude, with from three to six warps filled with proportionately heavy wefts, sometimes in plain over–under weave, but more often twined.[6] It may be inferred that this was the first sort of sandal made by the Anasazi. However, in the earliest groups of specimens so far recovered, there are in association with the heavy crude examples,[7] others much more carefully constructed, with both warp and weft of twisted cords.[8] In fabric the latter are tight-woven,[9] hard and extremely durable. Some are without patterns. Others bear raised designs on the sole side,[10] usually produced by devious twistings and knottings of the weft, but complicated in the most involved examples by the introduction of supplementary strands in both warp and weft. Such specimens exhibit some of the most intricate hand weaving[11] that the world has known at any time or place. They give us our first glimpse of an art that was to be practiced for a surprisingly long time.

Why the Anasazi should have chosen the making of footgear that would be worn out in little more time than it took to produce it, as the avenue in which to express their utmost in inventive skill and artistic genius, we shall never know. Nevertheless, that is exactly what they did. In the great efflorescence of Basketmaker III, sandal making outstripped all the other arts. The weave[12] became finer and the raised patterns on the soles were more delicate and intricate. Still further embellishment was attained by the introduction of colored designs on the upper surface. These began as narrow transverse stripes but soon were elaborated into patterns fully as complicated as the raised ones on the soles and in one style, spread to cover the entire length of the sandal.[13] The principal colors used were black, two shades of red, brown, yellow, white and the varying tawny hues of the natural fiber.

By the end of Basketmaker III sandal making had reached and perhaps passed its zenith. In shape, the original truncated wedge[14] became progressively indrawn at the sides toward the toe end with a proportional scalloping of that extremity. The scallop became ever and ever deeper until it was a V–like notch. And finally the notch was eliminated by a change in the arrangement of the warps. They were brought from the heel up one side, across and down the other, producing a fully rounded toe.[15] Sole patterns passed through a stage of extreme complexity and variety, then became more standardized and were restricted in area to the heelward half of the sandal. Colored decoration crystallized into transverse zones occupying the part of the sandal forward of the patterned portion of the sole.

Practically no perishable materials representative of Pueblo I and II have been recovered to date, hence there is no empirical evidence as to the prevalence or character of cross-woven sandals during those periods. But that the art of making them survived this long hiatus is shown by specimens from early Pueblo III refuse deposits, notably in the Aztec Ruin.[16] These are shaped for left or right foot, have the characteristic Pueblo III offset of the position of the little toe,[17] carry more warps per inch than the Basketmaker III examples, are thinner and lighter in texture, but are just as tightly woven.[18] Both colored and raised patterns are less elaborate than in the earlier specimens. Then finally cross-woven sandals ceased to be made altogether, for not one has been found in the Mesa Verde horizon of Pueblo III.

The earliest dated site from which cross-woven sandals have been taken is du Pont Cave and the latest is the Aztec Ruin. The cave dates at 217 A.D. The Aztec Ruin was built between 1110 and 1121 A.D. It would seem reasonable to suppose that the first-occupation refuse dumps in unused parts of the buildings were in process of deposition as late as 1200 A.D. Hence the life span of the cross-woven sandal is shown to have been in round numbers at least one thousand years.

Spread out on the work tables of our shop in Boulder are three hundred sandals, mostly of Basketmaker III age, taken in 1931 from caves in the western edge of Red Rock Valley, northeastern Arizona.[19] With few exceptions so worn and tattered that they were thrown away by their owners, at first glance they give little hint of their original magnificence. Yet very few are so badly frayed that their patterns, both structural and colored, cannot be recovered by careful scrutiny. And being too dilapidated for museum display, we feel free to dissect as many as desirable in order to work out the variations in weave.[20] For nearly a year Miss Jean G. Zeigler[21] has brought high skill to bear on the recovery and rendering of designs and the analysis and graphic depiction of weaves.[22] Months more must pass before the study of the present series will have been completed. That done we propose to go over two other collections, one of Basketmaker II sandals from the lower Chinlee,[23] the other of Pueblo III examples from the Aztec Ruin. Then some day we expect to have ready for the press a detailed description of cross-woven sandals that will show not only the sequence and variations of the processes by which they were produced, but which will also, through copious illustration, reveal to the degree that the remarkable patterns deserve, the rich beauty which the Anasazi wrought into the ephemeral bits of fabric that were to afford their feet brief protection against mud and stones and thorns.[24]

Clearing House for Southwestern Museums News-letters
No. 68–69, January–February 1944, pp. 239–241

Annotations to the Earl Morris 1944 Article
[Ann Cordy Deegan]

1. "Vegetable" substances refers to fibers obtained from plant sources, such as yucca plants.

2. Throughout this article, plaited means braiding. Braiding in these sandals involves the diagonal interlacing of leaves from toe to heel of a sandal. There are no cross-elements such as wefts.

3. Earl Morris uses "cross-woven" here to mean sandals made of warps (elements running toe to heel in sandals) and wefts (elements running side to side in sandals).

4. Cord is used as a general term for yarn in this article. The modern textile term "cord" refers to complex yarns made from other plied yarns.

5. "Woven" here could mean either woven or twined.

6. The plain weave sandals Morris mentions use coarse elements (wide diameter twisted leaves or yarns). The plain over–under weave is plain weave with warps and wefts interlacing over–1, under–1. Some twined sandals may also have used coarse elements. However, except for a brief mention in this paragraph of plain weave sandals as being cross-woven, cross-woven sandals in the remainder of this article refer exclusively to twined sandals made of yarn.

7. "Heavy crude examples" refers to plain or twined sandals made of large diameter yarn or twisted leaves.

8. Refers to the Basketmaker II square toe–square heel twined sandals made of yarn.

9. The term "tight-woven" refers to tightly packed yarns in twined sandals.

10. All diagrams of Basketmaker II square toe–square heel twined sandals drawn by the Morris team and seen by me do not show any raised design patterning on the sandal sole, just a cross-wise corrugation.

11. Here the use of the term "hand weaving" encompasses more than actual weaving; it also includes twining.

12. Weave here is predominantly twining.

13. The style referred to is Ann Morris' "burial sandal" (see Chapter 4, p. 44).

14. A truncated wedge is a scalloped toe.

15. This is the round toe–puckered heel twined sandal style. More recent dating indicates that the round-toe sandal coexisted with the scalloped-toe sandal. No definitive chronological dating has been done to determine if the shallower scalloped-toe sandals predate the deeper scalloped-toe sandals.

16. These are the shaped toe–cupped heel twined sandals (see Chapter 4, pp. 47–48).

17. This offset is called a toe jog.

18. The Aztec Ruin sandals are predominately twined.

19. These are the Prayer Rock District sandals on which the analyses in this book are based.

20. Remaining Morris laboratory data indicate that only four sandals were actually dissected from the hundreds found in the Prayer Rock District. The Morris laboratory diagrams and notes from these four are extremely detailed, with information on each weft row inserted into the sandals.

21. Miss Jean G. Zeigler was an art student at the University of Colorado, Boulder, who worked with Earl Morris on the Prayer Rock District sandals from 1942 or 1943 to about the summer of 1944, when she joined the WACS (letter from E. H. Morris to A. V. Kidder, June 12, 1944).

22. Here "weaves" means any textile fabric construction that was found, whether woven, twined, or some other construction technique.

23. The sandals of the lower Chinlee were probably from Broken Roof Cave, Arizona, mentioned in correspondence (Kidder 1944a, 1944b; E. H. Morris 1944b); some Morris laboratory diagrams are of these sandals (see Table 2.1).

24. Earl Morris and his team did not finish a "detailed description" of twined sandals. The only written portions that remain include the two documents by Ann Morris noted on page 15 (one of them printed above), this 1944 published article, and the Carnegie Institution report mentioned earlier (which is essentially the same as the 1944 article). A few of Earl Morris' laboratory diagrams were made into copper and zinc plates to determine how to print them, but they were never published. Many of the Morris team's beautiful laboratory diagrams and illustrations are incorporated into this book.

CHAPTER THREE

Excavation and Dating of the Prayer Rock Caves

Kelley Ann Hays-Gilpin

Although radiocarbon dating had not yet been invented, and tree-ring dating was still in its formative years when the Morrises developed their ideas about how sandals changed from one era to the next, their chronology is essentially correct. Ann Axtell Morris states in her manuscript (Chapter 2) that "The Post Basket Maker era is divisible into 3 time units." In his 1944 article, Earl Morris refers to Early, Middle, and Late Basketmaker III sandals.

This developmental scheme rests on two kinds of support, internal evidence and associational evidence. First, the Morrises proposed an evolutionary sequence of sandal construction based on the variation of shapes, techniques, and styles they saw in the hundreds of sandals collected from sites in several parts of the Four Corners region. Both Morris sandal manuscripts focus on this evolutionary sequence.

Ann Morris' sandal study concentrated on collections from Grand Gulch, where sites were excavated without adequate record-keeping, and from Canyon del Muerto, where sites had been occupied and reoccupied so many times it was impossible to tell which artifacts belonged to the same time period. To clarify this dating problem, Earl Morris wanted to examine the depositional contexts of the sandals: which artifacts and architectural styles were associated with each kind of sandal.

The Prayer Rock District rockshelters presented ideal locations for collecting the kind of evidence needed to reconstruct and date Basketmaker lifeways, because the dry, sheltered soils preserved organic materials, including sandals; occupations were short; and later uses of the caves did minimal damage to Basketmaker period remains. Morris intended to incorporate the relative and absolute dates of structures and other deposits that contained sandals into his study, but the painstaking work of tree-ring analysis was not completed and incorporated until his daughter, Elizabeth, undertook the task after her father's death.

SITE CHRONOLOGY

The basic chronology of structures and artifacts in the Prayer Rock caves proposed by Earl Morris was later refined by other archaeologists (Ahlstrom 1985; Bannister and others 1966; Hays 1992; E. A. Morris 1959a, 1980) in three ways: (1) tree-ring dating; (2) stratigraphic relationships among structures and deposits; and (3) a known ceramic sequence, from no pottery prior to about A.D. 450, to rare occurrences of undecorated polished gray and brown wares, to the appearance of rough but well-fired gray ware that included painted bowls by the A.D. 620s. These relationships are not explicit in the 1944 Morris article, but they can be reconstructed from field notes and the subsequent investigations in the area.

Tree-rings provide clusters of precise cutting dates that indicate the time of construction of many pit houses (Table 3.1). The dates presented here have been carefully examined by Richard Ahlstrom (1985), who sorted out the effects of stock-piling timbers for later use, reusing old timbers, and repairing structures with new beams. Ahlstrom finds the collection of samples from Prayer Rock, especially Broken Flute Cave, to be exceptionally reliable for deriving construction dates, and his determinations do not differ in any significant way from those of Bannister and others (1966) and Elizabeth Morris (1980).

Dating the abandonment of these pit houses is not possible, but consensus among researchers using tree-ring evidence together with experimental and ethnoarchaeological methods is that any one pit house probably was not used for much longer than about 15 to 20 years (Ahlstrom 1985). Many of the Prayer Rock pit houses burned while in use and they may have been inhabited for even shorter spans of time.

Stratigraphic relationships among deposits in the Prayer Rock caves were not well recorded by today's

Table 3.1. Chronology of Prayer Rock District Sites with Sandals or Tree-ring Dates

Locality	Constructed in A.D.	Sandal Shapes
Broken Flute Cave		
Pit House 1	501, 508?	Burned, indeterminate
Pit House 2	499	None on floor, scalloped-square in fill (1)
Pit House 3	(505 noncutting)	None on floor, scalloped-square in fill (6)
Pit House 4	628	Scalloped-puckered (4); with La Plata Black-on-white pottery
Pit House 5	629	Round-puckered (3), scalloped-puckered
Pit House 6	623 or 624	Scalloped-puckered (19) and round-puckered (1); with La Plata Black-on-white pottery
Pit House 7	625 or 626	Round-puckered, scalloped-puckered child's sandal; with La Plata Black-on-white pottery
Below Pit House 7	No date	Scalloped-square
Pit House 8	625	Scalloped-puckered (1); round-puckered and scalloped-puckered in fill
Pit House 8A	494	None
Pit House 9	624	Round-puckered (2), scalloped-puckered (6); with La Plata Black-on-white pottery
Pit House 10	No date	Round-puckered (3), scalloped-puckered (6)
Pit House 11	625 or 635	Round-puckered "winter sandal" on floor; scalloped-puckered in fill
Pit House 12	623	None
Pit House 16	(about 500)	Scalloped-square (fill above); underlies great kiva
Pit House 17	489 or 605	Scalloped-square (fill above)
Cist 9	No date	Scalloped-square (1), scalloped-puckered (1), round-puckered (1)
Cists 6, 16, 20, 52	No date	Scalloped-puckered, round-puckered
Cist 44	No date	Braided whole-leaf yucca sandal, with Pueblo I pottery
Cist 57	No date	Scalloped-puckered (2) and round-puckered (1)
Cave 1		
Pit House 1	(657 noncutting)	Scalloped-puckered; with La Plata Black-on-white pottery
Pit House 3	(658 noncutting)	Sandals not described; with La Plata Black-on-white pottery
Cave 2		
Pit House 1	669	Sandals not described; with La Plata Black-on-white pottery
Pit House 2	669	Twined scalloped-puckered and round-puckered sandals, braided whole-leaf sandals; with La Plata Black-on-white pottery
Pit House 4	670	Sandals not described; with La Plata Black-on-white pottery
Cave 3	(646 noncutting)	Scalloped-square, scalloped-puckered, round-puckered
Cave 8	(668 noncutting)	Scalloped-puckered (1), possibly scalloped-square (1)
Cave 10	No date	Scalloped-puckered, round-puckered
Pocket Cave	(438 noncutting)	Scalloped-square. Later reoccupation, twined scalloped-puckered and braided whole-leaf sandals; with La Plata Black-on-white pottery
Obelisk Cave	470–489	Scalloped-square; with Obelisk Utility and Lino Gray pottery

NOTE: Numbers of sandals in parentheses are compiled from a combination of collections and excavation notes. Noncutting dates in parentheses indicate that outer tree-rings are missing and construction took place an unknown number of years after this date. Tree-ring dates are from Ahlstrom 1985.

expectations. By the standards of 1931, however, Earl Morris' notes and maps of Broken Flute Cave were excellent. Many instances of superpositioning of structures were recorded there, but no such information exists for most of the other sites in the district.

Broken Flute Cave contains strong evidence of two occupations and numerous episodes of reuse for storage only. Broken Flute Cave apparently sheltered at least three households around A.D. 500 (Fig. 3.1). The first occupation dates to the late 400s or early 500s and includes Pit Houses 1, 2, 8A, and probably 3, 16, and 17. No pottery was found in them. Ceramics were introduced to the area sometime in the 400s, but were not numerous and do not appear in all sites of that period.

According to Paul Reed of the Navajo Nation Archaeology Department, there is an apparent occupational

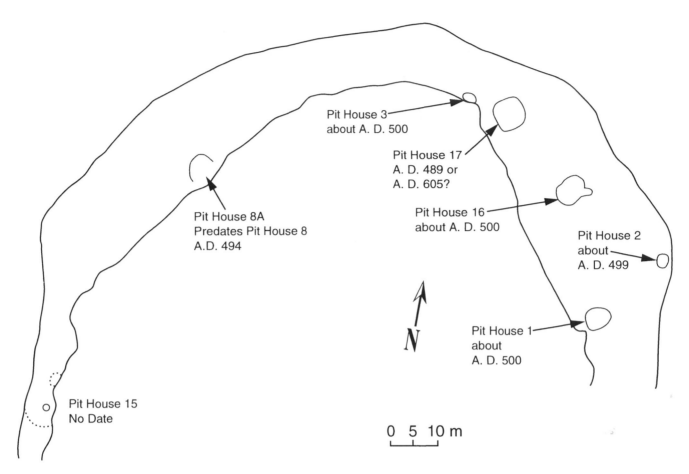

Figure 3.1. First pit house occupation of Broken Flute Cave. (Adapted from Elizabeth Ann Morris 1980, Fig. 5.)

hiatus in the Prayer Rock District, and the Red Rock Valley area in general, between A.D. 520 and 580 when the population was probably living in a different drainage system. The Zuni Archaeological Program excavated two Basketmaker III sites in the Red Rock Valley, east of Prayer Rock near the New Mexico border (Hildebrant 1989), and the Navajo Nation Archaeology Department excavated several sites on the Cove to Red Rock Valley (N33) road, about 7 km (4.4 miles) south and southeast of Broken Flute Cave (Reed and Wilcox 1996). Sites from both projects date to the Obelisk phase (A.D. 470–520) and the Broken Flute phase (A.D. 580–700). Sites belonging to both phases have structures similar to some of the architecture in Broken Flute Cave, Pocket Cave, Morris Cave 2, and sites in Canyon de Chelly (Hildebrant 1989: 638).

Between 7 to 12 households began moving into Broken Flute Cave in the year A.D. 623 (Ahlstrom 1985; Bannister and others 1966; E. A. Morris 1980). This second occupation is reliably dated with tree-rings. Some pit houses incorporate beams reused from the ear-

lier occupation, but most beams were cut between the years 623 and 629; the latest dates probably represent repairs.

Six, and possibly seven, pit houses were built in Broken Flute Cave between A.D. 623 and the winter of 625–626 (Fig. 3.2). Four pit houses were built in or after 628 and may represent additional families or replacements for pit houses that had burned. One pit house is undatable, but if contemporaneous would bring the total seventh-century population to 12 households. Most of the storage cists probably also date to this occupation, as well as the large, circular structure Earl Morris called a great kiva.

People may have started leaving shortly thereafter; three pit houses were abandoned and filled with trash, and three burned while in use and were filled with trash. One of these trash-filled houses, Pit House 11, appears to have been built in A.D. 625, remodeled in 635, abandoned sometime thereafter, and partly dismantled. The trash inside it, then, most likely dates after 635. There are four pit houses that were not trash-

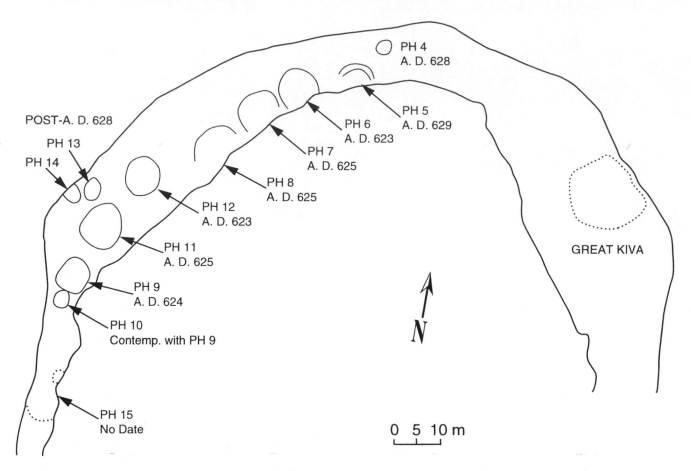

Figure 3.2. Second pit house occupation of Broken Flute Cave. (Adapted from Elizabeth Ann Morris 1980, Fig. 5.)

filled; they probably represent the last occupation of the cave. Their inhabitants must have contributed much of the trash in the abandoned pit houses. One of these late-used pit houses burned while in use, one was abandoned and then burned, and two were abandoned but not burned. The last tree-ring cutting date recorded is A.D. 652, but this sample was not recovered in a structure. No construction or repair is evident in the pit houses after 635, the latest cutting date in Pit House 11. It is likely, therefore, that this occupation of the cave lasted from 12 to 20 years.

ARTIFACT CONTEXTS

Pit houses that burned while in use contained many pottery vessels, coiled baskets, sandals, and textiles. Also preserved were joints of meat, corn and beans, and a wide variety of stone and wooden artifacts. Fire destroyed whatever designs existed on the baskets, textiles, and sandals that were in these pit houses when they burned. Decorated pottery survived, and most of the examples seem to have come from "in-use" assem-

blages. Much of the perishable material, including sandals, came from trash deposits in pit houses and cists or refuse near the surface and represent discarded items. Sometimes sandals were found near the base of the entry ladder, where Morris noted their charred remains but was unable to recover them intact. Apparently Basketmakers left their sandals on the roof or at the base of the ladder (Fig. 3.3) and entered their houses barefoot. Soot-blackened muddy footprints on the floor of a pit house in Pocket Cave are eerily personal testimony to this practice (Fig. 3.4). Notably well-preserved items unearthed where they were carefully stored were a whole basket full of turkey feathers cached below Pit House 8; two basket fragments; a bag; two women's string aprons; and some sandals in slab-lined cists (Cists 6, 16, and 20). Several sandals from pit house floors also escaped burning (Fig. 3.5).

In general, dates from the other Prayer Rock caves were reported by site only and not by individual structure. Pit houses and cists were present in all sites except Obelisk Cave, which may have held only cists. Still, datable wooden beams and sandals were collected from

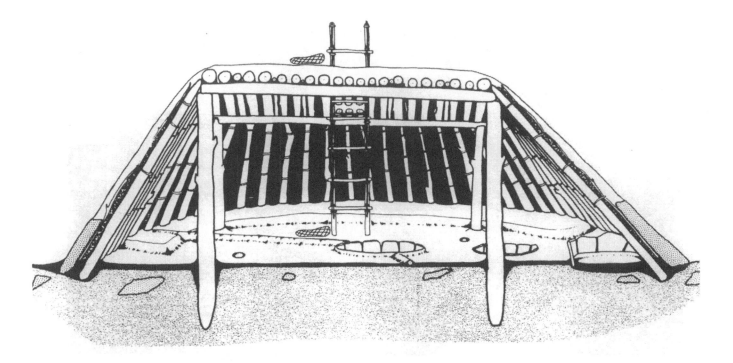

Figure 3.3. Reconstruction of a pit house with sandals piled on the roof and near the ladder base. The drawing by Elizabeth Ann Morris has been computer scanned, with sandals added.

Figure 3.4. Burned muddy footprints on the floor of a pit house in Pocket Cave. (Photo by Earl H. Morris; Arizona State Museum Neg. 5988.)

Figure 3.5. Intact round toe–puckered heel sandal near the juncture
of the roof and bench in a burned pit house in Broken Flute Cave.
(Photo by Earl H. Morris; Arizona State Museum Neg. 6329.)

many of these sites and information about association
with particular kinds of sandals at different time periods
corroborates the Broken Flute Cave evidence.

SANDAL CHRONOLOGY

How well does the Morris sandal chronology correlate with stratigraphic and tree-ring evidence? The
Prayer Rock District collections, excavation records,
and tree-ring analysis suggest the following relationships
between chronology and sandal morphology. To inte-
grate these comments with the standard terminology
used in the rest of this book, I illustrate in Figure 3.6
a simple classification scheme for Basketmaker twined
sandals based on the shape of the toe and the heel.
Morris' "early" Basketmaker III sandals are termed
"scalloped–square" because they have scallop-shaped
toes and square heels. His "middle" and "late" types
are described as "scalloped–puckered" and "round–

puckered." One reason for this change is to provide
terms that coincide with the shape of the footwear.
Secondly, as we later explain, Morris' "late" sandals
are not necessarily any later than the "middle" ones.

The Morrises' assertion that scalloped–square sandals
dated earlier than scalloped–puckered ones seems
sound. There is evidence that scalloped–square sandals
predate A.D. 600 and that scalloped–puckered twined
sandals were the dominant type of the 600s. Scalloped–
square twined sandals were the only kind of footwear
recovered from Obelisk Cave, where tree-ring cutting
dates range from A.D. 470 to 489. Scalloped–square
sandals also came from Broken Flute Cave, in refuse
filling two early-occupation rooms. Pit House 2 had a
beam with a cutting date of 499, and Pit House 3 yielded a single noncutting date of 505. These kinds of sandals also appeared on the surface in the great kiva,
which overlay the undated but aceramic Pit House 16;
in the fill of Pit House 16; in Cist 9; and in mixed de-

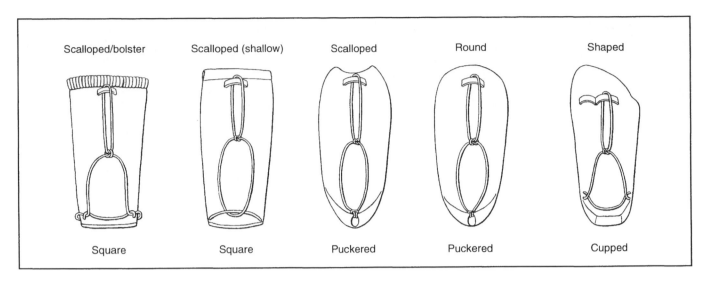

Figure 3.6. Classification of twined Basketmaker sandals by toe shape (*top*) and heel shape (*bottom*).

posits where they were sometimes associated with later types. Such a mixture results from later occupants churning up trash left by earlier inhabitants, mixing in their own debris.

Scalloped–square sandals appeared in two sites that also contained later sandals, Pocket Cave and Cave 3. Pocket Cave had a single noncutting date of A.D. 438, indicating it could have been used sometime in the later 400s. The early sandals were not associated with the pit houses, which architecturally and ceramically resembled those dated to the 600s in Broken Flute Cave and which contained scalloped–puckered sandals. In this case, scalloped–square sandals were probably deposited in the late 400s, when at least one structure was constructed in Pocket Cave. Later, probably in the 600s, traces of that structure were wiped out and the old beams were recycled in building a new one.

Both scalloped–square and scalloped–puckered sandals came from Cave 3, which yielded a single non-cutting date of A.D. 646. No traces of earlier structures appeared in this tree-ring assemblage, but the scalloped–square sandals found in mixed trash suggested that this cave had an earlier Basketmaker III occupation as well as the later one indicated by the tree-rings. Unfortunately, excavation notes for this site are meager, and perhaps were lost, but this example shows how the Morris sandal chronology can provide archaeologists with an additional line of evidence for site dating.

All the sites with occupations that dated in the A.D. 600s from which sandals were described contained scalloped–puckered sandals. Broken Flute Cave, Cave 2,

Cave 3, and Cave 8 are dated by tree-rings, and the style of pottery in Pocket Cave suggests it was re-occupied in the 600s. Scalloped–puckered sandals were also found in undated Ram's Horn Cave and Cave 10.

Scalloped–square and scalloped–puckered sandals appeared together in only a few Broken Flute Cave proveniences: in mixed trash behind Pit House 8 (built in A.D. 625 over an earlier structure, probably dredging up old trash in the process) and in refuse above Pit House 2 (built in A.D. 499 and probably only partly filled in, leaving a handy depression for later inhabitants to fill with trash). Cist 9 contained a scalloped-square, a scalloped-puckered, and a round-puckered sandal. In most of the Broken Flute Cave deposits and in Pocket Cave, scalloped-square and scalloped-puckered sandals were not found in association.

In summary, scalloped–square and scalloped-puck-ered sandals were recovered together only in excavations where two temporally separate occupations were present, or at least plausibly present, and scalloped–square sandals were the only type at the single-component site of Obelisk Cave. Although contemporaneity of the two sandal types cannot be ruled out completely, the evidence indicates that scalloped–square sandals date at least to the A.D. 400s and probably 500s, and scalloped–puckered sandals date to the 600s.

Although Earl Morris called round-puckered twined sandals "Late Basketmaker III," and in the first manu-script Ann Axtell Morris called them "Prepueblo," the evidence from the Prayer Rock District does not show that round-puckered sandals replaced scalloped–puckered ones. Sandal assemblages that clearly date to the A.D. 600s because they were deposited in structures that were tree-ring dated to that century contain varying proportions of the two types. The production of round–puckered twined sandals clearly overlaps with the production of scalloped–puckered twined sandals. When the two types are associated, there are always far fewer round–puckered sandals than scalloped–puckered ones. The proportion of round–puckered sandals does not appear to increase in structures with late construction dates.

Scalloped–puckered and round–puckered sandals occurred together in Broken Flute Cave Cists 6, 16, 20, 52, and 57; in fill over Pit Houses 5, 7, 8, and 9; and in Pit Houses 8, and 10. In Pit House 11 a round–puckered sandal was on the floor and a scalloped-puckered sandal was recovered from fill. A round–puckered sandal was on the floor of Pit House 7, and a child's scalloped–puckered sandal was on the bench of the same structure. Round–puckered sandals came from Caves 3 and 10, which also contained scalloped–puckered sandals. Round-puckered sandals did not appear by themselves in any context.

Morris' placement of round–puckered sandals after scalloped–puckered ones is possible, but supporting evidence must come from some other area. More information is needed on sandals in pit houses dating after the A.D. 630s. There is no demonstrable increase in the proportion of round–puckered sandals between the occupation of Broken Flute Cave in the 630s and the occupation of Cave 8 around 670, because only two sandals were reported from Cave 8 and neither is round–puckered. (One is scalloped-puckered; one is scalloped-square and probably indicates an earlier habitation there.) Occupation of rockshelters in the area ends by about 700. Archaeologists do not yet know if round–puckered sandals eventually increased in popularity and replaced scalloped–puckered sandals, as Morris proposed, or if round–puckered sandals were simply a variant and contemporaneous style throughout the seventh century.

Finally, undecorated braided yucca leaf sandals probably postdate the Basketmaker III occupation of the Prayer Rock sites. The few recorded specimens could all date to Pueblo I through Pueblo III use of the caves for storage, but there are no absolute dates associated with these sandals. A small number of them could plausibly have been in use at almost any time, but none occur in well-dated Basketmaker contexts such as pit house floors. As we shall see, braided leaf sandals would have been far less time-consuming to make than twined sandals. Shifts through time in the proportions of the different kinds of sandals made and used eventually may tell us a great deal about changes in the lives of Basketmaker and Pueblo people.

CHAPTER FOUR

Prehistoric Puebloan Footwear

Ann Cordy Deegan

Sandals are only one solution to the problem of protecting the human foot from hazards such as sharp rocks, gravel, cold mud, hot sand, thorns, stickers, burrs, and substances most unsanitary. Through the centuries, this purpose was filled by various kinds of footgear. At the time of European contact, Native people of the American Southeast, Pacific Northwest, and Caribbean spent most of their time barefoot. Seri people of the Sonoran coast walked barefoot on hot sand until their feet calloused into the so-called "Seri boot." Arctic peoples developed hard-soled boots (Wissler 1950). Soft-soled moccasins, together with snowshoes in winter, were favored in the Subarctic, Northeast, and northern prairie regions. The hard-sole moccasin appeared in the Great Basin and Plains (Driver and Massey 1957). Most Puebloans wore such hard-sole moccasins at the time of the Spanish contact, but archaeological finds like the footwear described in this volume show that sandals were most common from the Archaic period to an unknown time between the fourteenth and sixteenth centuries A.D. Use of sandals extended from the Southwest through Mesoamerica and south to Chile (Driver and Massey 1957: 329, Map 116; Wissler 1950: 63, Fig. 20).

Sandals appear in the traditional dress of peoples in many parts of the world, but New World sandals have a unique feature: the toe ties usually enclose more than one toe, often the second and third toes, as reported for the Basketmaker examples described herein. Old World thong toe ties, as seen in ancient Egyptian examples, emerge between the first and second toe. Europeans brought their thong tie sandals to the New World, and this form replaced the traditional toe loop (Mason 1896: 310, 319–320, 361–365).

Mesoamerican artisans made leather and fiber sandals, but favored leather at the time of the Spanish Conquest. Fibrous sandals were overwhelmingly dominant in the Southwest. Some were made simply, of braided whole leaves, yarn in plain weave, or what appear to be fiber mats stitched together. These types were frequent in the Hohokam area (Fulton 1941: 25–29, 31–33, Figs. 4, 5, 6; Haury 1950: 433–439, Plates 44–46). Classic Mimbres Mogollon pottery, dating about A.D. 1000–1150, shows men and women wearing sandals (Shaffer and others 1997). The depictions probably represent sandals made of braided yucca leaves or plain weave sandals, the most frequent types of footwear recovered from dry sites of this region (Cosgrove 1947: 82–90; Martin and others 1952: 266–276, 294–295). The Basketmaker twined sandals described here are among the most complicated and labor-intensive sandals known anywhere.

Leather sandals also appear in early Southwest assemblages, but rarely. Moccasins, too, are rare in prehistoric Puebloan sites, but date as early as the Basketmaker II period and appear in southern Utah, northern Arizona (Ambler 1968: 74–77; Guernsey 1931: 52, 66–68, Fig. 20, Plate 47f), and southwestern Colorado (Fewkes 1909: 51, Fig. 37; Nordenskiöld 1979: 102, Plate 46–4). Puebloan people, then, knew how to make leather moccasins, leather sandals, and fibrous sandals, but the overwhelming proportion of fibrous sandals in their houses and trash middens show this is the footgear they favored.

Why, then, did the art of making fibrous sandals decline and all but disappear sometime between about A.D. 1300 and 1540? The archaeological evidence for footwear from this period is meager, but we do know that trade between Rio Grande Pueblo farmers and bison-hunting Plains peoples increased during this interval. Western Pueblo people, such as Hopi, Zuni, and Acoma, obtained bison hides by trading with Rio Grande people. Some early Puebloan moccasins preserve prehistoric sandal features. Earlier Puebloan hide and fiber sandals that had side-loop ties pulled the sandal edges up as their lacings attached up and over the foot. This upturned sole edge, from earlier sandals, is a feature preserved in later Puebloan moccasins. The moccasin leather upper was stitched to this hard up-turned sole, suggesting that moccasin makers based their new designs on the already familiar sandal (Hatt 1916; Salwen 1960: 225–226), rather than adopting a whole new design from the Plains. New materials, then, rather than new designs, seem to have inspired the change.

At no time before was durable leather so easy to obtain (Salwen 1960). Antelope and mountain sheep, the large-game prey of earlier Puebloan peoples, including the Basketmakers, have smaller, thinner hides and were not always plentiful or easy to hunt. It is possible, then, that the often time-consuming art of twined sandal making gave way to market forces; once leather was readily available, perhaps moccasins were easier to make. Still, braided leaf sandals, the dominant type in the A.D. 1200s, should have been even quicker and easier to produce. We shall probably never know what other forces were involved in their replacement. Did leather take longer to wear out? Did the hard-sole moccasins protect the foot better than sandals? Did changing aesthetics play a role? Whether it happened in a generation or gradually over several centuries, the art of twined sandal making disappeared. Some kind of yucca fiber or leaf sandal is still known to Hopi elders, however. The Hopi name is *moototsi,* "shoe made of yucca." Hopi people say their ancestors, the *Hisatsinom,* wore sandals, and *Maasaw,* the deity of death, fire, and the earth surface is said to wear them still (Hopi Dictionary Project 1997).

FOOTWEAR AND FUNCTION
Kelley Ann Hays-Gilpin

The Basketmaker twined sandal would have provided excellent foot protection and comfort in several ways. The extra thickness of the doubled-warp toe protected the front of the foot from thorns and bruises. Few holes were worn in this area, but the toe loop often pulled loose, breaking the colored wefts and producing ragged holes. The 2/2 twill twining over four or two warps provided fewer interlacing points than did plain weave, in which each weft crossed one warp. As a result, twill-twined sandals were more flexible than plain weave ones, and this flexible construction was placed under the toes and ball of the foot, just where the foot needs to bend when walking or running. The raised sole designs extending under the ball of the foot provided traction in climbing rocky slopes or muddy trails. Twined sandals,

like today's rubber soles, were soft and pliable; they deformed under pressure to grip hard surfaces like the expanses of red slickrock surrounding the Basketmakers' rockshelter homes.

A recent study by the American Society for Testing and Materials (Wilson 1990: 122) recommended features for slip-resistant soles that included rounded and patterned heels, not unlike that of the late Basketmaker sandals. Sole patterns of channels and cleats should cover the heel and as much of the rest of the shoe surface as possible. Patterns should include leading edges in many directions to reduce slipping in more than one direction. Basketmaker sandal sole patterns have raised and recessed areas oriented in several directions, and they include many "leading edges," such as several series of short ribs filling spaces between diagonal ridges. Raised areas also provided extra padding for heels, but heels nonetheless showed the heaviest signs of abrasion and often bore gaping holes. Sandal midsections were the most likely to bear colored decoration and the least likely to wear out. Construction techniques used in the midsection served no apparent functional purpose other than to incorporate detailed decoration into the sandal. All in all, Basketmaker sandals seem over-engineered for the primary purpose of protecting the foot, suggesting to us that these sandals are about more than walking and running. The subsequent switch to leather footwear meant the abandonment of an art form that provided much beauty to the lives of prehistoric Native Americans.

Basketmaker sandal construction techniques are notably complicated and were probably learned by watching a skilled person at work, not by simply examining a sandal obtained in trade or found discarded on a trail. Thus far, each sandal is unique, and researchers have detected almost no flaws. Sandal makers must have invested many hours in learning their craft and in practicing it.

Before beginning to twine a sandal, the maker had to gather long leaves from wild yucca plants and soften their fleshy tissue (parenchymal tissue) by soaking, boiling, baking, or pounding the leaves. Fibers had to be removed from softened leaves by scraping or perhaps chewing (although chewing yucca leaves has an emetic effect on the chewer and chewing tends to tangle fibers). For narrow diameter yarns, fibers were probably combed to remove tangles and to break down fiber bundles into thinner elements. The artisans were skilled spinners; yarns are evenly spun, tightly twisted, and often 2–plied or 3–plied. Picture a woman in the firelight, after a hard day's work, arranging two handfuls of yucca fiber, simultaneously rolling them up her thigh (Z–twist), then twisting them together and rolling them down the thigh (S–twist) for a 2–ply yarn. The 3–ply yarns required more skill, and would have been rolled as three clusters up the thigh to form singles and then plied. She repeats this process every evening until she has the nearly 7 meters (22 feet) of 3–ply warp and 28 meters (90 feet) of 2–ply weft yarn needed to make a single sandal. Even after spinning her yarn, our artisan may have had to prepare at least three dyes, perhaps three dyes and a bleach, dye the yarns, and plan out, at least in the mind's eye, up to three different symmetrical designs. Each artisan may have mastered as many as 21 different textile techniques during Basketmaker times.

An increase in elaboration of the design element and symmetry repertoire and an increase in the proportion of sandals that had colored decoration suggest an advancement in technical and artistic skill among sandal makers from Basketmaker II to the late Basketmaker III period. This time trend, together with an increasing standardization of color use and design placement, hints that fewer artisans were making more sandals, that craft specialization on some scale appeared in the Basketmaker economy. Craft specialists in nonmonetary economies are people who make more of an item than can be used by their own household in order to trade for basic subsistence resources, such as agricultural produce, game, and firewood. Craft specialization provides new roles for some individuals, roles that can enhance prestige, economic status, and connections, via trade, with individuals in other communities. Specialization is "social labor" that enriches, empowers, and creates social ties and networks (Costin 1996).

TYPES OF TWINED SANDALS
Ann Cordy Deegan

This brief overview of prehistoric Puebloan fibrous sandal types provides perspective on the specific Prayer Rock District sandal styles that are discussed in Chapters 5 and 6. These sandals date from about 500 B.C. to A.D. 1300. The chronological chain begins, however, with the early Archaic sandals (dating around 8030 to 5440 B.C.) recovered in areas that the prehistoric Puebloan people later occupied. Sandal and textile terminology is based on Emery (1980) and Deegan (1993) and is presented in Table 2.2 and Figure 2.1.

Archaic Twined Sandals

Archaic open twined sandals represent the earliest known twined footwear found in the area inhabited by the prehistoric Puebloans. These fragile appearing constructions (Fig. 4.1) consist of yucca leaves bent double at the toe, with six to ten total warps (Fig. 4.2). Four to six rows of widely spaced weft-twining extend down the sandal from the toe toward the heel (Fig. 4.2; Ambler 1968: 93). Ties are side-loops created by extending each row of weft twining out beyond the sandal edge before turning back to create the next row of body twining. To make these open structures useable as sandals, they were padded with grasses or juniper bark (Fig. 4.1; Ambler 1968: 94). The long side loops then were pulled up and over the foot with a lacing cord threaded through the loops to secure the sandal. Ambler (1968: 93–97, 117–119) and Geib (1995: 8–9, Figs. 1, 3) discuss Archaic open twined sandals in more detail.

Eleven sandals, from seven Archaic sites, have been dated by radiocarbon. The range of dates is from about 8030 to 5440 B.C., the early Archaic period (Geib 1995: 9, Fig. 3; Smiley and Robins 1997). Archaic sandals have been reported as far north as Rock Bar Alcove (near Green River in Utah), south to Atlatl Rock Cave (at the edge of Rainbow Plateau), east to Old Man Cave (Comb Wash, Utah), with a western boundary roughly following the Colorado River up into Utah (see Fig. 1.4; Geib 1995: 8, Fig. 1). It is in these dry rock-shelters with favorable preservation conditions that the Archaic open twined sandals survived; their original distribution was probably much wider.

High Density Twined Sandals

The twined, high density, yucca yarn sandals appearing at varying times within the Basketmaker II through Pueblo III periods (about 500 B.C. to A.D. 1300) are classified into five types. Herein, each type has been named for its combined toe and heel silhouettes, with the toe silhouette given first. For example, a twined sandal with a square toe and a square heel is called a square–square sandal. Earl Morris found sandals representing three of these five twined types in the Prayer Rock District: scalloped–square, scalloped–puckered, and round–puckered. These types are described in detail in Chapters 5 and 6.

High density twined sandal geographic distribution is presented here and is based on current literature and laboratory findings. Some sandal features could not be verified from the literature for each sandal so these data serve as an estimate of geographic distribution. There still remain other sandals in collections and mentioned in unpublished field reports that will aid in broadening our knowledge of the geographic distribution of prehistoric Puebloan twined sandals.

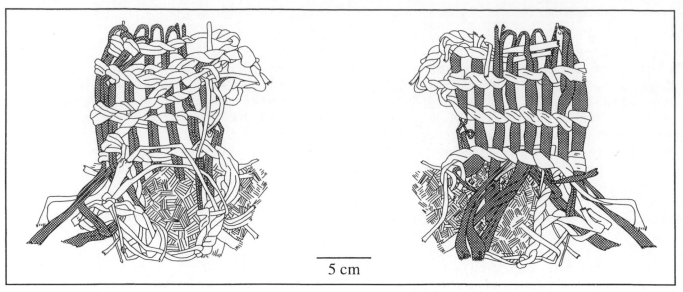

Figure 4.1. Top (*left*) and sole view of an Archaic open twined sandal. Cross-hatching represents sandal padding that probably extended over the entire sandal top when worn. Sandal length is 24 cm. Conventional ^{14}C age is 7590 ± 60 Beta 95281. (Edge of the Cedars Museum, Blanding, Utah: ECPR–96014; from Smiley and Robins 1997.)

Figure 4.2. Section of an Archaic open twined sandal. (Ambler 1968: 97, Fig. 76; reprinted with permission from The Northern Arizona Society of Science and Art.)

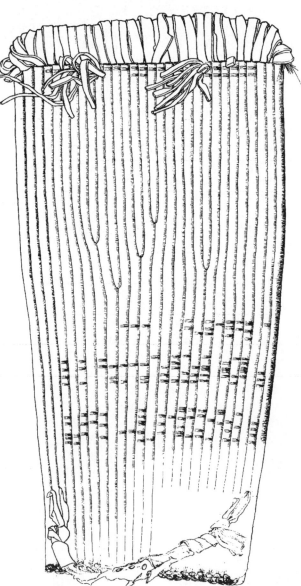

Figure 4.3. Square toe–square heel twined sandal with bolster toe, top view. Sandal length is 23.5 cm. A photograph of this sandal is in Deegan 1996, Fig. 2. (Broken Roof Cave, Sandal 72506–B.)

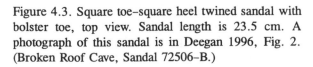

→

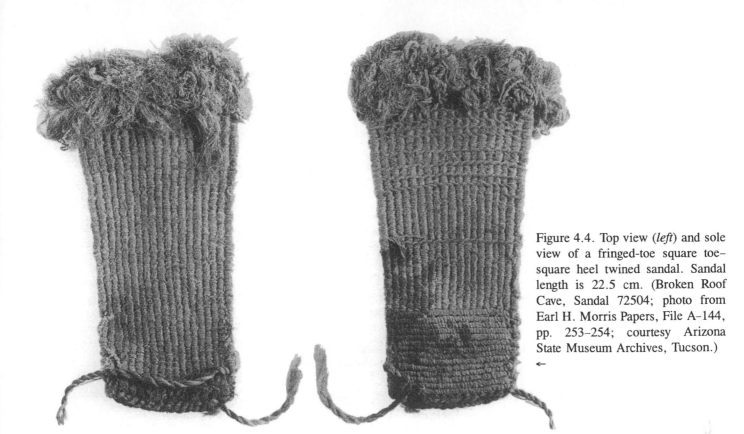

Figure 4.4. Top view (*left*) and sole view of a fringed-toe square toe–square heel twined sandal. Sandal length is 22.5 cm. (Broken Roof Cave, Sandal 72504; photo from Earl H. Morris Papers, File A–144, pp. 253–254; courtesy Arizona State Museum Archives, Tucson.) ←

Square Toe–Square Heel Sandal Type
(Basketmaker II Period)

The Basketmaker II period (about 500 B.C. to A.D. 400) twined sandal often has a fringe and sometimes a bolster toe of leather or fiber that does not occur on later sandals. The heel is square and flat (Figs. 4.3, 4.4). The body silhouette is a tapered rectangle, wider at the toe but without left or right foot shaping. The sole reveals patternless cross-wise raised tread lines. When colors are present, they are limited to black and red, and the few motifs are simple geometrics. Twining, wrapping, or complicated combinations of these two techniques create the raised tread. Nonraised portions of these sandals, between the raised rows, are either plain weave or simple weft twining. Leather, hair, or yucca yarn ties form a toe-heel fastening system with a toe loop over the second and third toes, ankle and heel loops, and a long cord connecting the toe loop to the ankle loop. Figure 4.5 is a later, round toe sandal, but it clearly illustrates this toe-heel tie system.

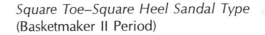

Figure 4.5. Toe-heel tie system on a round toe–puckered heel twined sandal, top view. Sandal length is 26.0 cm. (Sandal 113–C; photo by Elizabeth Ann Morris, Arizona State Museum Neg. 6066.) ←

[41]

Table 4.1. Basketmaker II Period Square Toe–Square Heel Twined Sandals

Location	Sandals n = 52	Sources
Broken Roof Cave, AZ	7	Earl Morris Papers, Arizona State Museum, Files A–136, A–144
		Guernsey 1931: 66, Plates 29e, 47d
Canyon del Muerto, AZ Tsea-hot-tso (Big Cave)	2	Earl Morris Papers, Arizona State Museum, Files A–143, A–144, A–145a, b
Kayenta area, AZ, Marsh Pass		
White Dog Cave	3	Guernsey and Kidder 1921: 15, 19
	1	Guernsey 1931, Plate 47g
Sunflower Cave	1	Kidder and Guernsey 1919, Plate 68b, c
	1	Guernsey and Kidder 1921: 3
Cave I	2	Kidder and Guernsey 1919: Plates 68d, 69a, b
Tseyi-Hatsosi Canyon, AZ	6	Guernsey 1931: 28, Plates 29a, b, d
	4	Guernsey and Kidder 1921: 36–38
	4	Cummings 1910: 14; Cummings 1953: 108–109
Grand Gulch, UT	11	Earl Morris Papers, Arizona State Museum, File A–144
	1	Deegan lab notes: Museum of Northern Arizona 12650.GSQ 23.7
Kanab area, UT		
Du Pont Cave	8	Nusbaum and others 1922: 73–79, Plates 36–39
Kanab Canyon	1	Kankainen 1995: 90 (Utah Museum of Natural History 8093)

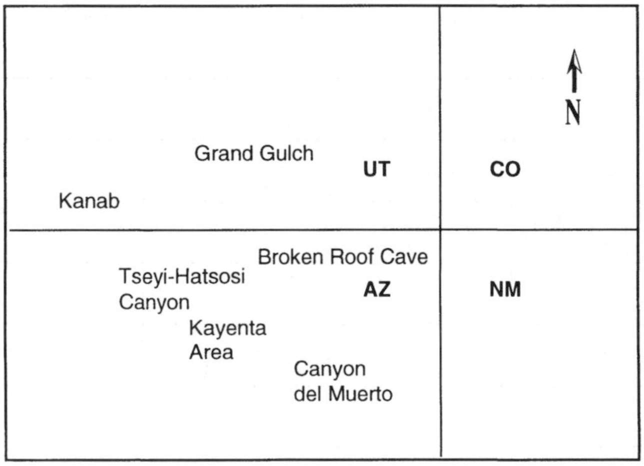

Figure 4.6. Schematic distribution of Basketmaker II square toe–square heel twined sandals.

The distribution of sites with square-square twined sandals centers on northeastern Arizona and southeastern Utah (Table 4.1, Fig. 4.6). Many of these sites date to the Basketmaker II period, such as Broken Roof Cave and White Dog Cave. No square-square twined sandals were found in the Prayer Rock District excavations.

Additional information on the square-square twined sandal type is in Deegan (1996), Guernsey (1931: 28, 66, Plates 29a, b, d, e and 47d, g), Kidder and Guernsey (1919: 159–160, Plates 68b, c, d, and 69a, b; their Basketmaker Type IIIb), Nusbaum and others (1922: 75, 79–80), and Talge (1995: 44–47).

Scalloped Toe–Square Heel Sandal Type
(Early Basketmaker III Period)

A change in toe appearance and in toe construction technique arises in the next sandal type, the Basketmaker III scalloped-square sandal, dating late in the A.D. 400s (Fig. 4.7). Like the Basketmaker II square-square twined footwear, this sandal has a flat, square heel and a body silhouette not shaped to the foot, but the toe is now scalloped (a concave indentation). Some symmetrical tapering from toe to heel does appear as early as Basketmaker II (see Fig. 4.3). During Basketmaker III, the raised sole of many sandals acquired geometric patterning (Fig. 4.8), instead of the patternless raised corrugation of the Basketmaker II square-square sandal. Some of the same raised construction techniques (see Figs. 5.9a1b, 5.9a2a, 5.9a2b) continued in use from the Basketmaker II era, but now the sandal maker had to visualize the raised sole design be-

Figure 4.7. Scalloped toe–square heel twined sandal, top view. Sandal length is 21.5 cm. (Sandal 803–D; photo by Elizabeth Ann Morris; Arizona State Museum Neg. 6066.)

Figure 4.8. Scalloped toe–square heel twined sandal with geometric raised sole, sole view. Portion is 22.5 cm long. (Sandal 41; photo by Elizabeth Ann Morris; Arizona State Museum Neg. 6092.)

fore or during sandal construction while manipulating the many yarns required to produce the raised sole: truly a skilled task!

The nonraised sandal areas, between the raised rows, are plain weave, simple weft twining, or both. More and larger areas are often covered with color motifs and additional, different construction techniques are introduced. The former toe-heel tie system continues in use but now the side-loop system is more prevalent than in Basketmaker II times. Figure 4.9 is a later, round-toe sandal, but it illustrates this side-loop tie system; it consists of a series of loops attached to the sandal sides with a cord laced through these loops up and over the top of the foot.

Additional information on the scalloped-square twined sandal type is in Elizabeth Morris (1980: 116–117; her Class A, Type 1) and Talge (1995: 48–54, 55).

The distribution of scalloped-square sandals is more restricted than that of square-square sandals. They have been recovered only from the Prayer Rock District and Canyon del Muerto (Table 4.2, Fig. 4.10).

Table 4.2. Basketmaker III Period Scalloped Toe–Square Heel Twined Sandals

Location	Sandals n = 59	Sources
Canyon del Muerto, AZ	9	Earl Morris Papers, Arizona State Museum, File A–143: 7–11, 14–15, 18, 26–27
	1	Earl Morris 1925: 300
	1	Amsden 1949: 54, Fig. 7
Prayer Rock District, AZ	48	Earl Morris Papers, Arizona State Museum (see Chapter 5 in this book)
		Elizabeth Ann Morris 1980: 116, 117, Figs. 76b–c, 77b (her Class A Type 1)

Figure 4.9. Side-loop tie system on a round toe–puckered heel twined sandal, top view. Sandal length is 26.4 cm. (Photo by Ken Matesich; Arizona State Museum Neg. 99790.)

The "Burial" sandal mentioned in the Ann Morris manuscript (Chapter 2, pp. 22, 23) is a construction variant of the scalloped-square sandal (see Fig. 5.3). It has the same toe and heel silhouettes and raised sole patterning, but reveals colorful geometric patterning over most of the sandal surface rather than in the more limited areas of other scalloped-square sandals. Construction techniques appear to be similar to those of the Basketmaker II period. Ann Morris (Chapter 2, p. 22) felt that this was a "ceremonial survival of Basket Maker [II] methods," because the sandals had been "found solely upon burials" in Canyon del Muerto. Ann Morris noted that the "Burial" sandal occurs throughout the time spans of the scalloped-square and scalloped-puckered twined sandals (during the A.D. 400–600s). The three Prayer Rock District scalloped–square sandals of the "burial" type (see Chapter 5) were discovered after Ann Morris' study and were not found with burials. Therefore, care must be taken not to assume that they all come from burials or that this type of sandal was made specifically as an offering for the dead.

UT	CO
AZ Prayer Rock District Canyon del Muerto	NM

Figure 4.10. Schematic distribution of Basketmaker III scalloped toe–square heel twined sandals.

Scalloped Toe–Puckered Heel Sandal Type
(Late Basketmaker III Period)

Another type of twined sandal appears late in the Basketmaker III period (A.D. 600s), again with a scalloped toe and no right or left foot shaping, but now with a different heel construction, the puckered heel (Fig. 4.11). The square, flat heel edges of the sandal were pulled together into a puckered heel that cradled the back of the foot. Colors, motifs, tie systems, and patterned raised constructions continued much as in the scalloped-square sandals, but with larger sandal surface areas covered by colored motifs. Several new color motif construction techniques appear during this period.

Scalloped-puckered sandals are recorded in greater numbers (Table 4.3) than are other types of prehistoric Puebloan twined sandals. We do not know whether this abundance represents favorable preservation and excavation conditions or, in fact, production of larger quantities of these sandals. Scalloped-puckered sandals appear in more sites than do the other twined sandal types (18 sites versus 2 to 10 sites; Fig. 4.12, Table 4.3).

Additional information about the scalloped-puckered twined sandal type is in Baldwin (1938: 467–479, 482–484, Plates 6, 7; 1939: 224–234, Plate 1; his Type 4), Deegan (1992, 1997), Kidder (1926), Earl Morris (1944a: 240), Elizabeth Morris (1980: 116–118; her Class A, Type 2), Nordenskiöld (1979, Plate 46–6), Rohn (1977: 227–229), and Talge (1995: 48–54, 55).

Round Toe–Puckered Heel Sandal Type
(Late Basketmaker III Period)

The round-puckered sandal marks another toe construction change (Figs. 4.5, 4.9). This kind of sandal apparently coexisted with the scalloped-puckered sandal, at least in the Prayer Rock area (A.D. 600s). The distinctive, symmetrically round toe, not shaped to the right or left foot, is attached to a sandal that still possesses a puckered heel. Although colored motifs are sometimes present on round-puckered sandals, they appear to be used less frequently. Types of motifs, colors, tie systems, patterned and nonpatterned raised sole constructions, and color motif structures continue from prior periods.

Round-puckered sandals appear in fewer sites than square-square, scalloped-puckered, or shaped-cupped sandals and are distributed mainly in northeastern Arizona (Table 4.4, Fig. 4.13), including the Prayer Rock District.

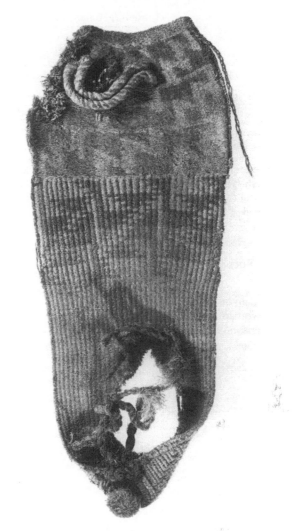

Figure 4.11. Scalloped toe–puckered heel twined sandal, top view. Sandal length is 24.0 cm. (Sandal 280–A; photo by Ken Matesich; Arizona State Museum Neg. 99791.)

	Alkali Ridge		
Cotton-wood Wash	**UT**	**CO** Lone Pine	Mesa Verde
Waterfall Ruin	**AZ** Prayer Rock District	**NM**	↑ N
Tseyi-Hatsosi Canyon			
Tsegi Canyon	Vandal Cave		
Kayenta Area	Deer Track Canyon		Tohatchi
	Canyon del Muerto		
	Black Creek		

Figure 4.12. Schematic distribution of Basketmaker III scalloped toe–puckered heel twined sandals.

Table 4.3. Basketmaker III Period Scalloped Toe–Puckered Heel Twined Sandals

Location	Sandals n = 274+	Sources
Black Creek, northeastern AZ	3	Deegan lab notes: Museum of Northern Arizona 5010.10B, 5010.61, 5010.62
Canyon del Muerto, AZ	2	Earl Morris 1925: 300
	5	Earl Morris Papers, Arizona State Museum, File A–143: 19–25
Kayenta area, AZ		
Marsh Pass: Cave 1	6	Guernsey 1931: Plates 9 and 47
Northeastern AZ* Marsh Pass, Kayenta area Vandal Cave and Deer Track Canyon in the Lukachukai Mountains Tseyi-Hatsosi Canyon	71	Baldwin 1938: 467–479, 482–484, Plates 6 and 7; Baldwin 1939: 224–234, Plate 1 (his Type 4)
Prayer Rock District, AZ	102	Earl Morris Papers, Arizona State Museum (see Chapter 5 of this book) Elizabeth Ann Morris 1980: 116–118 (her Class A Type 2)
Tsegi Canyon, AZ		
Batwoman Cave	1	Deegan lab notes: Utah Museum of Natural History 2845.1
Betatakin	1	Deegan lab notes: Utah Museum of Natural History 2847
Kiet Siel	1	Deegan lab notes: Utah Museum of Natural History 2519.352
Tseyi-Hatsosi Canyon, AZ	12	Cummings 1910: 10, 11; Cummings 1953: 109
	28	Deegan 1992; Deegan 1997 (some of the 28 may be duplicates of Cummings' 12)
	"many"	Guernsey 1931: 26
	2	Deegan lab notes: Museum of Northern Arizona A501, A502
Waterfall Ruin, AZ	1	Guernsey 1931: Plate 57b
Lone Pine, southwestern CO	2	Webster 1995: 1
Mesa Verde, CO		
Step House	1	Nordenskiöld 1979, Plate 46–6
Fewkes Canyon	1	Rohn 1977: 227–228, 229 (Fig. 83)
Tohatchi, NM	33	Webster 1996b: 10
Alkali Ridge, UT	1	Kankainen 1995: 33 (Utah Museum of Natural History AR328 85.1)
Cottonwood Wash, UT	1	Kankainen 1995: 66 (Utah Museum of Natural History 7169)

*Baldwin did not differentiate the number of sandals by each site, so all sites possible are listed.

Table 4.4. Basketmaker III Period Round Toe–Puckered Heel Twined Sandals

Location	Sandals n = 49	Sources
Prayer Rock District, AZ	38	Earl Morris Papers, Arizona State Museum (see Chapter 5 of this book) Elizabeth Ann Morris 1980: 117–118 (her Class A Type 3)
Northeastern Arizona* Marsh Pass, Kayenta area Vandal Cave and Deer Track Canyon in the Lukachukai Mountains Tseyi-Hatsosi Canyon	11	Baldwin 1938: 479–481, 484, Plates 6 and 7; Baldwin 1939: 234–236, Plate 1 (his Type 5)

*Baldwin did not differentiate the number of sandals by each site, so all sites possible are listed.

	UT	CO ↑N
Tseyi-Hatsosi Canyon	AZ Prayer Rock District	NM
Kayenta Area	Vandal Cave	
	Deer Track Canyon	

Figure 4.13. Schematic distribution of Basketmaker III round toe–puckered heel twined sandals.

Additional information about the round-puckered twined sandal type is in Baldwin (1938: 479–481, 484, Plates 6, 7; 1939: 234–236, Plate 1; his Type 5), Earl Morris (1944a: 240), Elizabeth Morris (1980: 117–118; her Class A, Type 3), and Talge (1995: 54, 56–60).

Shaped Toe - Cupped Heel Sandal Type (Pueblo Period)

A change to right and left foot shaping in sandal body silhouette occurred in the Pueblo period, dating from A.D. 900 to 1300 (Fig. 4.14). Some toe shaping includes the presence of a jog above the little toe (Fig. 4.14). The heel of these sandals changes; it still cradles the back of the foot, but now by creating a cupped form through sandal body construction, not by pulling together the heel edges. Raised sole patterning occurs and there is some use of colored geometric motifs but they are "less elaborate than in the earlier" types (Earl Morris 1944a: 240). Construction techniques in these shaped-cupped sandals have yet to be studied in detail. Both toe-heel and side-loop tie systems are seen among these sandals.

Shaped-cupped twined sandals have not been recorded from the Prayer Rock District, but they have been recovered in nearby prehistoric Puebloan sites such as Canyon del Muerto, Chaco Canyon, and Aztec Ruin. The type is second to the scalloped-puckered sandal in abundance and may have the widest geographic distribution of the five types (Table 4.5, Fig. 4.15). These sandals appear eastward into New Mexico and north into Colorado at Mesa Verde.

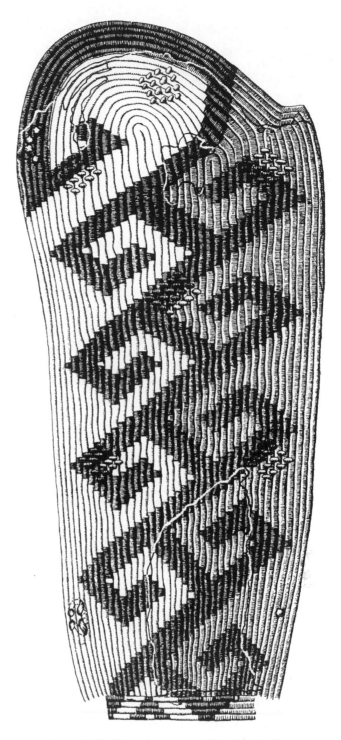

Figure 4.14. Shaped toe–cupped heel twined sandal with toe jog, sole view. Sandal length is 25.5 cm. (Pueblo Bonito, Sandal 3942.)

Additional information about the shaped-cupped twined sandal type is in Judd (1954: 74, 76–79), Kidder and Guernsey (1919: 103–106, Plate 39b, c; their Pueblo

Table 4.5. Pueblo Period Shaped Toe–Cupped Heel Twined Sandals

Location	Sandals n = 123	Sources
Canyon del Muerto, AZ		
Antelope House	78	Magers 1986: 257–259, 261, 264-265
Tsea-hot-tso	2	Earl Morris Papers, Arizona State Museum, File A–141
Kayenta area, AZ		
Marsh Pass: Cave 1	1	Guernsey 1931, Plate 57f
Monument Valley, AZ		
Ruin 1	2	Kidder and Guernsey 1919: 103–106, Plate 39b, c (their Pueblo Type IIb)
Northeastern AZ		
Site 37 North of Rock Point	1	Morss 1927, Plate 7a'
Tsegi Canyon, AZ		
Lem-o-ki	1	Deegan lab notes: Museum of Northern Arizona 2630.R5.1
Mesa Verde, CO		
Long House	1	Osborne 1980: 328–330
Aztec Ruin, NM	32	Earl Morris 1919: 49, 50–51
		Earl Morris Papers, Arizona State Museum, File A–141
Chaco Canyon, NM		
Pueblo Bonito	1	Earl Morris Papers, Arizona State Museum, File A–141
	1	Pepper 1920: 94–95
	2	Judd 1954: 74, 76–79
Cottonwood Wash, UT	1	Kankainen 1995: 67 (Utah Museum of Natural History 7172)

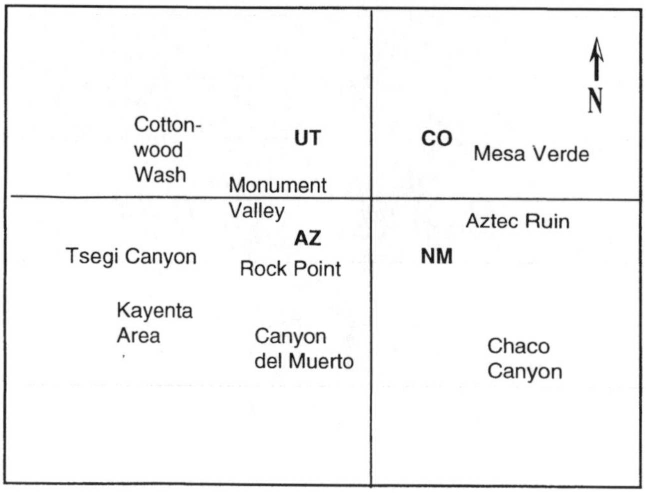

Figure 4.15. Schematic distribution of Pueblo period shaped toe–cupped heel twined sandals.

Type IIb), Magers (1986: 257–259, 261, 264–265), Earl Morris (1919: 49, 50–51; 1944: 240), Osborne (1980: 328–330), and Pepper (1920: 94-95).

TYPES OF NONTWINED SANDALS
Ann Cordy Deegan

Both plain weave and braided (plaited) sandals have been recovered in the Prayer Rock District. Although not discussed in detail in this volume, they indicate the range of fibrous sandal footwear available to the prehistoric Puebloans.

Plain Weave Sandals

During Basketmaker II through Pueblo III times, crude, more rapidly made, plain weave sandals (over-1, under-1 interlacing) coexisted with twined sandals (Fig. 4.16). Some were made from yucca leaves (with or without twisting) or thick yucca yarns that were quickly woven in a plain weave. Leaf or yarn ends were often allowed to protrude onto the sole where they frayed from abrasion, forming a thick pad. No color motifs or raised sole constructions appear in these plain weave sandals. Silhouettes were oval to rectangular with a rounded toe and flat, rounded heel. The toe-heel tie

Figure 4.16. Plain weave sandal, top view. Sandal length is 29 cm. (Sandal 1011; photo by Elizabeth Ann Morris; Arizona State Museum Neg. 6093.)

Figure 4.17. Shaped toe-cupped heel braided sandal, top view. Sandal length is 24.5 cm. (Sandal 1100; photo by Elizabeth Ann Morris; Arizona State Museum Neg. 6115.)

Figure 4.18. Square toe-square heel braided sandal, top view. Sandal length is 27.0 cm. (Sandal 560-A; photo by Elizabeth Ann Morris; Arizona State Museum Neg. 6115.)

system was used in this sandal type. Additional information on plain weave sandals is in Anderson (1969: 132), Kidder and Guernsey (1919: 103, 157, 158, Plates 38, 39, 67; their Basketmaker Types Ia and Ib and Pueblo Types Ib and IIa), Magers (1986: 259–260), Earl Morris (1944a: 239), and Elizabeth Morris (1980: 118, 120; her Class C, Types 1–3).

Braided (Plaited) Sandal Types

Braided sandals were particularly abundant during Pueblo III times (about A.D. 1100–1300) but may date back as early as Basketmaker III. Braided constructions include 2/2 (over-2, under-2) and 1/1 (over-1, under-1) interlacing patterns. These braided sandals contain flattened yucca leaves rather than spun yarn. Two shapes appear: one is similar to the Pueblo shaped-cupped twined sandal with a shaped toe and cupped heel (Fig. 4.17); the other type has a square toe and a square, flat heel (Fig. 4.18). Although these sandals tend to be undecorated, at least one has been found with geometric color motifs. Toe-heel and side-loop tie systems occur on braided sandals. In contrast to twined sandals, braided sandals would have been far less labor intensive to create.

Additional information on braided sandals is in Anderson (1969: 129–131), Baldwin (1939: 237–240), Kidder and Guernsey (1919: 101–103, Plates 35–37; their Pueblo Types Ia1 and Ia2), Magers (1986: 254–257, 261, 262–265), Earl Morris (1919: 49–50; 1944: 239), Elizabeth Morris (1980: 118, 119; her Class B, Types 1–4), and Nordenskiöld (1979: 102–103, Plate 46).

WINTER SANDALS
Ann Cordy Deegan

Another type of footwear mentioned in the manuscript by Ann Morris (Chapter 2, p. 22) is the "winter shoe," which actually is a sandal (Fig. 4.19). The identifying characteristics of the winter sandal include a common size, tie system, and use, rather than a common sandal body construction or toe and heel silhouette. Because the winter sandals are made in a variety of body constructions (such as twined or braided), they do not actually constitute a different "type" based on construction.

Winter sandals are often large and perhaps were made to wear over other sandals or to accommodate the juniper bark, corn husk, or corn leaf stuffing so often found with them. Their side loops have larger diameters and are sometimes longer than the normal side loops that extend up and over the top of the foot. A lacing cord, threaded through these loops, would hold the sandal on and the stuffing over the foot and under the laces. Seventeen twined Prayer Rock District winter sandals have been recorded (three scalloped-puckered and five round-puckered with raised patterned soles, and two scalloped-puckered and seven round-puckered with raised nongeometric tread soles). At least four braided (1/1 interlacing) winter sandals also came from the Prayer Rock District. Some winter sandals still have mud on the soles, along with the bark and leaf-husk padding for warmth, indicating usage during wet weather, cold weather or both.

Additional information on the winter sandal is in Kidder and Guernsey (1919: 107), Magers (1986: 232, 254), Earl Morris (1919: 50), Elizabeth Morris (1980: 118, 119; her Class B, Type 1), and Nordenskiöld (1979: 102–103, Plate 46).

Figure 4.19. Winter sandal, with padding, top view. Sandal length is 30 cm. (Photo by Elizabeth Ann Morris; Arizona State Museum Neg. 6087.)

In summary, the Prayer Rock District scalloped-square, scalloped-puckered, and round-puckered sandals attest to an era of remarkable diversity in sandal construction techniques for color and raised patterning. Despite their differences, techniques used in making these three types, plus the earlier square-square and later shaped-cupped twined sandals, continue through time with numerous similarities in yarn use, twining and wrapping techniques, and remarkable craftsmanship. Unfortunately, it appears that many of the sophisticated constructions in these twined sandals did not bridge the gap from about A.D. 1300 to the time of Spanish exploration in the 1500s (Salwen 1960). Early Spanish writings on Pueblo Indian footwear of the American Southwest speak only of leather moccasins, but not of the beautiful twined footwear of the Pueblo Indian's ancestors.

CHAPTER FIVE

Construction Techniques of Basketmaker III Twined Sandals

Ann Cordy Deegan

Earl Morris separated the Prayer Rock District Basketmaker III twined sandals into three divisions: "early," "middle," and "late." The classification herein is based on the distinctive toe and heel silhouettes of the sandals (see Fig. 3.6). The "early" Basketmaker III sandals, identified as scalloped-square (Fig. 5.1), probably date in the early Basketmaker III time period (late A.D. 400s). Earl Morris' "middle" Basketmaker III sandal type is scalloped-puckered (see Fig. 5.16) and the Prayer Rock specimens date in the A.D. 600s. Evidence from the Prayer Rock sites supports the idea that Morris' "late" Basketmaker III sandal, a round-toe type, coexisted with the scalloped-puckered sandal in the A.D. 600s. The round-puckered sandal derives its name from its distinctive round toe and puckered heel (see Fig. 5.26).

To understand the twined sandal construction techniques used by the prehistoric Basketmakers, I studied the laboratory notes made by Earl Morris' team, examined the team's drawings of 188 Prayer Rock sandals (see Appendix B and the Earl Morris Papers in the Arizona State Museum Archives), and analyzed the actual sandals. I gave zone numbers to those portions of sandals with shared body construction and color techniques to ease discussion and facilitate identification. These zones are defined in Table 5.1 and illustrated in Figures 5.2, 5.15, and 5.24 for the three types of twined sandals. Terminology is based on Emery (1980) and Deegan (1993) except as noted (see also Table 2.2 and Fig. 2.1).

The drawings made by Earl Morris' team represent many hours of analysis per sandal. The tight weft yarn packing obscures constructions, making the few dissections of sandals done by this team of irreplaceable value. These dissections were performed carefully, weft

Table 5.1. Sandal Construction Zones

Zone	Construction Type	Sandal Type
1a	2/2 twill twining over 4 warps Doubled warp* layer	1. All scalloped-toe types: a. All scalloped-square (48) b. All scalloped-puckered (102)
1b	2/2 twill twining over 2 warps Single warp layer	1. All round-puckered (38) (two of these sandals have two layers of warps in Zone 1b)
2	Single warp layer Color motifs No raised sole work	1. Scalloped-square (22) 2. Scalloped-puckered (66) 3. Round-puckered (10)
3a	Single warp layer Patterned raised sole	1. All scalloped-square (48) 2. Scalloped-puckered (101) 3. Round-puckered (26)
3b	Single warp layer Nonpatterned raised sole	1. Scalloped-square (3) 2. Scalloped-puckered (1) 3. Round-puckered (12)

NOTE: The number of Prayer Rock sandals examined that had laboratory data recorded by Earl Morris' team is in parentheses.
*In sandals, warp yarns run toe to heel, weft yarns side to side.

yarn by weft yarn, and recorded meticulously. Today we see faded colors and, in many cases, heavily abraded soles on these sandals, reinforcing a viewer's awe over the tremendous work these diagrams represent.

SCALLOPED TOE–SQUARE HEEL SANDALS

The 48 Prayer Rock District scalloped-square sandals that have construction data from the Morris study (see Appendix B) are characterized by a scalloped toe; a flat, square heel; an average total of 30 warps; plied warp and weft yarns; and two or three zones of differing construction in the same sandal. Thirty-one of these sandals (65%) contain color motifs ranging from solid color narrow bands to regions of geometric patterning.

There are two zones of construction in 23 (48%) of the scalloped-square Prayer Rock sandals (Figs. 5.1, 5.2*a*). All of them have a narrow, smooth region at the toe (Zone 1a) followed by a zone with raised geometric sole patterning (Zone 3a). The other 25 scalloped-square sandals (52%) have three zones of construction. Twenty-two of them have the narrow toe zone (Zone 1a) and the raised geometric sole pattern (Zone 3a) of the two-zone sandals, plus an additional narrow color motif zone (Zone 2) inserted directly after the toe zone and before the relief patterning starts (Fig. 5.2*b*1, 5.4). The three remaining three-zone sandals possess the same toe and heel shapes, yarn type, and number of warps as the two-zone and three-zone scalloped-square sandals (Zones 1a and 3a), but directly after Zone 1a and covering nearly the entire sandal is a color motif section (Zone 3b) with a nongeometric raised sole beneath it (Figs. 5.2*b*2, 5.3). These three represent the "fourth type of sandal" or so-called "burial" sandal mentioned by Ann Morris (Chapter 2, pp. 22, 23).

Scalloped-toe Construction
(Zone 1a)

The narrow toe zone (Zone 1a) on all scalloped-square sandals was probably created, as described by Ann Morris (Chapter 2, p. 21), by first laying all warps parallel to each other on a flat surface (Fig. 5.5*a*). A few rows of 2/2 twill twining over two warps (Fig. 5.6*a*3), labeled by Ann Morris as "over-under weave" (Chapter 2, p. 21) but described in later laboratory notes as 2/2 twill twining, were then inserted across these warps toward one end. Ann Morris observed (Chapter 2, p. 21) that this insertion was about 1.3 cm from one end (Fig. 5.5*b*). The warps were then folded over on themselves on a line through the center of the twining (one set of warps lying on top of the other; Fig. 5.5*c*). A cord placed inside this fold could have been attached to a support (such as a tree or post). After finishing the sandal, this same support cord was then cut flush at each side of the sandal toe. Whether the heel ends of the warps were ever attached to a belt (such as a backstrap) to provide constant warp tension or left free hanging is uncertain. Experiments by Talge indicate a need for warp tension during manufacture (Talge 1995: 48–54).

The 2/2 twill twining continued, extending over the doubled warps (over four warps rather than two; Figs.

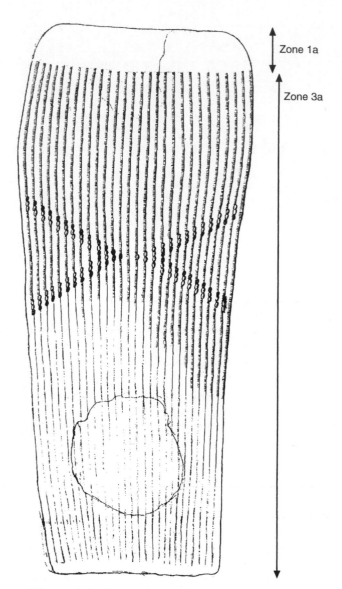

Figure 5.1. Two-zone scalloped toe–square heel sandal, top view. (Sandal 803–B, length is 22 cm.)

5.5*c*, 5.6*a*4). The gentle pull on the support cord, as twining proceeded, resulted in a shallow scalloped toe. To end the narrow toe zone, alternate warps were cut off (half of the warps) across the width of the sandal (Fig. 5.5*c*). The entire Zone 1a only extends a short distance in these sandals (an average length of 2.4 cm in 19 scalloped-square sandals, with a range of 1.5 cm to 3 cm). The remaining zones on all scalloped-square sandals consist of only one layer of warps with columns running toe to heel on the sandal top. No color motifs appear in Zone 1a of the scalloped-square Prayer Rock sandals. Talge (1995: 48–54), through replication studies, describes the possible steps taken in the manufacture of the scalloped toe.

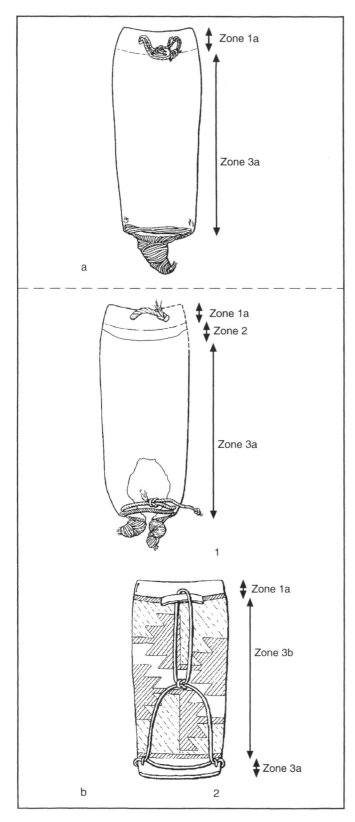

Figure 5.2. Scalloped toe–square heel sandal construction zones, top views: *a*, two-zone sandals (n = 23); *b*, three-zone sandals (n = 25).

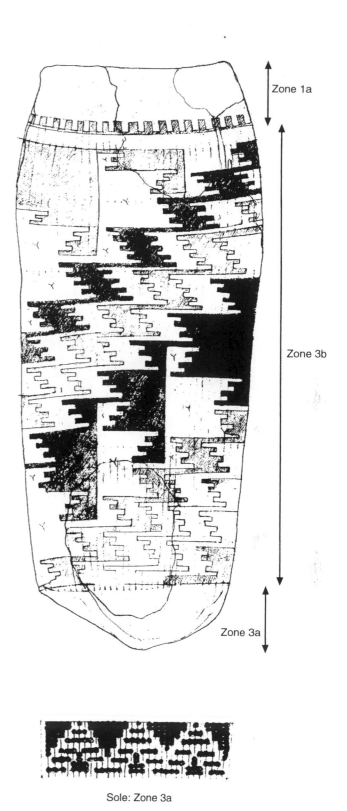

Sole: Zone 3a

Figure 5.3. Top view (*top*) and sole heel design of a three-zone scalloped toe–square heel sandal. (Sandal 1009–F; length is 24.5 cm.)

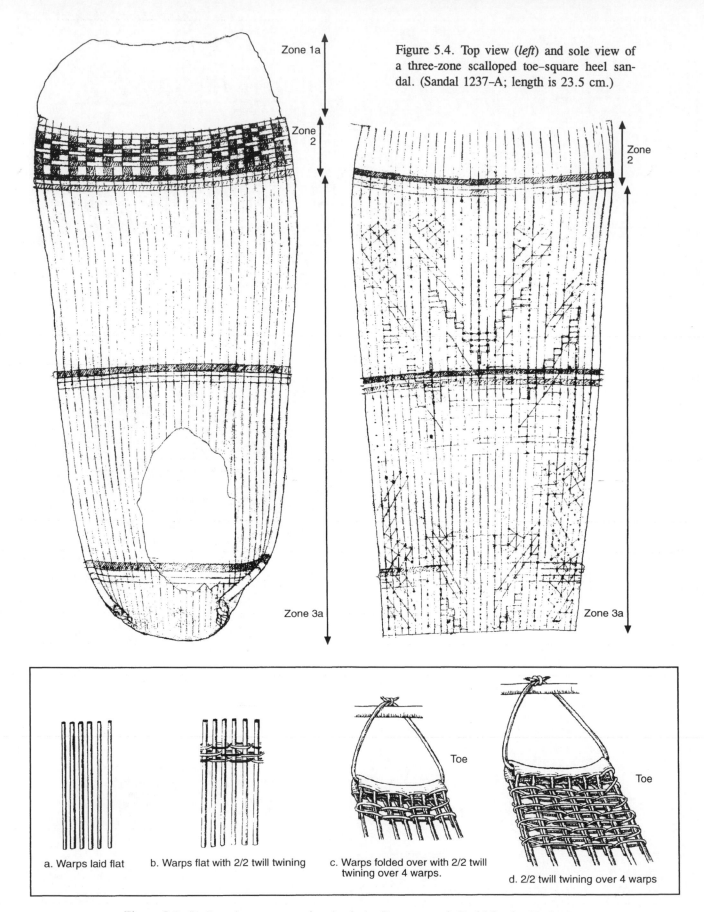

Zone 1a

Zone 2

Zone 3a

Zone 2

Zone 3a

Figure 5.4. Top view (*left*) and sole view of a three-zone scalloped toe–square heel sandal. (Sandal 1237–A; length is 23.5 cm.)

Toe

Toe

a. Warps laid flat

b. Warps flat with 2/2 twill twining

c. Warps folded over with 2/2 twill twining over 4 warps.

d. 2/2 twill twining over 4 warps

Figure 5.5. Scalloped-toe construction (*a*, *b*, by Deegan; *c*, *d*, Earl Morris sketches).

[54]

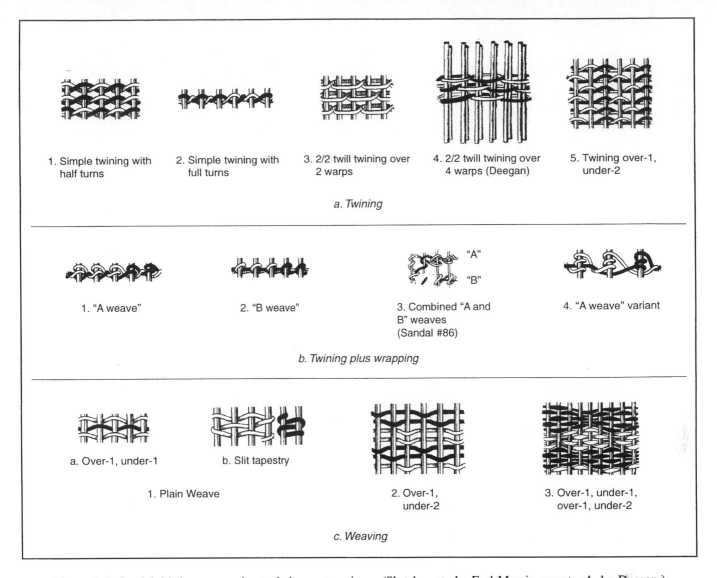

Figure 5.6. Sandal fabric construction techniques; top views. (Sketches are by Earl Morris except *a*4, by Deegan.)

The labels within the figure are:

a. Twining
1. Simple twining with half turns
2. Simple twining with full turns
3. 2/2 twill twining over 2 warps
4. 2/2 twill twining over 4 warps (Deegan)
5. Twining over-1, under-2

b. Twining plus wrapping
1. "A weave"
2. "B weave"
3. Combined "A and B" weaves (Sandal #86) "A" "B"
4. "A weave" variant

c. Weaving
a. Over-1, under-1
b. Slit tapestry
1. Plain Weave
2. Over-1, under-2
3. Over-1, under-1, over-1, under-2

Zone 2 Color Motif Construction

Twenty-two three-zone sandals contain a narrow color motif band (Zone 2) directly after the doubled toe zone (Figs. 5.2*b*1, 5.4). Some of the Zone 2 construction techniques created clear motifs on top that are blurred on the sole, whereas other techniques formed reversible motifs between sandal top and sole. As within Zone 1a, no raised structures appear beneath Zone 2. The color motif bands are narrow, averaging 1.6 cm for 19 sandals. Tight yarn packing makes it difficult to identify Zone 2 construction techniques. As described by Morris' team, a variety of twining and plain weave techniques were used for Zone 2 construction.

Two different twining techniques appear in scalloped-square sandals to create Zone 2 color bands. One is twining over–1, under–2, with two colors paired together (3 specimens; Fig. 5.6*a*5). Clear motifs appear on the sandal top with similar but indistinct motifs on the sole; the construction produces a float over two warp yarns on the sole that blurs the motifs. No relief patterning exists on the sole, because the very short floats are scattered on the sole.

The second technique is simple twining with half-turns and full-turns, using paired colors (5 specimens; Figs. 5.6*a*1, 5.6*a*2). This turning produces clear motifs on top, with the same motifs on the sole but in reversed colors. Half-turns of paired wefts between warps move a color from top to sole or vice versa. Introduction of a full twining twist allows the color to remain on the same surface, producing reversed colors top to sole. The full-twining twist is called "lock-weave" by Kidder (1926: 622, Fig. 4c) and "lock stitch" by Earl Morris (Earl Morris Papers, Arizona State Museum Archives, File A–145a, b: 36).

[55]

Analyses by Morris' team revealed that, in addition to twining, three different woven techniques produced Zone 2 motifs. One sandal contains slit tapestry (plain weave; Fig. 5.6*c*1b); when two different colored weft yarns meet in one row, they turn around adjacent warps, producing tiny warp-wise slits in the fabric. Three sandals have an over–1, under–2 woven pattern (top view; Fig. 5.6*c*2). Two sandals used over–1, under–1, over–1, under–2 weaving (top view) across the sandal (Fig. 5.6*c*3). Both the second and third woven techniques render a clear design on the top, but blur the sole motif through floats over two warps on the sole. Floats scattered on the sole prevent any organized raised sole patterning.

Raised Patterning Construction (Zone 3a)

All Prayer Rock scalloped-square sandals contain a geometric patterned raised sole section (Zone 3a; Fig. 5.7), the "bars and knots" Ann Morris describes in her manuscript (Chapter 2, p. 21). On two-zone sandals this raised patterning covers nearly the entire sole (Fig. 5.2*a*). Three-zone sandals vary in the extent of this patterned raised region, from nearly the entire sole in most of them (Fig. 5.2*b*1) to those that have a Zone 3b with only a narrow raised pattern strip at the heel (Fig. 5.2*b*2).

Actual geometric raised patterning was created through decisions on the location of a raised row on the sandal sole, on the placement of a wrap within a raised row, and on the type of wrap used. Raised zones do not consist exclusively of raised rows, rather these rows are thrown into relief by preceding and subsequent rows of plain weave, simple twining, or both. These nonraised rows probably served to accentuate and secure the raised rows.

It is difficult to identify sequences and wrap techniques in the tightly packed raised sole design areas, a situation made worse if the sandal sole is abraded from heavy use. Only 23 scalloped-square sandals (48%) have laboratory data on row sequencing, and only one raised row sequence is identifiable. This sequence is raised row (R), simple twining row (T), plain weave row (P), plain weave row (P), abbreviated as RTPP (Fig. 5.8*a*). This four row sequence repeats over and over down the length of Zone 3a.

The exact types of wraps used in a raised row vary and are difficult to determine without sandal dissection. Morris' team recorded two major categories of wraps: (1) interwarp wraps, which create a ball *between* toe to

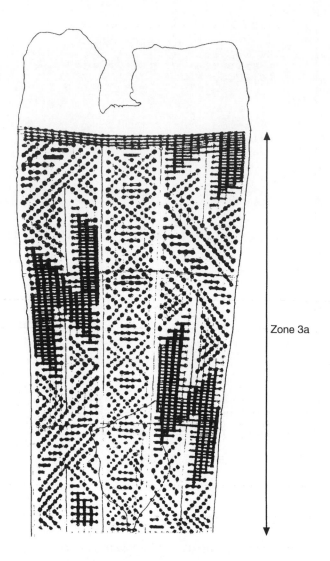

Zone 3a

Figure 5.7. Raised sole patterning; heel not shown in this diagram. (Sandal 1009–B.)

heel columns on the sandal sole (Figs. 5.9*a*1a–b, 5.10), and (2) twining with warp wraps, which form a ball *on top* of a toe-heel column (Fig. 5.9*a*2a–c). The Morris team identified interwarp wraps on 42 of the 48 scalloped-square sandals (88%; diagrams showing balls between warps). Interwarp wraps were formed by simple twining where paired wefts made one or more full turns about each other between adjacent warps (Fig. 5.9*a*1a, 1b). One full turn was called "lock-weave" by Kidder (1926: 622, Fig. 4c). The most common interwarp wrap had two full turns, Earl Morris' "double wrap" (Fig. 5.9*a*1b). Kidder (1926: 622, Fig. 4h) identified, described, and named this structure "double wrap" through dissection of a scalloped-puckered sandal from the Canyon de Chelly area.

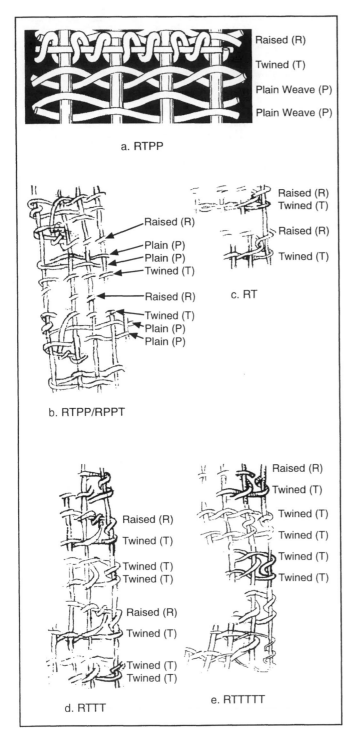

Figure 5.8. Raised row sequences: R, raised row; T, twined row; P, plain weave row.

by Earl Morris' team. Exact structures for these twined warp wraps were difficult to determine because only two techniques were diagramed from two sandals: (1) simple twining combined with warp wrapping where one of the paired wefts periodically wrapped around both a warp and the other twining weft (Fig. 5.9*a*2a), and (2) wrapping around a warp but anchored through the other paired weft (Fig. 5.9*a*2b). Earl Morris called the first "Kidder's single wrap" (Kidder 1926: 622, Fig. 4i) and the second "lock knot."

Color Use in Zone 3a

Color motifs are visible in Zone 3a raised sole patterning areas in 6 two-zone sandals and in 11 three-zone sandals. Motifs include narrow width-wise bands, diagonal lines, and other geometric shapes. Eleven (65%) of these sandals have narrow transverse solid or checkered bands of color in Zone 3a, made by using colored wefts within the raised sections (Fig. 5.4). The same color and line size are seen on the top and the sole within these bands (reversible motifs, top and sole), with relief patterns incorporated into the design areas through the use of dyed weft yarns in the regular raised patterning sequence of RTPP.

Diagonal line motifs, such as in zigzags, chevrons, and arrow heads (Fig. 5.1), required a staircase weft float technique (Fig. 5.11). A colored weft crossed in a staircase direction to the right or left behind one warp, turned 90 degrees toward the heel to run vertically between the next warp and over about three to four regular raised pattern weft rows, again turned ninety degrees to run behind the next warp to the right or left, repeating these steps down the sandal length. This technique can be identified by longitudinal short dashes of color between warps on the sandal top (Fig. 5.1). These patterns do not show on the sole, because they are covered with normal raised sole patterning. Simple twining anchors these steps as they proceed down the sandal (Fig. 5.11).

Slit tapestry (plain weave interlacing of over–1, under–1; Fig. 5.6*c*1b) produces reversible colors and motifs on the sandal top and sole. Slit tapestry created the shaft of an arrow motif in one sandal and geometric inserts on the sandal edges in another. The tapestry was inserted around and between regular relief patterning so the sole retained the raised pattern appearance.

Morris' team identified two sandals that contained painted motifs in Zone 3a. They do not involve a textile construction technique, so are not discussed here.

Thirty-one (65%) scalloped-square sandals reveal twined warp wraps, always found with interwarp wraps on the same sandal. These twined warp wraps are identifiable as a dot on top of the warps in diagrams drawn

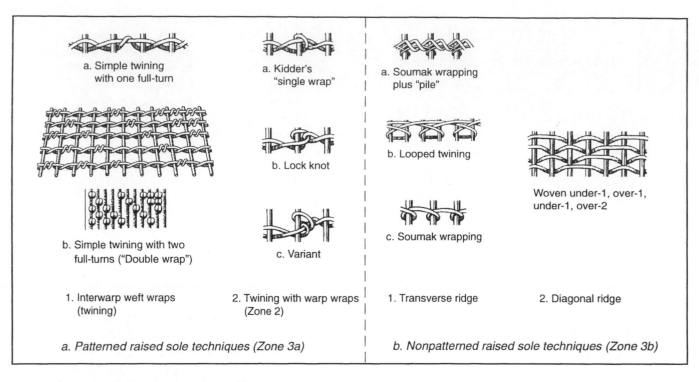

a. Patterned raised sole techniques (Zone 3a)

b. Nonpatterned raised sole techniques (Zone 3b)

Figure 5.9. Raised sole construction techniques; sole views (Earl Morris sketches).

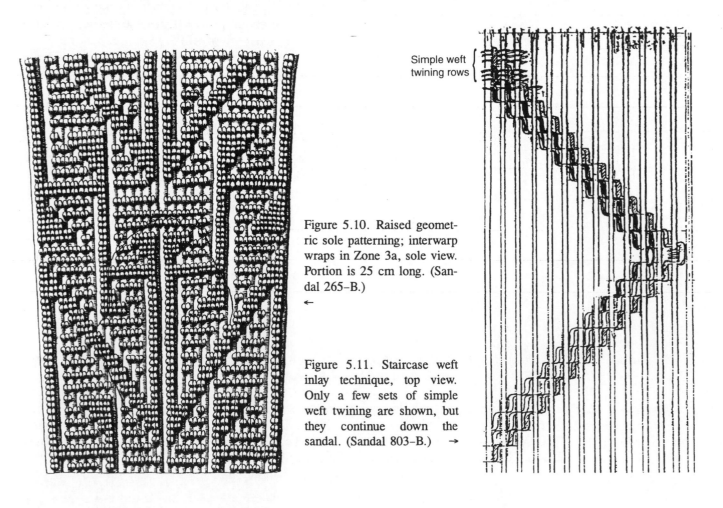

Figure 5.10. Raised geometric sole patterning; interwarp wraps in Zone 3a, sole view. Portion is 25 cm long. (Sandal 265–B.)

←

Figure 5.11. Staircase weft inlay technique, top view. Only a few sets of simple weft twining are shown, but they continue down the sandal. (Sandal 803–B.)   →

Zone 3b Color Motifs and Nonpatterned Raised Techniques

Three scalloped-square sandals contain stunning, long color motifs called Zone 3b (Fig. 5.3). The color motifs extend nearly the full length of each sandal, leaving about 2.5 cm to 5 cm at the heel for raised sole patterning (Zone 3a) and about 2.5 cm at the toe for the narrow, doubled warp toe zone (Zone 1a).

Slit tapestry creates the Zone 3b colored motifs in two of these sandals (Figs. 5.3 and 5.6*c*1b). A woven pattern with weft slit joins appears in the third sandal: over–1, under–1, over–1, under–2 (top view; Figs. 5.6*c*3 and 5.12). Short warp direction floats of colored weft yarn float over about three to four weft rows in the over–1, under–1, over–1, under–2 sandal's surface to connect similar color regions (Fig. 5.12). Raised soles without geometric patterning, visible under Zone 3b of these three sandals, create either transverse or diagonal raised lines.

Transverse raised lines, called "pile" by Earl Morris (Earl Morris Papers, Arizona State Museum Archives, File A–138: 24), are on the soles of the two tapestry sandals (Fig. 5.9*b*1a). The raised "pile" cross-bands pack so tightly between the tapestry rows that the tapestry patterning is not visible on the sole. Thin wefts wrap around warps in an over–2, back under–1 soumak wrapping while encircling a long coil made of two thicker wefts (which rest on the sole against the warps; Fig. 5.9*b*1a). The coiled wefts produce the "pile" ridges. This complicated technique apparently involved cutting the coiled weft strands at the ends of each row and securing them under the weft involved in tapestry as it made its edge turn.

Faint, short, diagonal raised lines appear in Zone 3b on the sole of the third sandal. The same construction technique that created the color motif pattern, a woven interlacing pattern of over–1, under–1, over–1, under–2 (top view) also produced a short float over two warps on the sole (Figs. 5.9*b*2, 5.12). Only a lightly textured surface is visible; no distinct diagonal lines occur because of the noncontinuous float patterning.

Heel Finishing

The scalloped-square sandal has a flat, square heel (Fig. 5.1). After all zones of construction were completed, the warp ends had to be secured. If a backstrap had been used for warp tension, the heel ends of the warps had to be let loose from the backstrap to manipulate the heel finish. On sandals with laboratory data on heel finishes, warp ends carried over one warp to the

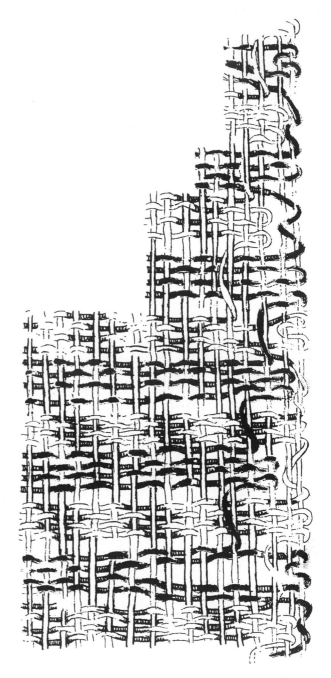

Figure 5.12. Three-zone "burial" sandal Zone 3b structure (over–1, under–1, over–1, under–2); top view. Portion is 21 cm long. (Sandal 1412–B.)

right or left and tucked under or wrapped around the neighboring warp, producing a braided appearance (Fig. 5.13). Warp ends were cut short (Fig. 5.14*a, b*) or used as heel loops. On some sandals, warp ends were gathered into a trailing braid (Fig. 5.14*c*) or knotted (Fig. 5.14*d, f*).

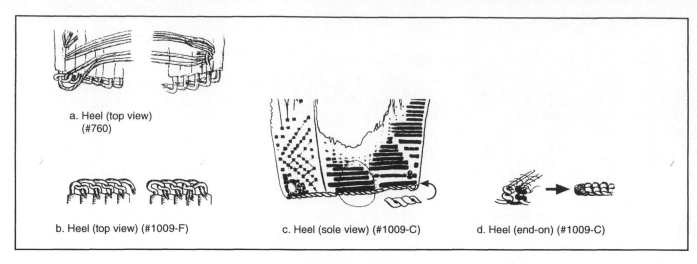

a. Heel (top view)
(#760)

b. Heel (top view) (#1009-F)

c. Heel (sole view) (#1009-C)

d. Heel (end-on) (#1009-C)

Figure 5.13. Earl Morris team sketches of heel finishes on scalloped toe–square heel sandals.

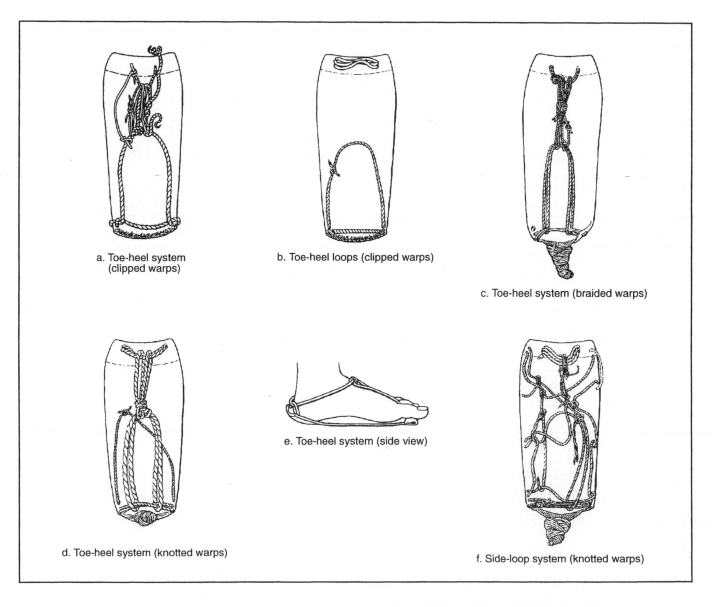

a. Toe-heel system
(clipped warps)

b. Toe-heel loops (clipped warps)

c. Toe-heel system (braided warps)

d. Toe-heel system (knotted warps)

e. Toe-heel system (side view)

f. Side-loop system (knotted warps)

Figure 5.14. Tie systems for scalloped toe–square heel sandals, top views and side view (e).

Ties

The overall tie systems on scalloped-square sandals include toe-heel (Fig. 5.14*a–e*), which predominates, and a few sandals with the side-loop tie system (Fig. 5.14*f*).

SCALLOPED TOE–PUCKERED HEEL SANDALS

The Prayer Rock scalloped-puckered sandal type is based on Earl Morris' laboratory construction information on 102 sandals. Like the scalloped-square sandals, these specimens have plied warp and weft yarns, an average of 29 total warps, a scalloped toe (varying in depth, most of them deeper than the scalloped-square sandals), and at least two shared zones of construction: the toe area (Zone 1a) and the raised patterned sole (Zone 3a; Figs. 5.15, 5.16). However, unlike the scalloped-square sandals, the scalloped-puckered type has a distinctly different heel finish, the puckered heel. Sixty-six (65%) scalloped-puckered sandals have colored designs.

Thirty-five two-zone scalloped-puckered sandals have the smooth, Zone 1a double warp toe region that extends nearly halfway down the sandal (Figs. 5.15*a*, 5.17), followed by the Zone 3a raised geometric sole pattern section. One additional two-zone sandal has a raised sole but without geometric patterning (Zone 3b instead of Zone 3a).

All but one of the Prayer Rock three-zone scalloped-puckered sandals (99%) have a long Zone 1a toe region, a narrow Zone 2 color motif band in the arch area, and a Zone 3a with raised geometric sole patterning (Figs. 5.15*b*1, 5.16, 5.18). One three-zone scalloped-puckered sandal has an Extended Zone 2 (Fig. 5.19).

Scalloped-toe Construction (Zone 1a)

Toe construction of the scalloped-puckered sandals followed the same process as for the toes of scalloped-square sandals (Fig. 5.5). After all of the warps were laid flat, a few rows of 2/2 twill twining over two warps were then inserted, probably at a point more midway down the length of the warps than in the scalloped-square sandals to create a longer doubled warp toe section. The doubled warp zone extends to just above the arch of the sandal, unlike the narrow Zone 1a of the scalloped-square sandal (Fig. 5.5*d*).

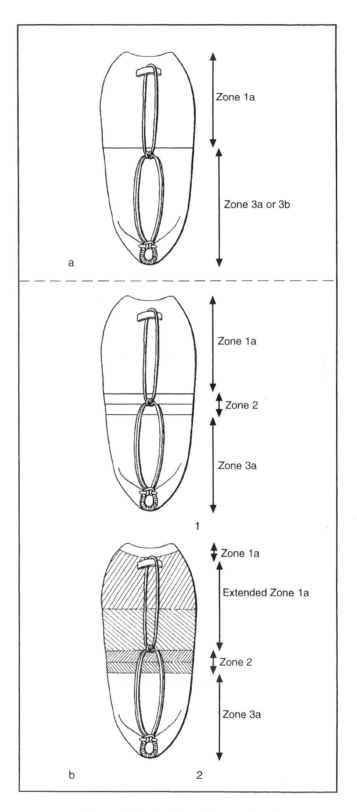

Figure 5.15. Scalloped toe–puckered heel sandal construction zones.

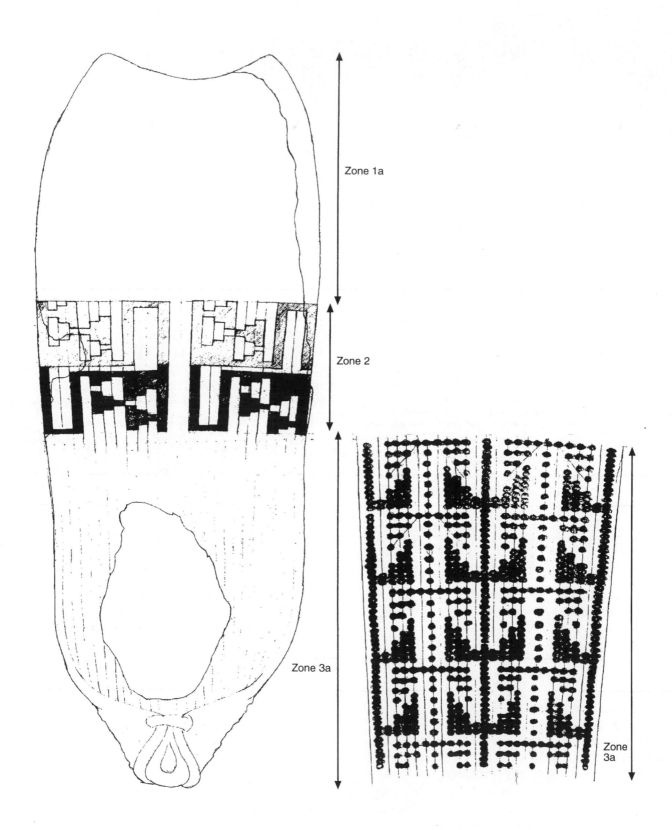

Figure 5.16. Three-zone scalloped toe–puckered heel sandal (Zones 1a + 2 + 3a), top view (*left*) and sole view. (Sandal 387–D, length is 24.5 cm.)

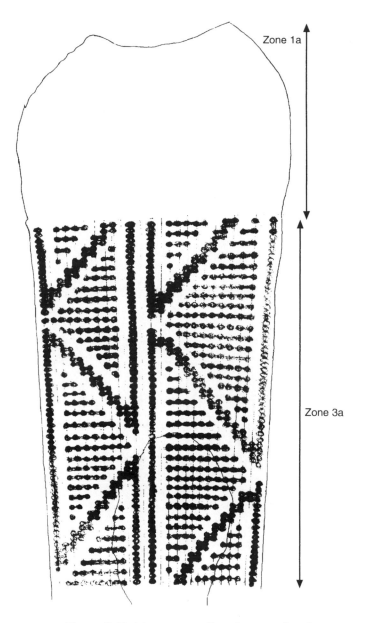

Zone 1a

Zone 3a

Figure 5.17. Two-zone scalloped toe–puckered heel sandal (Zones 1a + 3a), sole view. (Sandal 1058, length is 22 cm, heel missing.)

Thirty-seven (56%) three-zone scalloped-puckered sandals contain colored geometric designs in Zone 1a, placed after an initial narrow band without colored motifs (Figs. 5.15*b*2, 5.20). As the construction is essentially the same as in Zone 1a, it is called Extended Zone 1a. Paired colored wefts in 2/2 twill twining over four warps are used but with full-turns, as well as half-turns, between warps (Fig. 5.6*a*4). This causes the same motif to appear in this zone on both the top and sole but in reversed colors. Extended Zone 1a can be

identified without dissection of the sandal by checking for the same motif on both sides but in reversed colors, by the presence of a smooth surface, and, if colors are faded, by the appearance of full twined turns between warps. (Full twined turns are not necessary unless color is introduced.)

After the desired length of doubled warps was attained, then alternate warps were cut off with the remainder of each sandal containing only a single layer of warps with toe to heel columns, as in the scalloped-square sandals.

Zone 2 Color Motif Construction

All three-zone Prayer Rock scalloped-puckered sandals (66) have a Zone 2 color motif band in the area of the sandal covered by the arch of the foot (see Figs. 5.15*b*1 and *b*2, 5.16, 5.18, 5.19, 5.20). Construction in Zone 2 is difficult to identify without dissection. Only three Zone 2 construction techniques for scalloped-puckered sandals appear in Earl Morris' papers. In one, two sandals use the same construction technique described by Kidder (1926: 622, Fig. 4f, g) for a scalloped-puckered dissected sandal. Paired colored wefts twined across the sandal from left to right for one row, with the top yarn making one full wrap over and around each warp between each twining twist (Fig. 5.6*b*1, *b*3), called "A weave" by Kidder (1926) and illustrated by Earl Morris (Earl Morris Papers, Arizona State Museum Archives, File A–138: 36, 38). Then the same pair of yarns twined back across for one row with the top yarn making one full wrap under and around each warp between each twining twist (Fig. 5.6*b*2, *b*3), called "B weave" by Kidder (1926). The two rows packed together, "A" and "B," made one "row" of color pattern (Fig. 5.6*b*3). A full twist in twining kept the same color on top, a half-twist transposed the two colors. This construction creates a clear top motif that is blurred on the sole. Identifying characteristics of this construction, without dissection of the sandal, include no raised work on the sole under Zone 2, the presence of a single layer of warps, toe to heel columns on top, and clear top motifs with blurred motifs on the sole. The second construction technique (1 sandal) involved a variation of the "A" weave (Fig. 5.6*b*4). The final technique is in a sandal with a Zone 1a and narrow Zone 3a, but with a longer or Extended Zone 2 of colored motifs (Fig. 5.19). The colored geometric motifs of this Zone 2 were constructed by tapestry and are visible on the top and sole of the sandal without color reversals (Fig. 5.6*c*1b).

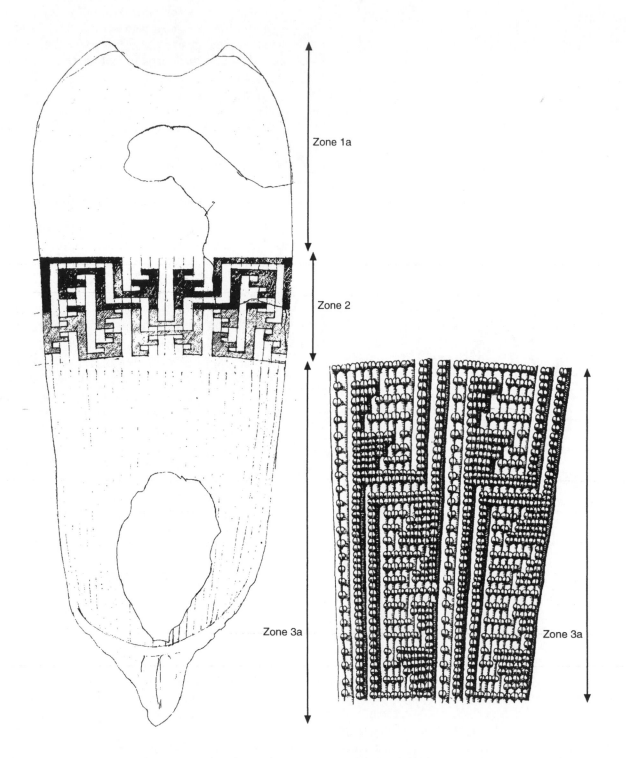

Figure 5.18. Three-zone scalloped toe–puckered heel sandal (Zones 1a + 2 + 3a), top view (*left*) and sole view. (Sandal 87–A, length is 24 cm.)

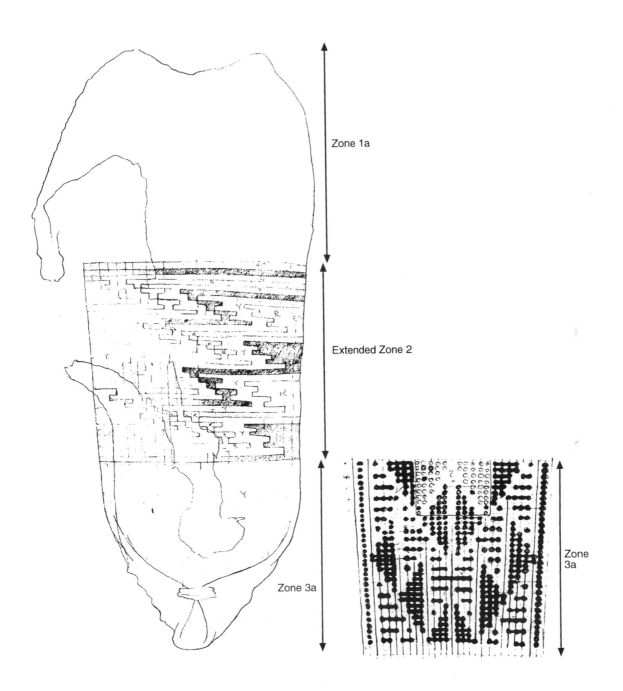

Figure 5.19. Three-zone scalloped toe–puckered heel sandal with Extended Zone 2, top view (*left*) and sole view. (Sandal 114–G, length is 24 cm.)

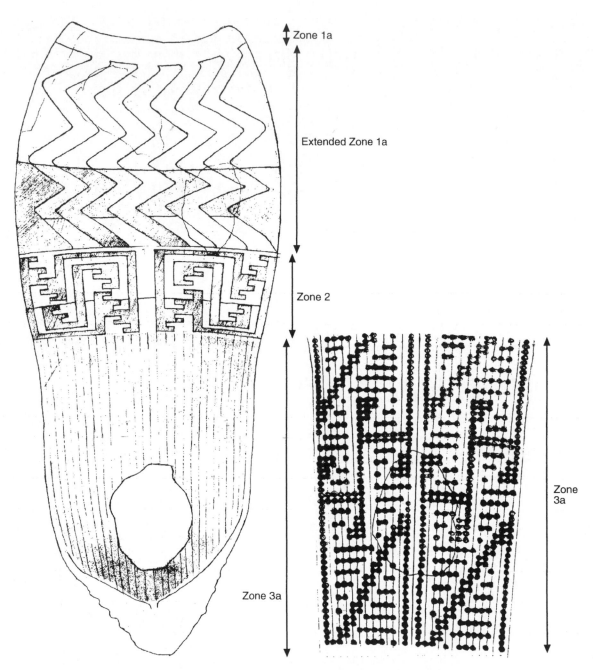

Figure 5.20. Three-zone scalloped toe–puckered heel sandal with Extended Zone 1a (Zones 1a + Extended Zone 1a + 2 + 3a), top view (*left*) and sole view. (Sandal 114–D, length is 26.0 cm.)

Geometric Raised Patterning Construction (Zone 3a)

Zone 3a raised patterning occurs in all 102 scalloped-puckered sandals, sharing with scalloped-square sandals the basic principle of placing raised rows in relief through row sequencing. Twenty-two sandals with laboratory analysis notes on raised row sequencing

reveal more sequence variety than among the scalloped-square sandals. The most common sequence (17 sandals) is again RTPP (Fig. 5.8*a*), recorded in all 23 scalloped-square sandals that have raised row sequence data. For scalloped-puckered footwear, five sandals use RTTT (raised row, three rows of simple twining; Fig. 5.8*d*), with one of these alternating RTTT with RTPP. One sandal switches two different four-row sequences

(RTPP alternating with RPPT; Fig. 5.8*b*), and one uses the sequence RTPP + TTPP (no illustration available).

Interwarp wraps, present in 97 percent of the scalloped-puckered sandals, include simple twining with two full turns, the "double wrap" visible on three sandal diagrams (Fig. 5.9*a*1b). Twined warp wraps (on 22% of the scalloped-puckered sandals) always occur on sandals that also have interwarp wraps. Kidder's "single wrap" appears in one sandal (Fig. 5.9*a*2a).

Color Use in Zone 3a

Two three-zone scalloped-puckered sandals reveal transverse colored lines in Zone 3a. I found no information on this line construction in the Morris notes. I examined the actual sandals and it is probable that dyed weft yarns were used in forming the raised techniques, because raised soles are visible under these lines with no reversal of color from top to sole, the same structure as in scalloped-square sandal lines in Zone 3a (see Fig. 5.4).

Zone 3b Nongeometric Patterned Raised Techniques

One two-zone sandal has a Zone 3b with transverse ridges. This Zone 3b was made using looped twining (Fig. 5.9*b*1b) with 5 to 11 rows of simple twining between each raised row.

Heel Finishing

The general heel finish for scalloped-puckered sandals has warp ends that fasten in a ring, or pucker, at the heel (Fig. 5.21). Some puckered heels were created by laying the outside warp from each edge across all other warps, pulling up on these two warps until the

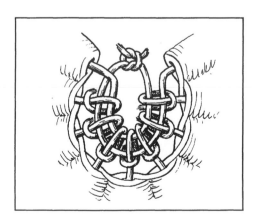

Figure 5.21. End-on view of puckered heel construction.

outside corners met, and then fastening each intervening warp end around the two warps to secure them in place (Fig. 5.21). This technique created the puckered heel silhouette that, in combination with the scalloped toe, quickly defines this sandal type.

Ties

Both side-loop and toe-heel loop tie systems appear among scallop-puckered sandals (Fig. 5.22). After finishing the puckered heel, uncut warps were sometimes used to form heel loops.

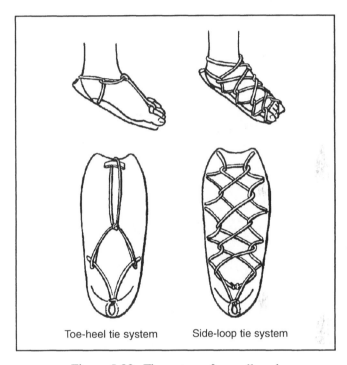

Toe-heel tie system   Side-loop tie system

Figure 5.22. Tie systems for scalloped toe–puckered heel sandals.

ROUND TOE–PUCKERED HEEL SANDALS

Round-puckered sandals (38 with Morris laboratory construction data) share several features with scalloped-square and scalloped-puckered sandals. These features are use of yarn, raised sole patterning, and a minimum of two construction zones: a smooth surface toe area (Zone 1b) and a raised sole (Zone 3a or 3b). These sandals possess the puckered heel seen on scalloped-puckered sandals. The round-puckered sandal, however, has a distinctive, symmetrically round toe that is not shaped to the foot (Fig. 5.23). Round-toe sandals appear

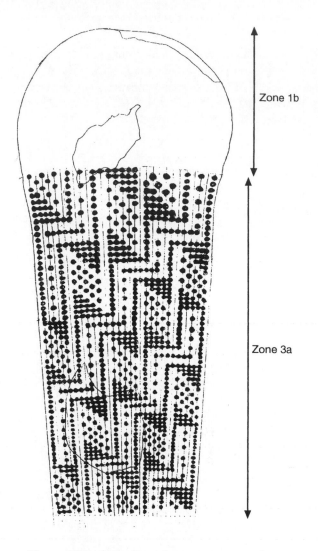

Figure 5.23. Sole view of a two-zone round toe–puckered heel sandal (Zones 1b + 3a). Portion is 27 cm long, heel missing. (Sandal 168.)

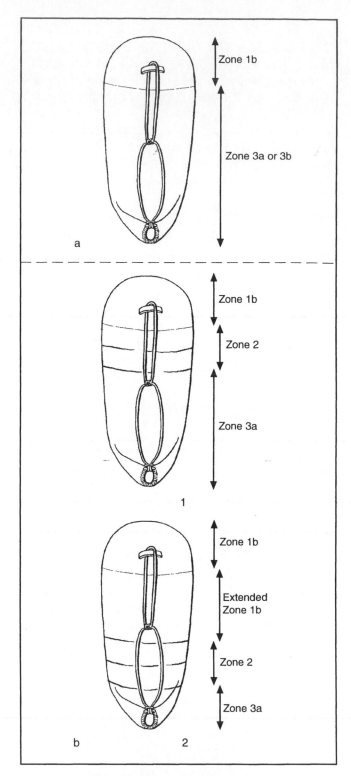

Figure 5.24. Round toe–puckered heel sandal construction zones.

to have fewer total warps (averaging 26) than scalloped-puckered sandals (averaging 29). Because of the toe construction method, round toes lack folded over, doubled warps (no Zone 1a), with the exception of two unusual sandals. Only ten round-puckered sandals (26%) have colored patterning.

Round-puckered sandals have two zones or three zones (Fig. 5.24*a, b*). Two-zone sandals (28, 74%) have a round-toe section, usually extending to the base of the toe rounding (Zone 1b), followed either by a Zone 3a geometric patterned raised sole region (16 sandals; Figs. 5.23, 5.24*a*) or by a Zone 3b nongeometric raised sole region (12 sandals; Figs. 5.24*a*, 5.25). Eight three-zone sandals (21%) have a round-toe section (Zone 1b), followed by a Zone 2 band of color motif in or above the arch area and a final Zone 3a of raised sole patterning (Figs. 5.24*b*1, 5.26). Two three-zone

sandals possess an Extended Zone 1b with geometric color motifs, a Zone 2 color motif band near the heel, and a very narrow Zone 3a raised sole pattern section at the heel (Figs. 5.24*b*2, 5.27).

[68]

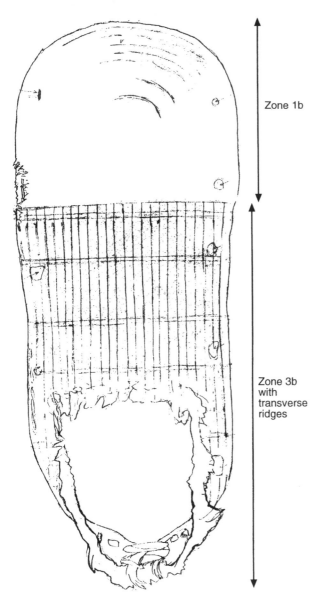

Figure 5.25. Two-zone round toe–puckered heel sandal with transverse sole ridges (Zones 1b + 3b), sole view. (Sandal 265–A, length is 26 cm.)

Round-toe Construction (Zone 1b)

Ann and Earl Morris were mindful of the difference in how scalloped-toe and round-toe sandals were started (Chapter 2, pp. 22–23, 27). Whereas the scalloped-toe sandals probably were made using a suspension cord (tension could be supplied by pulling), the round-toe sandals had no such built-in tensioning device.

Based on the sandal laboratory notes (Earl Morris Papers), the Ann Morris manuscript, the 1944 Earl Morris article (Chapter 2), and the replicative work of Talge (1995), the most probable start to a round toe was to lay half as many warps as needed parallel to one an-

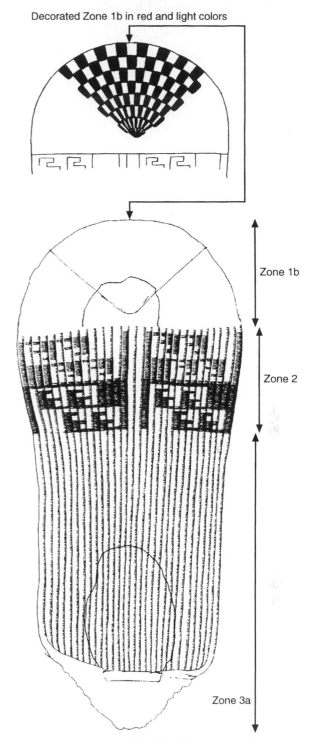

Decorated Zone 1b in red and light colors

Figure 5.26. Three-zone round toe–puckered heel sandal (Zones 1b + 2 + 3a), top view. (Sandal 265–B, length is 25 cm.)

other on a flat surface (Fig. 5.28a). As with the scalloped-toe sandal types, a few rows of 2/2 twill twining over two warps were then added, here mid-way down the warps (Fig. 5.28a). Instead of folding along the twined portion and inserting a suspension cord within

[69]

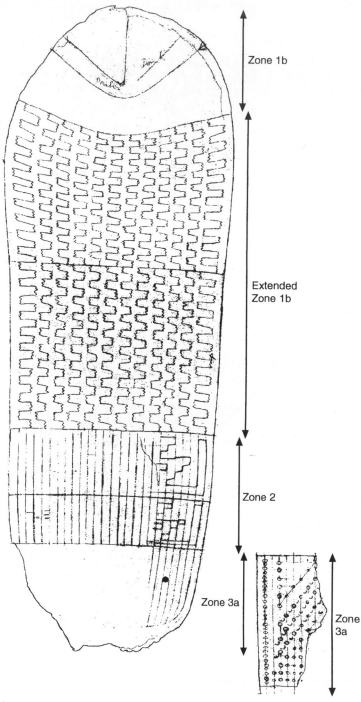

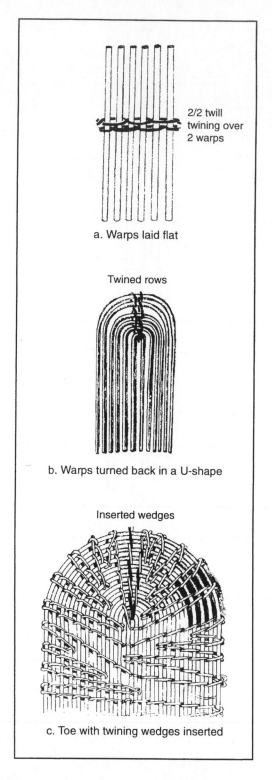

Figure 5.27. Three-zone round toe–puckered heel sandal with Extended Zone 1b (Zones 1b + Extended 1b + 2 + 3a); top view (*left*) and sole view of Zone 3a. (Sandal 455–F, length is 24.5 cm.)

Figure 5.28. Round-toe construction steps. (*a*, *b*, by Deegan; *c*, Earl Morris sketch; Sandal 213–A.)

the fold, the round-toe sandal warps bent back on themselves into a U shape (Fig. 5.28*b*). The 2/2 twill twining around two warps continued, now, however, inserted in wedges to fill in until the twining reached a point where all weft rows extended from selvage to selvage at ninety degrees to the warps (Fig. 5.28*c*). No

folding over of warps meant no doubled warps within the toe region. Talge's (1995: 54–59) sandal toe replication study provides more extensive discussion of round-toe construction techniques.

Two sandals have color motifs in an extension of Zone 1b (Fig. 5.27), with a highly unusual double layer of warps. Morris' team hypothesized that the double layer in Zone 1b and Extended Zone 1b came from overlaying a second set of U-shaped warps on top of the first (Earl Morris Papers, Arizona State Museum Archives, File A–140: 21).

Color patterns in Extended Zone 1b resulted from using 2/2 twill twining over four warps with full and half twists to control the placement of color within the design (Fig. 5.6*a*4). Motifs are the same on the top and sole but in reversed colors. Identifying features for the round-puckered Extended Zone 1b include a smooth top surface; no raised patterning underneath; a double layer of warps; the same motif on top and sole in reversed colors; and the presence of full, weft-twining twists.

Zone 2 Color Motif Construction

All ten three-zone sandals have a Zone 2 arch color motif band (Figs. 5.26, 5.27). There was no information in Earl Morris' laboratory notes on the construction of these motifs. They possess columns like the Zone 2 motifs of scalloped-square and scalloped-puckered sandals and they have no raised work beneath them on the sole. The similar Zone 2 single warp layers in scalloped-square and scalloped-puckered sandals present numerous construction possibilities, necessitating further analysis on round-puckered sandals to determine these Zone 2 techniques.

Zone 3a Raised Geometric Patterning Construction

Geometric patterned raised soles (Zone 3a) appear on 16 two-zone and all 10 three-zone round-puckered sandals. Not all the laboratory notes for these 26 sandals with this zone contain construction data.

Raised row sequencing involves raised rows alternating with plain weave, with twining rows, or both, similar to all the scalloped-toe sandal types. The popular sequencing of RTPP again appears, here in five round-puckered sandals (Fig. 5.8*a*). A repeated sequence of raised row followed by five rows of simple twining (RTTTTT; Fig. 5.8*e*) occurs alone in one sandal and in another sandal that also has a three-row twining sequence (RTTT; Fig. 5.8*d*). Two sandals have a repeated sequence of one raised row followed by a simple twined row (RT; Fig. 5.8*c*).

Types of wrapping used in round-puckered sandals repeat types on the scalloped-toe sandals. Morris' team recorded interwarp wraps on 25 sandal illustrations but did not diagram the exact types. Four of the sandal diagrams exhibit twining with warp wraps on sandals with interwarp wraps. The only twining with warp wrap technique diagramed in the laboratory notes for round-puckered sandals appeared in just one sandal. The technique remains unnamed, but consisted of one weft with a full twist around its paired weft and then a wrap back around the previous warp (Fig. 5.9*a*2c).

Zone 3b Nongeometric Patterned Raised Sole Techniques

Eleven two-zone, round-puckered sandals have only nongeometric patterned raised soles (Zone 3b). Nongeometric patterned raised rows appear in two distinct forms: either as transverse ridges (five sandals) or diagonal ridges (two sandals); four sandals have both kinds of ridges.

Transverse ridges were made in two ways in these round-puckered sandals. In six sandals a single weft yarn wraps over–2 and then back around each successive warp across one weft row, a technique called soumak wrapping (Fig. 5.9*b*1c). One or more rows of plain weave appear between each soumak row. A second technique, occurring in one sandal that also contains soumak, used weft twining with wrapping, where each paired weft wrapped over three warps and back under one warp, thereby alternating wrapping around warps (each skipped a warp; Fig. 5.9*b*1b). This technique is called looped twining. Simple twining and plain weave rows are interspersed between these rows, producing a transverse ridge.

Diagonal ridges were created in Zone 3b in five sandals by weaving single weft yarns in a plain weave pattern (over–1, under–1), with occasional short floats over two warps on the sole. These floats are offset by one in each row, producing a distinct diagonal ridge (similar to Fig. 5.6*c*2). Plain weave rows are between these raised rows on some of the sandals.

Heel Finishing

The puckered heels of round-toe sandals were probably created in a manner similar to the construction of scalloped-puckered heels (see Fig. 5.21), but no information was obtained from the Morris papers on this feature.

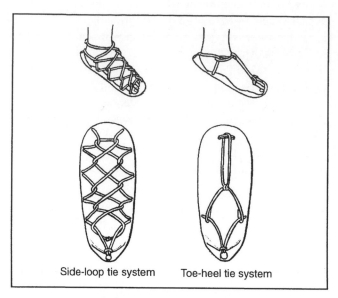

Figure 5.29. Side-loop and toe-heel tie systems on round toe–puckered heel sandals.

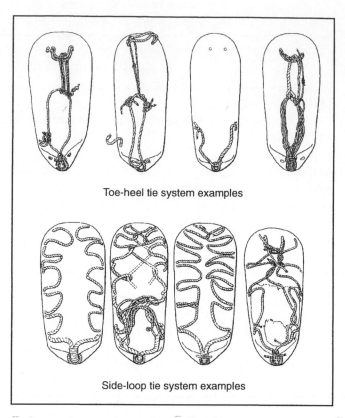

Figure 5.30. Tie systems on round toe–puckered heel sandals.

Ties

Both side-loop and toe-heel overall tie systems appear among round-puckered sandals (Figs. 5.29, 5.30).

COMPARISON OF TWINED SANDAL TYPES

There are more than twice as many Morris team diagrams of scalloped-puckered sandals (102) from Prayer Rock than of scalloped-square (48) or round-puckered (38) sandals. These quantities may represent conditions of preservation or of excavation in deposits reflecting the high population density of the A.D. 600s. Morris' team did not analyze all the construction techniques in all zones of sandal structure, perhaps because tight weft yarn packing would have required more sandal destruction through dissection. One scalloped-square and one round-puckered sandal from the Prayer Rock District were dissected, plus two additional sandals without provenience, a scalloped-puckered sandal and a sandal fragment without a toe but with a puckered heel. The two unprovenienced dissected sandals are included in this study only when construction illustrations overlap with provenienced sandal data.

Some comparisons and trend analyses cannot be made because lack of identification of a structure in one type may result from anomalies of sample size or lack of data. It is particularly difficult to compare construction techniques among the three sandal types within Zone 2 (information is especially lacking in scalloped-puckered and round-puckered sandals), among raised sequences in Zone 3a, and between types of relief wrappings in Zone 3a. Relative sizes of zones and types of zones, along with toe and heel silhouettes, can be compared based on their consistency within a type and their contrast between types. The numbers of sandals with interwarp and intrawarp wraps and type of Zone 3b structures can be used for comparisons, because nearly all the sandals with Zones 3a and 3b possess this information. The numbers of sandals with additional color motifs (Zones 1a, Extended 1a, 1b, Extended 1b, and 3a) cannot be compared definitively because, again, total numbers of sandals in each type may represent sampling biases.

Sometime in the A.D. 600s, artisans added round toes to their sandal repertoire. Why this happened may be answered through research like that of Talge (1995), which demonstrated that round-toe construction is much easier than scalloped-toe construction, with the change from 2/2 twill twining over four warps in scalloped toes

Table 5.2. Comparison of Zones for Three Types of Twined Sandals

Sandal Type	Zone 1a	Zone 1b	Zone 2	Zone 3a	Zone 3b
Scalloped–Square (48)	All (48)	None	All 3-zone except three sandals (22)	All (48)	3-zone sandals (3)
Scalloped–Puckered (102)	All (102; 37 with Extended Zone 1a)	None	All 3-zone (66)	All but one (101)	2-zone sandal (1)
Round–Puckered (38)	None	All (38; 2 with Extended Zone 1b)	All 3-zone (10)	All 3-zone (10) and 16 2-zone (26 total)	2-zone sandals (12)

NOTE. Numbers in parentheses indicate number of Morris sandals with laboratory data.

to over two warps with round toes. A round toe may be more comfortable and less clumsy to wear than a scalloped toe, because the round shape better fits the contours of the foot.

Heel silhouettes changed from flat and square to puckered. This technique may have provided a better fit to the foot, but required an extra step to create the puckered heel.

All three sandal types have two or more zones of construction (Table 5.2). Zone 1a construction and size changed through time. The earlier scalloped-square sandals used 2/2 twill twining over four warps, but for a very short length and with no color extensions. The scalloped-puckered sandals used the same construction, but 37 of them had extensions of Zone 1a using a full twist in the twining. The craftsperson had to pay attention to the placement of the motifs while the sandal was being constructed. There was also a lengthening of Zone 1a in the scalloped-puckered and round-puckered sandals. The round-puckered sandals, coexistent with the scalloped-puckered ones, did not use doubled warps in the Zone 1 region, thereby decreasing the complexity of construction (2/2 twill twining over two warps, not four), except in two exceptional cases.

All three sandal types include some sandals with a Zone 2 (scalloped-square, 46%; scalloped-puckered, 65%; round-puckered, 26%; Table 5.3). This zone lies approximately under the arch of the foot where the colored motifs would not have been visible when worn. Many sandals with a Zone 2 are well worn, with ragged holes in the heels and tearing where the toe loop attaches, indicating that they were not simply admired off the foot. In Zone 2 construction, the scalloped-square sandal had a narrow band that was widened on both the scalloped-puckered and round-toe sandals, representing a trend toward greater complexity. It was hard to determine Zone 2 constructions because of the tight packing of weft yarns. Morris' team identified 55 percent of the scalloped-square sandal Zone 2 constructions, but only 6 percent of the scalloped-puckered and none of the round-puckered (Table 5.3), although they did draw the colored designs (Chapter 6). One scalloped-square sandal was dissected, revealing one of the five structures identified from Zone 2 for scalloped-square sandals.

Almost all the Prayer Rock sandals (except 32% of the round-puckered and 0.01% of the scalloped-puckered sandals) had a Zone 3a geometric raised patterned

Table 5.3. Comparison of Zone 2 Constructions

Sandal Type	Construction Category: Twining	Construction Category: Weaving
Scalloped–Square (22; 12 with data)	1. Over–1, under–2 (top) (3 sandals) 2. Simple twining (1/2 and full turns) (5 sandals)	1. Tapestry (1 sandal) 2. Over–1, under–2 (top)* (3 sandals) 3. Over–1, under–1, over–1, under–2 (top)* (2 sandals)
Scalloped–Puckered (66; 4 with data)	1. 'A' and 'B' twining (2 sandals) 2. Variant of 'A' twining (1 sandal)	1. Tapestry (1 sandal)
Round–Puckered (10; no data)	No data	No data

* Following weft yarns.

Table 5.4. Comparison of Zone 3a among Sandal Types

Sandal Type	Raised Sequence	Interwarp Wraps	On-warp Wraps
Scalloped–Square (48 with Zone 3a)	1. RTPP (23 sandals)	42 sandals (6 without data)	31 sandals (always with interwarp wraps)
Scalloped–Puckered (101 with Zone 3a)	1. RTPP (15 sandals) 2. RTTT (4 sandals) 3. RTPP + RTTT (1 sandal) 4. RTPP + RPPT (1 sandal) 5. RTPP + TTPP (1 sandal)	99 sandals (3 without data)	22 sandals (always with interwarp wraps)
Round–Puckered (26 with Zone 3a)	1. RTPP (5 sandals) 2. RTTTTT (1 sandal) 3. RT (2 sandals) 4. RTTTTT + RTTT (1 sandal)	25 sandals (1 without data)	4 sandals (always with interwarp wraps)

section. This amazing consistency probably reflects the usefulness of a raised tread for traction, but does not explain the desire for geometric patterning. Corrugation through transverse ridges (Zone 3b of round-puckered sandals and one scalloped-puckered sandal) would have been sufficient for practical needs. All Zone 3a sections used a sequence of raised plus plain weave, simple twining, or both to throw the raised rows into relief (Table 5.4). The sequence RTPP was the most common and persistent through time (46 of all the sandals, 26%, had this sequence). A greater variety of sequences occurred among the scalloped-puckered sandals (5 types), but only one type, RTPP, was present in scalloped-square sandals, and four sequence types were in round-puckered sandals (Table 5.4). Of the sandals with a Zone 3a, 94 percent had data about the use of interwarp and on-warp wrap techniques, and all of them revealed use of the interwarp wrap. On-warp wraps appeared only when interwarp wraps were also present in a sandal. Scalloped-square sandals used more on-warp wraps (74%) than scalloped-puckered (22%) or round-puckered (16%) ones. Again, there seems to be a trend toward less work through time by dropping an additional relief structure, the on-warp wrap, and by decreasing the total space devoted to raised patterning (Zone 3a size) from scalloped-square to the later scalloped-puckered and round-puckered sandal types.

Ann Morris observed in her manuscript (Chapter 2, p. 22) that after scalloped-square types, the sandals "stressed the color effect [increased Zone 2 area] to the detriment of the knotted sole patterns [decreased Zone 3a area] which become...less intricate [fewer sandals contain on-warp wraps] as time went on." Round-toe sandals show the least use of geometric raised patterning (68% versus nearly 100% of scalloped-square and scalloped-puckered sandals) and the most use of the cor-

rugated style, nongeometric raised patterning (32% versus 0.01% of scalloped-puckered and 6% of scalloped-square sandals). Ann Morris noted (Chapter 2, p. 23) that "the knotted and barred sole patterns [geometric patterning] so degenerate as to nearly lose their function as design [in round-puckered sandals]." However, the assumption that round-toe sandals have less geometric patterning may be skewed by the total number of each type of sandal found at Prayer Rock and may not reflect actual manufacture. Data on the structures used for interwarp and on-warp wraps were scanty, probably because the tight construction in Zone 3a made analysis difficult. Only 5 percent of all sandals with a Zone 3a had information on Zone 3a structures (Table 5.5). Three of four techniques were identified from sandal dissection.

Although only 16 sandals had a Zone 3b (scalloped-square, 3; scalloped-puckered 1; round-puckered 12), all but three had details about their Zone 3b construction technique (Table 5.6). Transverse lines were more common (13 sandals) than diagonal lines (7 sandals), with four sandals having both. The most complex technique was the soumak wrapping with "pile" of the scalloped-square time period. Diagonal lines are visible on round-puckered sandals but less so on the scalloped-square sandal, resulting from differences in the placement of the sole floats.

There appears to be a trend toward decreasing color motif use from scalloped-square (65% with color) and scalloped-puckered sandals (65% with color) to round-puckered sandals (26%). No extension of Zone 1a occurred in scalloped-square sandals, but 37 scalloped-puckered sandals had these increased areas of color motif decoration. There were also more sandals with a Zone 2 in the scalloped-puckered sandals (66 specimens versus 22). Round-puckered sandals showed overall less

Table 5.5. Comparison of Interwarp and On-warp Wraps Used in Zone 3a

Sandal Type	Interwarp Wraps	On-warp Wraps
Scalloped–Square (48 with Zone 3a)	1. Double-wrap (5 sandals) (42 sandals with interwarp wraps)	1. Single wrap (2 sandals) 2. Lock knot (1 sandal) (31 sandals with on-warp wraps)
Scalloped–Puckered (101 with Zone 3a)	1. Double-wrap (3 sandals) (99 sandals with interwarp wraps)	1. Single wrap (1 sandal) (22 sandals with on-warp wraps)
Round–Puckered (26 with Zone 3a)	No data (25 sandals with interwarp wraps)	1. Full twist over paired and wrapped warp (1 sandal) (4 sandals with on-warp wraps)

coloring with fewer Zone 2 sandals (10), only two extensions of Zone 1b, and only two sandals with other color patterning (Zone 1b). Ann Morris noted this trend toward using less color in round-puckered sandals (Chapter 2, p. 23). "Colored decoration was practically obsolete [with round-puckered sandals]," but she felt that the round-puckered sandal followed the scalloped-puckered type chronologically. As noted in Chapter 3, tree-ring evidence unavailable to Earl Morris when he wrote his 1944 article (Chapter 2), suggests that the round-puckered sandal type coexists with the scalloped-puckered sandal type, at least in the Prayer Rock District.

Besides Zone 2, there were other zones with occasional use of color motifs: Zones 1a, 1b, Extended 1a and 1b, and Zones 3a and 3b (Table 5.7). A normal zone construction was used to create transverse lines, checker patterns, and wedge shapes by the insertion of dyed weft yarns in Zones 1a and 1b (regular 2/2 twill twining) and Zone 3a (regular geometric raised sequencing). Motifs in Extended Zones 1a and 1b used the regular zone 2/2 twill twining but with the addition of full twists. The only nonnormal zone constructions for color motif incorporation were in the scalloped-square sandal Zone 3a, with the use of staircase weft insertion (for diagonals) and tapestry weave (for lines and blocks), and Zone 3b with tapestry (2 sandals), and over–1, under–1, over–1, under–2 weaving (one sandal).

Table 5.8 summarizes all the construction techniques recorded among these three sandal types and the zones in which they are located. Twenty-one different construction techniques were identified among the 188 Prayer Rock sandals that possessed laboratory analysis data. Thirteen types of twining were used, from simple twining to the complex "a and b" twining with wrapping for Zone 2 and the lock knot and variant for relief wrapping in Zone 3a. Five woven structures were present, with fewer varieties than in twining and with the majority of plain weave. Other techniques included wrapping (soumak and soumak plus "pile") and staircase weft inlay. The soumak with "pile" was one of the most complex techniques in terms of finger manipulation. Ann Morris stated (Chapter 2, p. 21) that "during the elapse of the Post Basket Maker period [A.D. 400-700] 29 different manipulations of warp and weft were utilized for the production of the completed sandal and of these, the majority occur in the earliest part of that period [scalloped-square type] before custom had determined upon these stitches best adapted to need." (Of the Morris team diagrams used in this study, only 21 of the 29 techniques were noted, perhaps because Ann Morris' manuscript is not based on the Prayer Rock District sandals portrayed in these diagrams but on Canyon del Muerto and Grand Gulch sandals.) Of the 21 different structures in the Prayer Rock District sandal diagrams,

Table 5.6. Comparison of Zone 3b Raised Sole Structures

Sandal Type	Tranverse Ridges	Diagonal Ridges
Scalloped–Square (3 sandals)	1. Soumak with "pile" (2 sandals)	1. Over–1, under–1, over–1, under–2 weaving (top) offset by one warp but with scattered floats (1 sandal)
Scalloped–Puckered (1 sandal)	1. Looped twining (1 sandal)	None
Round–Puckered (12 sandals)	1. Soumak (6 sandals) 2. Looped twining (1 sandal)	1. Over–2 with under–1, over–1 weaving with patterning offset by 1 with distinct diagonal lines on the sole (5 sandals)

Table 5.7. Comparison of Color Motif Construction within Zones 1a, 1b, 3a, and 3b

Zone	Scalloped–Square Sandal	Scalloped–Puckered Sandal	Round–Puckered Sandal
Zone 1a	None	Lines of dyed wefts in 2/2 twill twining over–4 warps with half turns (2 sandals)	None
Extended Zone 1a	None	Dyed wefts in 2/2 twill twining over–4 warps with half and full turns (37 sandals)	None
Zone 1b	None	None	2/2 twill twining with half and full turns (1 sandal over–2 warps; 1 sandal over–4 warps)
Extended Zone 1b	None	None	2/2 twill twining over–4 warps with half and full turns (2 sandals)
Zone 3a	1. Lines of dyed wefts in raised sole sequence (11 sandals) 2. Tapestry (2 sandals) 3. Staircase weft inlay (4 sandals)	Lines of dyed wefts in raised sole sequence (2 sandals)	None
Zone 3b	1. Tapestry (2 sandals) 2. Over–1, under–1, over–1, under–2 weaving (top view; following weft yarns) (1 sandal)	None	None

14 of them were recorded in the scalloped-square sandals, 11 in the scalloped-puckered, and 8 in the round-puckered sandals. However, the total number of sandals in each type varied and for certain zones no analysis of structures was undertaken by Morris' team. One cannot assume, then, that a greater variety of construction techniques was used during the early scalloped-square period of the A.D. 400s.

Some of the 21 construction techniques used in these sandals, such as slit tapestry, soumak wrapping, and looped twining, are evident today in various parts of the world. However, several other techniques do not appear to have survived after A.D. 1300, including raised techniques like the lock knot (Fig. 5.9a2b), the lock knot variant (Fig. 5.9a2c), and soumak wrapping with two yarns caught under every soumak loop (Fig. 5.9b1a). Color constructions that did not persist are the staircase weft inlay (Fig. 5.11) and the variant of the "A weave" twining technique (Fig. 5.6b4). The color structure of "A" and "B" weaving (Fig. 5.6b1–b3) was noted in Kidder's work (1926: 622, Fig. 4f, g). Several raised structures appeared in a sandal studied by Kidder (1926: 622, Fig. 4h, i) that are not recorded elsewhere, including the raised structure called by Earl Morris "Kidder's single wrap" (Fig. 5.9a2a) and double wraps with ½

turns for spacing (Fig. 5.9a1b). The detailed diagrams presented here should enable the modern fiber artist to resurrect these "lost" techniques.

The overall trend among these three sandal types is toward less complexity of construction and silhouette through time. Although contemporary, the round-toe shape and construction is easier to produce than the scalloped toe. The area of Zone 3a raised geometric patterning decreases from scalloped-square to later scalloped-puckered and round-puckered types. Complexity of technique also decreases as a result of fewer on-warp wraps in the two later types. The areas devoted to Zones 1a or 1b increase from scalloped-square to later types, but these zones represent easier construction techniques compared with Zone 3a. Zone 2 increases in area with scalloped-puckered and round-puckered sandals, but lack of information about total numbers of structures prevents any trend analysis of structure complexity. Use of Extended Zones 1a and 1b, which required either preplanning or more attention during construction by the sandal maker, increased markedly during the scalloped-puckered period, with none appearing in the earlier scalloped-square period. As indicated, however, the quantities of each type of sandal may not represent the actual number of sandals manufactured.

Table 5.8. Comparison of Fabric Construction Techniques

Structure	Scalloped-Square Sandal	Scalloped-Puckered Sandal	Round-Puckered Sandal
Twining			
Simple twining:			
Half turns	Zone 3a	Zones 3a and 3b	Zones 3a and 3b
Half turns and full turns	Zone 2		
2/2 Twill twining over–2 warps:			
Half turns	Zone 1a	Zone 1a	Zone 1b
2/2 Twill twining over–4 warps:			
Half turns	Zone 1a	Zone 1a	
Half turns and full turns		Extended Zone 1a	Extended Zone 1b
Twining over–1, under–2 (top view)			
Scattered floats	Zone 2		
'A' and 'B' twining with wrapping		Zone 2	
Variant of 'A' twining		Zone 2	
Looped twining		Zone 3b	Zone 3b
Double wrap	Zone 3a	Zone 3a	
Single wrap	Zone 3a	Zone 3a	
Lock knot	Zone 3a		
On-warp variant of lock knot			Zone 3a
Weaving			
Plain weave	Zone 3a	Zone 3a	Zones 3a and 3b
Tapestry	Zones 2, 3a, 3b	Zone 2	
Over–1, under–2 weaving (top view)*			
Scattered floats on sole	Zone 2		
Over–1, under–1, over–1, under–2 weaving (top view)*			
Scattered floats on sole	Zones 2 and 3b		
Diagonal ridges on sole			Zone 3b
Miscellaneous			
Soumak wrapping			Zone 3b
Soumak wrapping plus "pile"	Zone 3b		
Staircase weft inlay	Zone 3a		
Number of structures per sandal type	14	11	8

* Following weft yarns.

The presence of elaborately decorated scalloped-square sandals (3) and the lack of such later may, again, be a sampling bias.

CHRONOLOGICAL COMPARISONS

Interestingly, the temporally preceding square-square twined sandal of Basketmaker II bears both striking similarities and dissimilarities to the Basketmaker III twined sandal types. No square-square sandals were reported from the Prayer Rock District, but they were recorded in neighboring areas such as Grand Gulch, Broken Roof Cave, Canyon del Muerto, and the Kayenta area, and, more distantly, in the Kanab region (see Table 4.1, Fig. 4.6). These comparisons are based on 52 square-square twined sandals (Table 4.1), some extensively analyzed by Earl Morris and his team. The team provided construction information on only 20 square-square twined sandals (Deegan 1996), compared with analyses of 48 scalloped-square, 102 scalloped-puckered, and 38 round-puckered Prayer Rock District sandals.

Like the Basketmaker III twined sandals, the Basketmaker II twined sandal is made of yarn, usually 2-ply or 3-ply. Its total number of warps ranges from 19 to 35, with an average of 25 (for 8 recorded sandals) compared to 26 to 30 average warps for the Basketmaker III twined sandals. The square-square sandal has a raised sole without geometric patterning and only cross-wise corrugation, with spacing between the raised rows using plain weave or simple twining as occurs later. Several raised construction techniques appear in Basketmaker II twined sandals that continue in later types. Soumak wrapping (Fig. 5.9*b*1c) was used for transverse raised line construction, also seen later in Zone 3b of round-puckered sandals (6 specimens). Looped twining (Fig. 5.9*b*1b) created transverse raised lines in two Basketmaker II sandals and later in one scalloped-puckered sandal and one round-puckered sandal.

For color constructions, the slit tapestry technique (Fig. 5.6*c*1b) extends from Basketmaker II (1 sandal) into Basketmaker III times for Zone 3b of two scalloped-square sandals, for small designs in Zone 3a (2 scalloped-square sandals), and for Zone 2 of one scalloped-puckered sandal. Simple twining using full turns occurs in both Basketmaker II (2 sandals with checkerboard designs) and Basketmaker III scalloped-square sandals in Zone 2 (5 sandals).

Despite these similarities, the Basketmaker II sandals have no raised geometric sole patterning as do the Basketmaker III sandals. There is no Zone 3a in Basketmaker II sandals, only Zone 3b with transverse lines predominating. Spacing row sequences center on either simple twining or plain weave, less mixing as occurs later, and no evidence of the combined RTPP sequence that later becomes popular. Two raised techniques share some features with later Basketmaker III techniques.

Ann Morris stated (Chapter 2, p. 22) that "owing to the similarity of certain detailed features of construction, obsolete in Post Basket Maker [Basketmaker III] times, [her scalloped-square "burial" sandals] are thought to be a ceremonial survival of Basket Maker [Basketmaker II] methods. . . . " Perhaps one of these obsolete construction techniques includes Basketmaker II soumak wrapping with a weft yarn caught under every other soumak loop (Deegan 1996). This technique is similar to the catching of two weft yarns under every soumak loop (Fig. 5.9*b*1a) observed in two scalloped-square Basketmaker III sandals that are similar to Ann Morris' "burial" sandal. Additionally, the Basketmaker

III double wrap (Fig. 5.9*a*1b) with its occasional ½ turns was used for raised sole geometric patterning. During Basketmaker II times, the double wrap appears but without any use of ½ turns that would have spaced the sole "knobs" for patterning. Instead, transverse rows of continuous raised "knobs" appear. Perhaps the Basketmaker III sandal makers received their idea for raised "knobs" from the earlier technique and spaced them in patterns by using occasional ½ turns. Several unnamed combined twining and wrapping techniques were used in square-square sandals for transverse line construction that apparently did not survive into later sandals (Deegan 1996). Finally, an extremely complex double warp and double weft structure appears in Basketmaker II sandals that did not persist later (Deegan 1996).

Compared to Basketmaker III sandals, little use was made of colored designs in square-square twined sandals. No Zone 2 or Extended Zones 1a or 1b exist in these early sandals. Occasional dashed lines appear in Zone 3b, and some sandals have red cross-bands or checkerboarding near the toe. Two sandals had more extensive colored geometric patterning in red or in red and black in the midsection. Slit tapestry continued from Basketmaker II into Basketmaker III, but the slit twining of Basketmaker II did not appear in the Prayer Rock Basketmaker III sandals. Slit twining is more time-consuming to create and may have been abandoned in preference for slit tapestry.

Not to be overlooked is the obvious difference in toe shape. The square toe sandal, sometimes fringed, bolstered, or both does not repeat in later twined sandals. Talge (1995: 59–67) discovered the square toe was easier to make than the scalloped toe and about equal to the round toe in ease of manufacture. Although the square shape might have been more awkward to wear than a pulled-in scallop or round toe, the fringing would have definitely created more difficulties in movement, a possible reason for abandoning the square toe.

As a group, few scalloped-square sandals have survived. The bulk of those recorded came from the Prayer Rock District and are included in this study (48). Eleven more scalloped-square sandals came from the Canyon del Muerto area, but they have not been studied extensively (Table 4.2).

Table 4.3 lists the large numbers of scalloped-puckered twined sandals that came from numerous sites in northeastern Arizona and those recorded from southwestern Colorado, southeastern Utah, and northwestern New Mexico (Table 4.3, Fig. 4.12). These complex sandals are remarkably similar from site to site. Those from Tseyi-Hatsosi Canyon (Deegan 1992, 1997) and other northeastern Arizona scalloped-puckered sandals (Kidder 1926; Baldwin 1938, 1939) share many similar construction features and zone layouts, including use of Zone 1a, Extended Zone 1a, Zone 2, and Zone 3a. Baldwin (1938: 467) called these "the most common and the most characteristic sandal of the Basket Maker III period." Because the zone layouts are similar and complex construction techniques and other features are shared, it seems unlikely that these features simultaneously sprang independently from different groups. Although these techniques are complicated, few sandals show errors, perhaps hinting at craft specialization and trade.

Like the scalloped-square sandals, the round-puckered sandals appear in small quantities and in few sites. The highest number in one area is again from Prayer Rock (38 specimens; Table 4.4, Fig. 4.13). Baldwin (1938: 479–481, 1939: 224, 234–236) has described similar construction features in the 11 round-puckered sandals he analyzed from northeastern Arizona.

Although not reported from the Prayer Rock District, the Pueblo shaped-cupped twined sandals were found widely scattered in the Four Corners region. Few of them have been analyzed for construction details so they cannot be fully compared with the earlier prehistoric Puebloan twined sandals (Table 4.5, Fig. 4.15). Earl Morris (1919: 49, 50–51) briefly discussed 20 sandals from Aztec Ruin and Magers (1986: 257–259, 261, 264–265) analyzed 78 sandals from Antelope House. Earl Morris' team did study the Aztec Ruin sandals (32) at about the same time as they worked on the Prayer Rock footwear. A few details from the Aztec Ruin laboratory sheets are included here (Earl Morris Papers, File A–141). Magers findings corroborate those of Earl Morris.

The shaped-cupped twined sandal is made of yarn, has numerous warps (average of 32 among the 25 Aztec Ruin sandals with data), and usually contains raised patterned soles with raised structures of interwarp double wraps and transverse geometric patterning in looped twining. Like the earlier twined sandals, raised rows are spaced by simple twining. Decorative colors are similar to earlier sandals, including red, yellow, and black. The few color geometric patterning constructions are not new and include slit tapestry (1 sandal), slit twining (not recorded in those sandals that date between Basketmaker II and Pueblo times; 3 slit, 2 interlock, and 1 dovetail twining), and simple twining with ½ turns in solid color cross-bands (7 sandals).

The toe and heel silhouettes differ from earlier twined sandals. Probably the toe construction was similar to that for round-puckered sandals but the toe was pulled in to a right or left foot shape, with many sandals having added warps for a toe jog. This same shaped toe occurs in braided sandals of the Pueblo period. The heel cupping of the Pueblo twined sandal was created while finishing the heel, not after the heel was completed as in puckered heel sandals. Both toe and heel shapes provided better comfort during wear because they followed the contour of the foot.

The raised geometric patterned sole designs in Pueblo twined sandals are often spread all over the sandal with wide spaces between the raised patterns. There is no real Zone 3a in these sandals, because the raised portions continue under colored patterning. It would seem that the raised sole lost much of its value as tread during this period. There is a trend from Basketmaker II of all-over tread without patterning in square-square sandals, to Basketmaker III with large areas of raised patterning in scalloped-square sandals, to Basketmaker III heel use in scalloped-puckered and round-puckered sandals, to Pueblo times with almost no tread construction. Magers (1986: 259) also noticed that 24 percent of the sandals she analyzed did not have raised patterning "on the more vulnerable heels and toes."

Of the 32 Aztec Ruin sandals with data sheets from Morris' team, only 5 have geometric colored patterns. Most color designs spread the length of the sandal (3 specimens) or center on the mid-section (7 specimens with cross-bands). Magers' analysis also revealed 9 sandals with cross-bands of color, again often spread nearly the length of the sandal (Magers 1986: 259). There is no real Extended Zone 1b or Zone 2 in these shaped-cupped twined sandals. A brown color remains in these sandals. I do not know whether it is an altered dye color or if the yarns were originally brown.

Three Pueblo period twined sandals were constructed in allover 2/2 twill twining with no raised sole work. One had a complex geometric pattern in black and white, achieved by executing full turns. Magers (1986: 257) reported four sandals at Antelope House in 2/2 twill twining.

Earl Morris (1944a: 240) observed that the Pueblo twined sandals were "less elaborate than in the earlier specimens" in both colored and raised patterning. The Basketmaker III use of Extended Zones 1a and 1b and Zone 2 for colored patterning is absent in these Pueblo sandals. The raised patterning that tightly covered the sole in Basketmaker III sandals became widely spaced, allover raised patterning in Pueblo sandals.

OVERVIEW

Toe and heel silhouette changes through time show marked improvement in efforts to shape the sandal to the foot, culminating in Pueblo times with the shaped-cupped silhouette that mimics the shape of the foot (see Fig. 3.6). Raised soles develop from a practical, non-slip, nondecorated tread in Basketmaker II to an apex of decoration in Basketmaker III on to less area of decoration and widely spaced tread with little practical value in Pueblo times. The elaborate Basketmaker III twined sandals also exhibit the greatest variety of spacing sequences, with Pueblo times showing the least. Basketmaker II transverse sole ridges, although not geometrically patterned, incorporate numerous construction techniques and the period could be considered a time of experimentation (Deegan 1996). Basketmaker III raised sole patterning continued some of the Basketmaker II techniques, but with spacing to create geometric patterning. The Pueblo twined sandals show that continuity existed in raised construction techniques, some of which are similar to Basketmaker II techniques and some to Basketmaker III techniques, with only a few minor additions to the repertoire.

The addition of color is limited in Basketmaker II twined sandals to red or red and black, expanding to paired color decoration in Basketmaker III times of red and yellow or black and tan. These colors may reflect an increased knowledge of dyes and pigments. A brown color dye apparently was added in Pueblo times, but colors were no longer paired.

Basketmaker II twined sandals contain bands of color and a few geometric patterns, but there is an explosion of designs and arrangements in Basketmaker III footwear. Pueblo sandals have simple color motifs, again revealing bands and a few geometric patterns. The limited but similar techniques of color motif structures in Basketmaker II and Pueblo sandals contrast with the greater variety of Basketmaker III color structures.

The prehistoric Puebloan craftspeople of the Prayer Rock District were skilled in a wide variety of techniques that they incorporated into their sandals, in some cases using as many as four or more different structures per sandal. Twenty-one different techniques appear among the 188 sandals with analytical data. These craftspeople had to plan the placement of color motifs and geometric raised patterning before or while the sandal structures were created in Zones 2, 3a, and Extended Zones 1a and 1b. Thirty-nine sandals even possessed an Extended Zone 1a or 1b, Zone 2, and a Zone 3a. No identical sandals and almost no flaws occur among these 188 specimens. Additionally, each sandal required yards of spun and plied yarn, representing time devoted to the gathering and processing of plant materials, to gathering dye materials, and to dyeing yarns for use in colored motifs—truly remarkable workmanship and a highlight of Southwestern prehistoric textile accomplishment.

CHAPTER SIX

Decoration of Basketmaker Twined Sandals

Kelley Ann Hays-Gilpin

Basketmaker twined sandals are among the most elaborately decorated artifacts ever made and used by prehistoric Pueblo people. This art form reached its peak of technical and stylistic complexity in the late Basketmaker III period, between about A.D. 600 and 700. Sandals were not the largest nor the most highly visible artifacts in use at that time; that distinction most likely belongs to baskets. The quantity of worn out and discarded remnants found by archaeologists suggest that sandals did not last very long. Yet the time, skill, and creativity invested in making intricate textured and colored designs attest to the unusual importance the Basketmaker people attached to their footwear.

For the study of decoration, I was able to analyze 198 whole or nearly whole Basketmaker III period twined sandals in the Prayer Rock District collections in the Arizona State Museum. These sandals were excavated by Earl Morris in 1931, the year in which the most detailed provenience records were kept. The designs on nearly all the sandals recovered that year were drawn by Morris' students and colleagues at the University of Colorado. To find out what proportion of sandals were decorated, what parts of sandals were decorated, and how designs were structured, I recorded sandal shape, location of decorated zones, design elements and motifs, and basic symmetry categories. For research on construction techniques (Chapter 5), Ann Deegan used only the 188 sandals from Prayer Rock that had been drawn and diagramed by Earl Morris' team; thus the numbers of sandals described in these two chapters and the cited proportions of sandal types vary slightly.

Many of the Earl Morris worksheets include notes on symmetry. Ink drawings being prepared for publication were grouped into general symmetry categories and many were annotated with comments and questions about the correct classification of designs according to their structures. Earl Morris' interest in symmetry was probably stimulated by the work of Anna O. Shepard, his colleague at the University of Colorado and the Carnegie Institution. Best remembered today for her highly technical analyses of pottery materials and their geological sources, Shepard was also especially interested in pottery decoration in the Southwest and Mesoamerica. Her monograph entitled *The Symmetry of Abstract Design with Special Reference to Ceramic Decoration* was published by the Carnegie Institution in 1948 (see also Shepard 1956: 267–281). In it, Shepard points out that only a limited number of design structures are mathematically possible and that out of all possible structures, artisans of a given culture and era are likely to select only a few. Unless a figure is asymmetrical and appears only once, any design can be broken down into fundamental, asymmetrical figures that are repeated in identifiable ways.

A few years prior to Shepard's work, George Brainerd applied symmetry analysis to middle Pueblo III period Anasazi pottery of the Monument Valley area (dating about A.D. 1200 to 1259) and to Maya Fine Orange pottery from Chichen Itza in the Yucatan, where Earl and Ann Morris spent many field seasons. Earl Morris may have read Brainerd's work as well as Shepard's. Brainerd (1942) discovered that the Anasazi potters used a more limited repertoire of design structures than did Maya potters and that they consistently preferred one symmetry category: bifold rotation. The Morris sandal collection shows that centuries before the pots Brainerd studied were made, the potters' Basketmaker ancestors already preferred bifold symmetry and they used it in complex ways and in combination with other motions.

The four motions Earl Morris used to sort sandal designs are: translation (sliding along a line), rotation (turning around a point), mirror reflection (as in the human body's left and right sides), and glide reflection

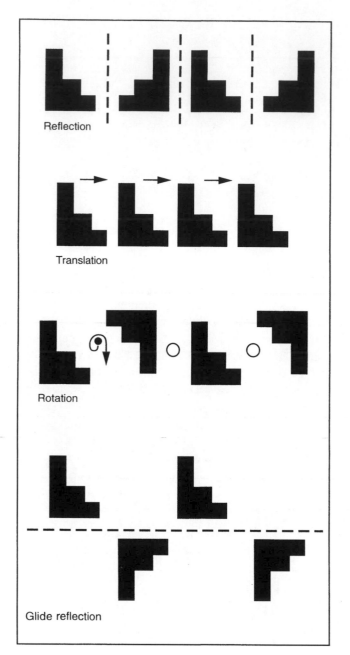

Figure 6.1. Motions by which elements repeat to form symmetrical designs.

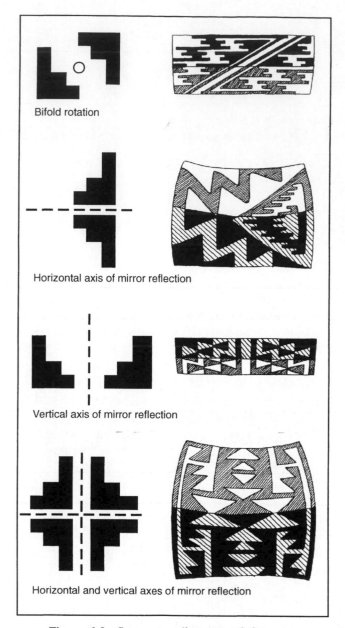

Figure 6.2. Symmetry diagrams of frequent finite sandal design structures.

(as in human footprints alternating right and left along a line). Figure 6.1 illustrates these motions (Shepard 1948: 219; Washburn and Crowe 1988: 44). Three axial categories (finite, one-dimensional, and two-dimensional) describe the way figures can be repeated on a plane surface. Figures can rotate around a central point or they can reflect across one or more axes that intersect at a central point, forming a *finite* design like those shown in Figure 6.2. Figures with more than one axis

of mirror reflection also admit rotation. Although such figures are structured by *both* rotation and reflection, I emphasize reflection here, to distinguish them from figures that admit only rotation.

Figures can rotate, reflect, translate, or glide reflect in 7 combined ways along a single linear axis, forming a one-dimensional or band pattern (Fig. 6.3). Figures can repeat using the same four motions combined in 17 ways in two directions, forming a two-dimensional or "wallpaper" pattern (Fig. 6.4), where the basic element, a stepped triangle, rotates in two directions. The design

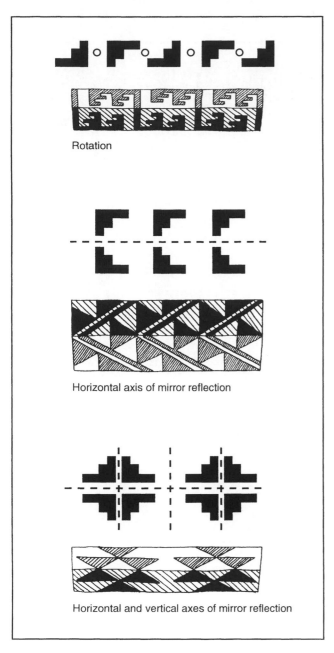

Figure 6.3. Symmetry diagrams of frequent one-dimensional sandal design structures.

Figure 6.4. Symmetry diagram of a two-dimensional sandal design structured by rotation and reflection. (See Figure 6.42, 503–H, for an example.)

could continue on infinitely with these same motions to cover a wall, a blanket, a pottery jar, or the sole of a sandal. Even more categories can be generated by alternating colors. Basketmaker artisans rendered all three classes of designs in sandals, many of them with color changes, but Earl Morris never completed a detailed symmetry analysis of them. In this study, I have done little more than he did, identifying points of rotation and lines of reflection to classify designs according to combinations of the four basic motions and according to finite, one-dimensional and two-dimensional classes. I

have not explored the nuances of combinations of different elements and movements, color changes, and frequencies of the different symmetry classes.

During the last two decades, archaeologist Dorothy Washburn has brought the study of symmetry far beyond Shepard's original explorations. She has developed a precise, standardized terminology for describing all possible plane patterns (symmetrical designs on flat surfaces, including curved surfaces that can be viewed as flat, such as bowls and jars). She bases her work on the sciences of crystallography and pattern mathematics, and she has produced a handbook for symmetry analysis in collaboration with mathematician Donald Crowe (Washburn and Crowe 1988; see also Zaslow 1981; Zaslow and Dittert 1977).

Washburn and Crowe argue that although anthropologists agree that artifact style communicates information about social identities, and even that individuals actively use style to negotiate identities and to create new roles and statuses, anthropology lacks an appropriate set of methods for studying style. Style is a term usually used to describe general similarities, for example, "style is a way of doing things." Each researcher tends to define style a little differently. Anthropologists have thus far failed to develop adequate methods for comparing stylistic behavior through time, across space, and among populations. Symmetry analysis provides a precise, replicable, scientific method for studying one important aspect of style. Washburn and Crowe (1988: 38) write:

The different kinds of symmetry are not artifact specific, but are based on a universal system of motion classes that may appear on any type of artifact with a repeated design. We can observe whether they occur consistently or not in a number of bodies of data and in this way observe trends which enable us to make general statements about the relationships of certain structures with certain types of behavior. Should we wish to use the concept of style, we could say that the consistent use of a certain symmetry is a stylistic behavior.

Symmetry analysis "is a powerful tool to organize and objectively present these cultural preferences. It does not explain these preferences, but it does organize the data in such a way that hypotheses may be formulated and tested and, ultimately, theories developed" (Washburn and Crowe 1988: 40). Before we can understand style and what it means for its users, we must "define and study the very universal properties which are the fundamental components of the perceptual process." Symmetry is one such property, and "Studies to date have clearly and consistently shown that a given culture preferentially uses only certain of these structural transformations and how the consistencies and changes in such structural aspects of style directly relate to cultural consistencies and changes" (Washburn and Crowe 1988: 268).

This chapter introduces only the basics of Basketmaker symmetry and other aspects of decorative style. Perhaps perceptual psychologists, clothing and textile specialists, and fine artists, as well as anthropologists, can contribute more insight by studying these facets in greater detail.

SCALLOPED TOE–SQUARE HEEL SANDALS

Fifty-two sandals in the Prayer Rock collection have scalloped toes and flat, square heels. Scalloped-square sandals have been reported from Broken Flute Cave, Cave 3, Pocket Cave, and Obelisk Cave, and they date to the late A.D. 400s, in the early Basketmaker III period. This type of sandal is very rare in deposits that contain sandals of the other two major decorated types discussed below.

Ann Deegan (Chapter 5) defines distinct zones in sandals based on construction technique. Scalloped-square sandals have two zones or three zones. The front of the toe area on all scalloped-square sandals contains an area of doubled warps with 2/2 twill twining, designated Zone 1a. This zone is never decorated.

All but nine of the scalloped-square sandals examined have raised patterns on their soles, designated Zone 3a. Sketches of 36 of these relief patterns appear in the Morris archives (Figs. 6.5–6.8). Triangles, stepped lines, parallel bars, dots, rectangles, and other small repeated elements cover almost the entire sole.

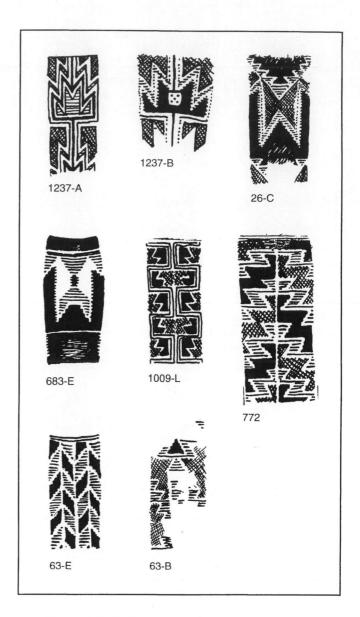

Figure 6.5. Scalloped toe–square heel sandal sole designs with vertical axes of mirror reflection.

These simple elements are arranged in a wide variety of symmetrical patterns. Most Zone 3a designs have a symmetry axis from the toe to the heel. Sometimes the design is reflected across this axis (Figs. 6.5, 6.9) and in other designs there is a thin central band flanked by elements that rotate around it (see Fig. 5.7). Less frequently, the design has a point of bifold rotation in the middle of the design field, resulting in a diagonal or stepped line across the sole (Fig. 6.10). Occasionally, there are cross-wise symmetry axes of mirror symmetry, that is, the mirror lines run perpendicular to the toe-to-heel symmetry axis (Figs. 6.6, 6.11).

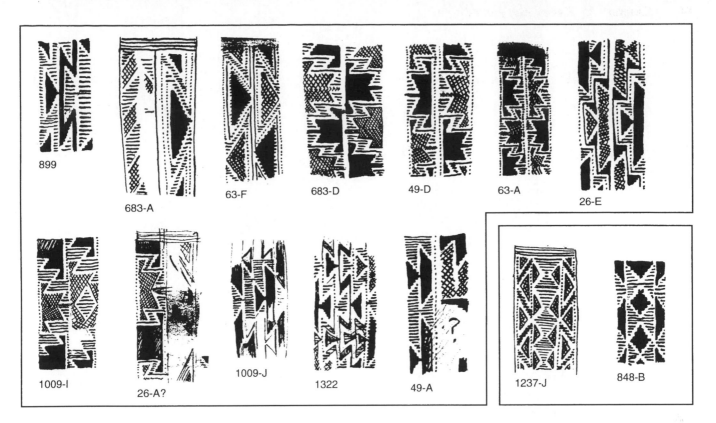

Figure 6.6. Scalloped toe–square heel sandal sole designs with horizontal axes of mirror reflection.

Figure 6.7. Scalloped toe–square heel sandal sole designs with horizontal and vertical axes of mirror reflection.

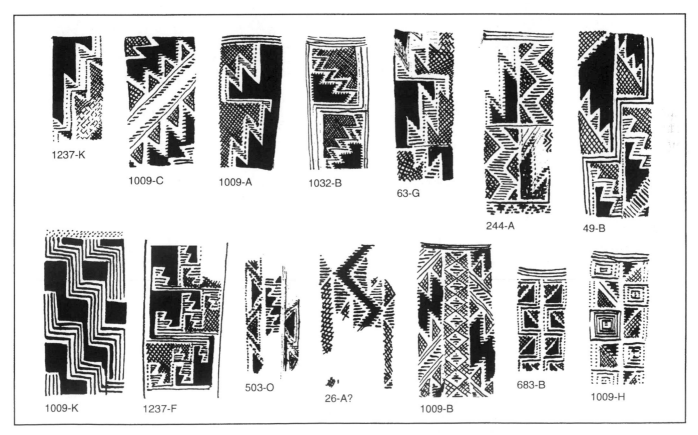

Figure 6.8. Scalloped toe–square heel sandal sole designs with point axes of bifold rotation.

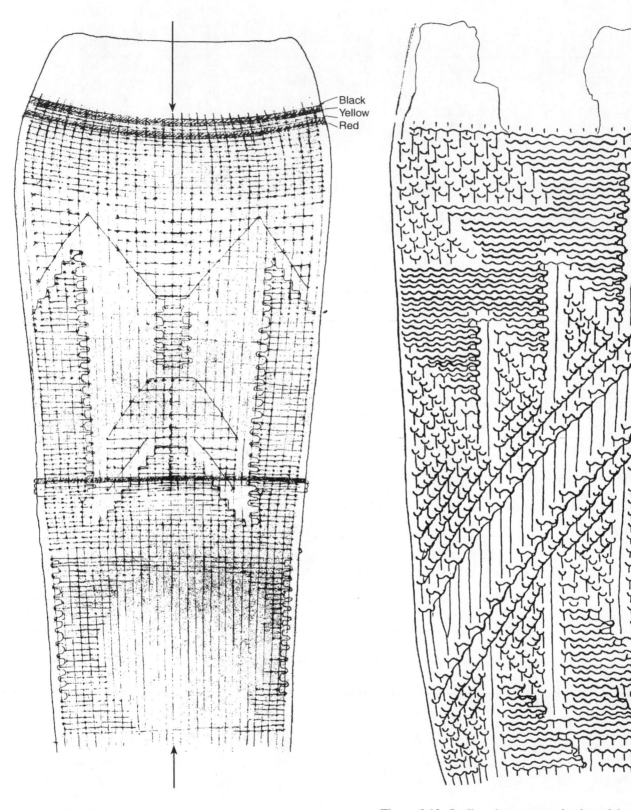

Figure 6.9. Scalloped toe–square heel sandal with sole design structured by a vertical axis of mirror reflection, sole view. (Sandal 683–E, length is 23 cm; Morris team sketch.)

Figure 6.10. Scalloped toe–square heel sandal with finite sole design structured by a central point of bifold rotation: design units rotated around a center point, sole view. (Sandal 1009–C, dissected, no length available; Morris team sketch.)

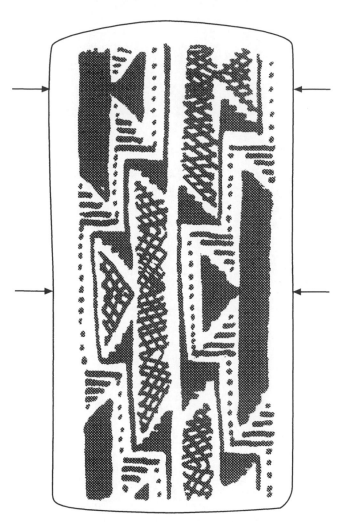

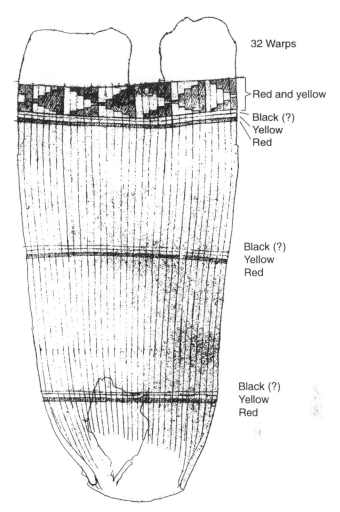

Figure 6.11. Scalloped toe–square heel sandal sole with one-dimensional design structured by horizontal axes of mirror reflection and point axes of bifold rotation. (Sandal 26–E, length is 22 cm; Morris team sketch.)

Figure 6.12. Scalloped toe–square heel sandal with narrow band of colored decoration structured by vertical and horizontal axes of mirror reflection, top view. (Sandal 1009–B, length is 22.5 cm; Morris team sketch.)

Of the 52 scalloped-square sandals, 28 have colored designs on the top surface, including 6 of the 9 that lack textured sole designs. Color appears primarily in the area designated Zone 2 (see Table 5.3 for construction techniques). No relief patterning appears in Zone 2. The 28 colored Zone 2 designs sketched for the Morris study are shown in Figure 6.13. Most often, simple, thin, solid or checkerboard stripes cross the toe. A few sandals have narrow bands of half terraces, stepped triangles, or diagonal fringed lines in Zone 2 (Fig. 6.12, for example). Sometimes thin lines appear on the instep and heel in Zone 3a. One sandal from the east end of Broken Flute Cave has a thin red line across the toe, a band of red, yellow, and black stripes across the instep, and another thin red line across the heel. Although many painted textiles, such as tump bands and women's

string aprons appear in Prayer Rock District and Canyon del Muerto Basketmaker sites, only two painted sandals appear in the Morris collections; both are scalloped-square sandals. One (1237–K) has painted rectangles and triangles in Zone 2 and the second (63–D) has several simple painted lines.

Three sandals have a color decorated Zone 3b that covers most of the sandal's top surface (items 1009–F, 760, and 1412–B in Fig. 6.13, Fig. 6.14, and see Fig. 5.3). These are among the most elaborate colored designs in the entire collection. The textured Zone 3a on these sandals is limited to a small strip along the heel. These sandals were in deposits of general refuse and were not associated with any identified or dated structure or feature. The Morrises suggested that they may have been mortuary sandals because a large proportion

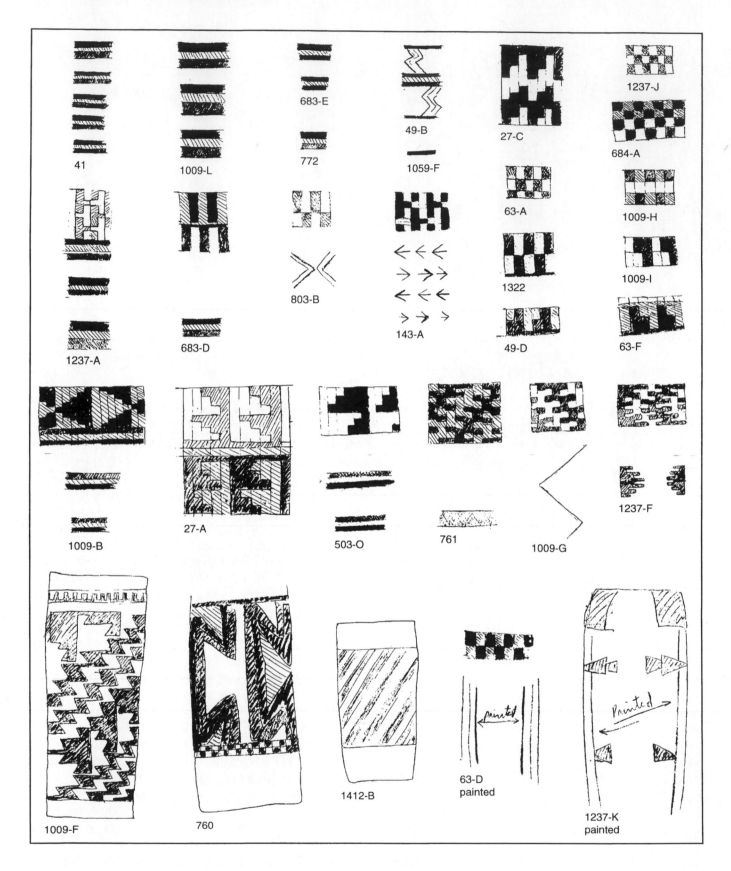

Figure 6.13. Colored designs on scalloped toe–square heel sandals.

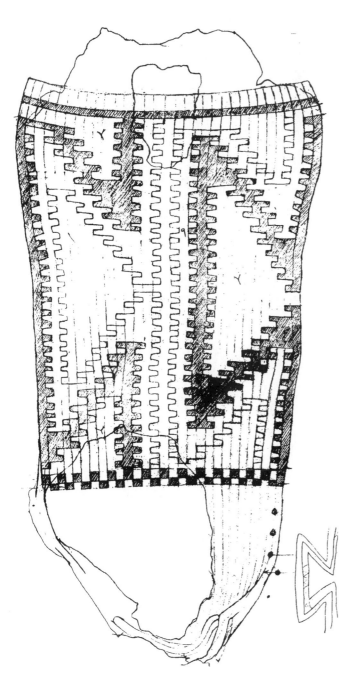

Color same, not reversed on bottom. Therefore, this weave is different from that in toe zones or middle zones. This has weaving gaps, as does 1009–F. [Earl Morris note.]

Figure 6.14. Scalloped toe–square heel sandal with colored design covering most of its top surface, top view. (Sandal 760, length is 23 cm; Morris team sketch.)

of the colored decoration resembles that on sandals Earl Morris found in human burials in Canyon del Muerto (E. H. Morris 1925). The three Prayer Rock examples

were not in graves and they have worn heels, suggesting that they were not made or used as grave offerings.

SCALLOPED TOE– PUCKERED HEEL SANDALS

The 121 scalloped-toe, puckered-heel sandals came from Broken Flute Cave, Cave 3, Pocket Cave, Cave 8, and Cave 10. They date to the A.D. 600s. All but two scalloped-puckered sandals have a raised design in the sole under the heel, designated Zone 3a. This zone is produced by combinations of weft-twining and weft-wrapping, similar to the techniques used in scalloped-square sandals (see Tables 5.4, 5.5).

Morris' team made sketches of 98 sole designs for scalloped-puckered sandals (Figs. 6.15–6.20). Design elements, mostly triangles, stepped lines, parallel bars, and dots, are the same as elements that appear on scalloped-square sandals. The same symmetry categories appear, but with different frequencies. Most scalloped-puckered Zone 3a designs have two identical side-by-side sections. Each section contains points of rotation and, sometimes, axes of reflection. The two sections are related to each other by rotation. That is, the whole design could be produced by simply translating a copy of one unit *or* by rotating the unit; each section may contain additional pivot points, producing a one-dimensional or two-dimensional pattern (for example, Figs. 5.20, 6.21–6.26). If a design admits rotation, I have, like Morris, classified it as rotational, even if it also admits translation. Some designs are bilateral (reflected across a central axis; see Figs. 5.16, 5.19) or biaxial (two perpendicular axes of reflection; Fig. 6.27).

Scalloped-puckered sandals whose only decoration is the textured sole Zone 3a are two-zone sandals. Zone 1a, doubled warps with 2/2 twill twining of the same color yarn as the rest of the sandal, extends from toe to midsole. Zone 3a, at the heel, is rectangular. There are more scalloped-puckered sandals with colored decoration than without it. In some colored sandals, the doubled-warp toe area is divided into a short undecorated Zone 1a and a decorated Extended Zone 1a. A decorated Zone 2 appears in the middle of the sandal. The textured Zone 3a heel is shortened to a square to make room for Zone 2. The Morris archival work sheets juxtaposing sandal sole designs and top designs illustrate this effect (see Fig. 5.16; compare Fig. 5.17, a two-zone sandal with a long Zone 3a, with the three-zone sandal in Fig. 5.18).

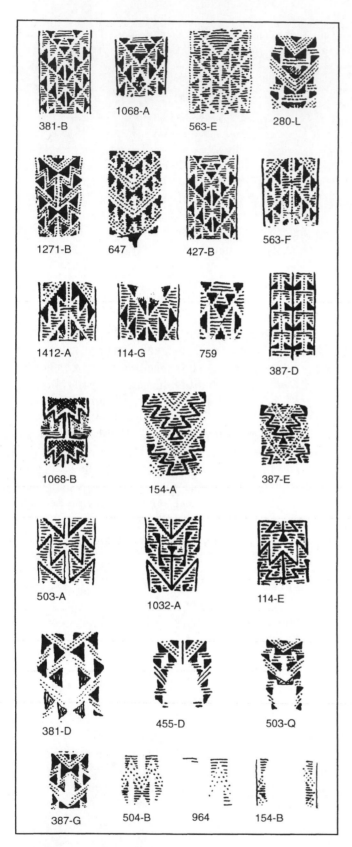

Figure 6.15. Scalloped toe–puckered heel sandal sole designs structured by a vertical axis of mirror reflection.

Figure 6.16. Scalloped toe–puckered heel sandal sole designs structured by horizontal axes of mirror reflection.

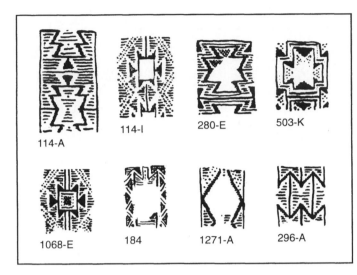

Figure 6.17. Scalloped toe–puckered heel sandal sole designs structured by horizontal and vertical axes of mirror reflection.

Figure 6.18. Scalloped toe–puckered heel sandal sole designs structured by multiple horizontal and vertical axes of mirror reflection.

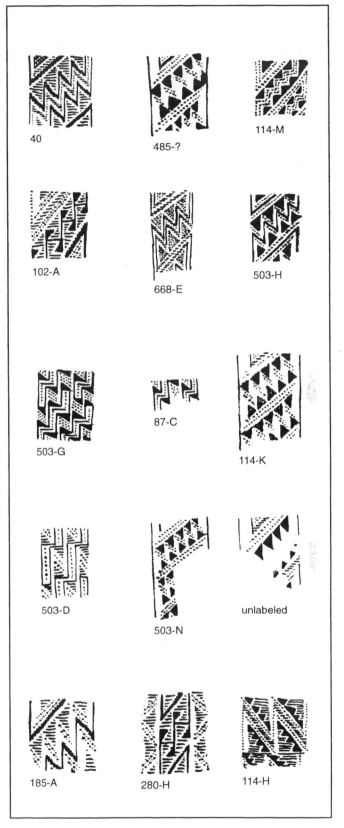

Figure 6.19. Scalloped toe–puckered heel sandal sole designs structured by bifold rotation.

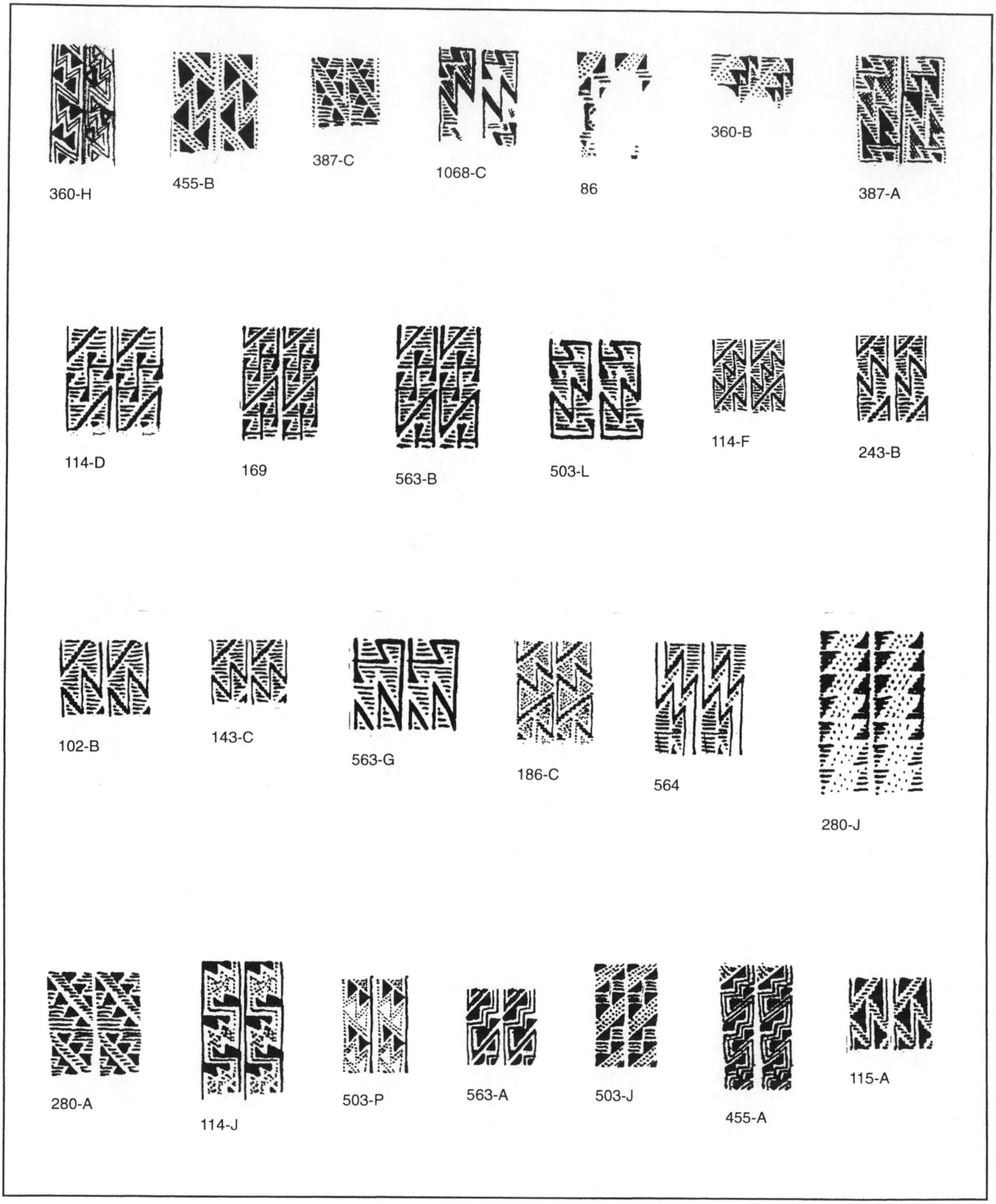

Figure 6.20. Scalloped toe–puckered heel sandal sole designs structured by bifold rotation.

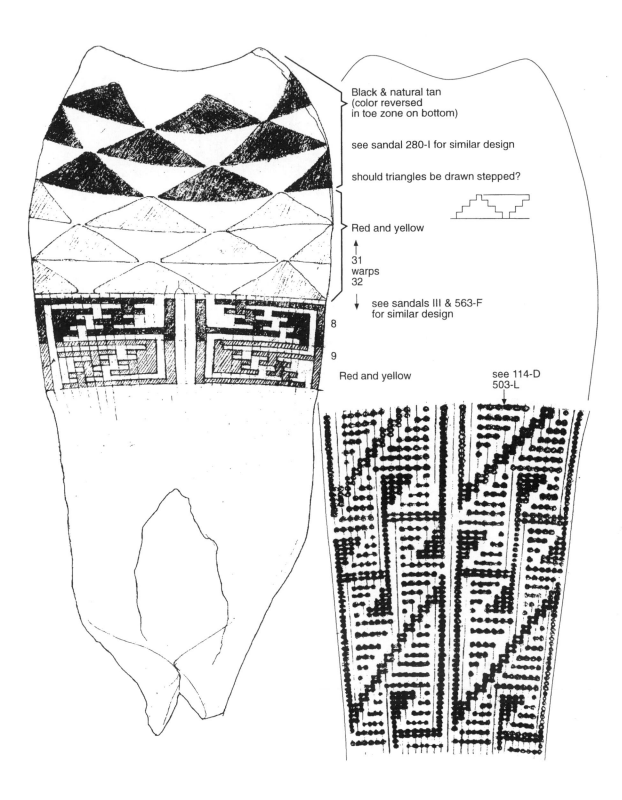

Black & natural tan
(color reversed
in toe zone on bottom)

see sandal 280-I for similar design

should triangles be drawn stepped?

Red and yellow

↑
31
warps
32
↓

see sandals III & 563-F
for similar design

8

9

Red and yellow

see 114-D
503-L

Figure 6.21. Scalloped toe–puckered heel sandal (top view) with two-dimensional sole design (*right*) structured by bifold rotation in two directions. (Sandal 563–B, length is 24.5 cm; Morris team sketch.)

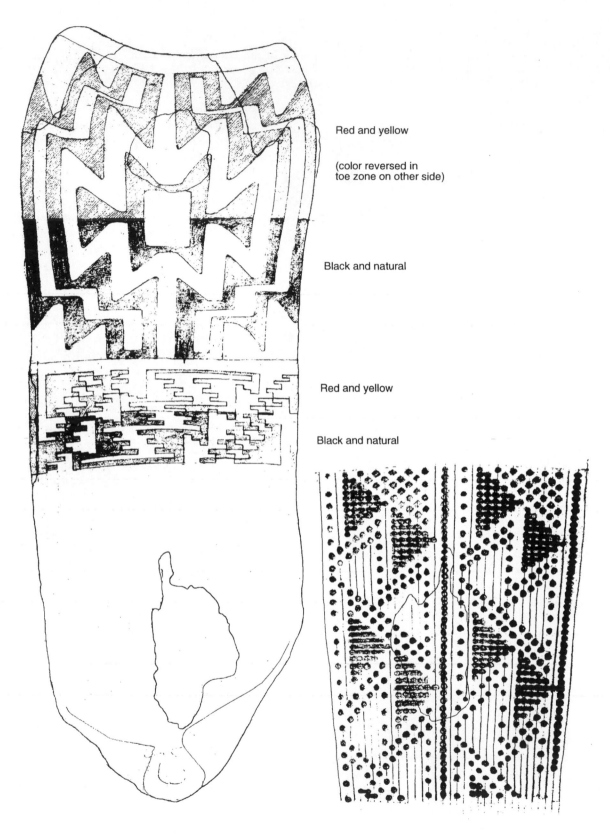

Red and yellow

(color reversed in
toe zone on other side)

Black and natural

Red and yellow

Black and natural

Figure 6.22. Scalloped toe–puckered heel sandal (top view) with two-color bifold sole design (*right*). (Sandal 503–P, length is 25 cm; Morris team sketch.)

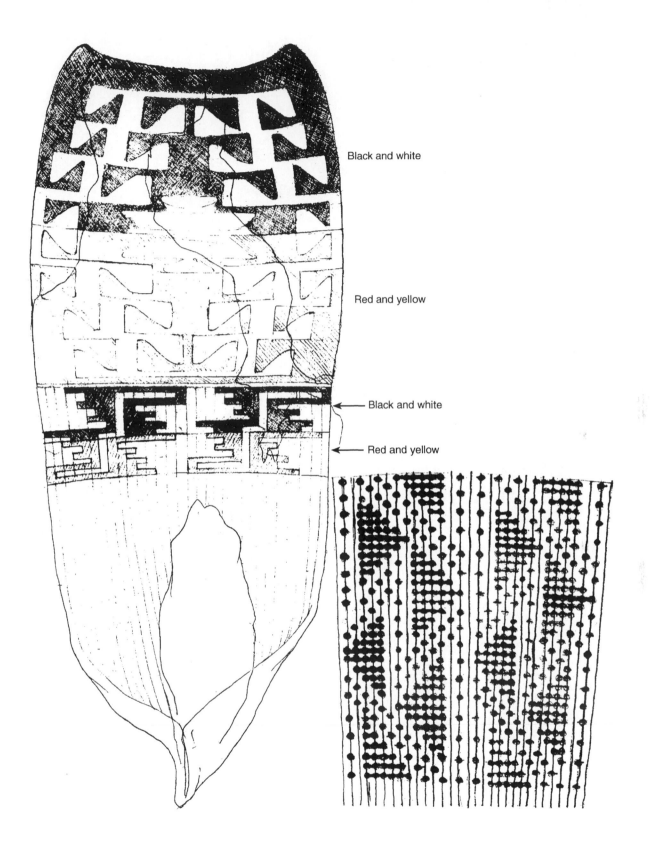

Black and white

Red and yellow

Black and white

Red and yellow

Figure 6.23. Scalloped toe–puckered heel sandal (top view) with one-color bifold sole design (*right*). (Sandal 455–B, length is 25 cm; Morris team sketch.)

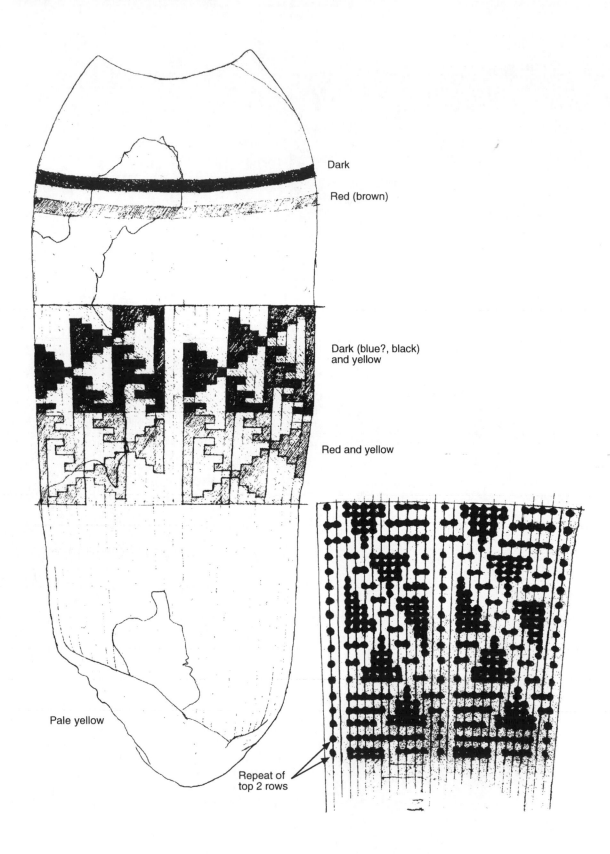

Dark

Red (brown)

Dark (blue?, black)
and yellow

Red and yellow

Pale yellow

Repeat of
top 2 rows

Figure 6.24. Scalloped toe–puckered heel sandal (top view) with bifold sole design (*right*). (Sandal 387–C, length is 24.5 cm; Morris team sketch.)

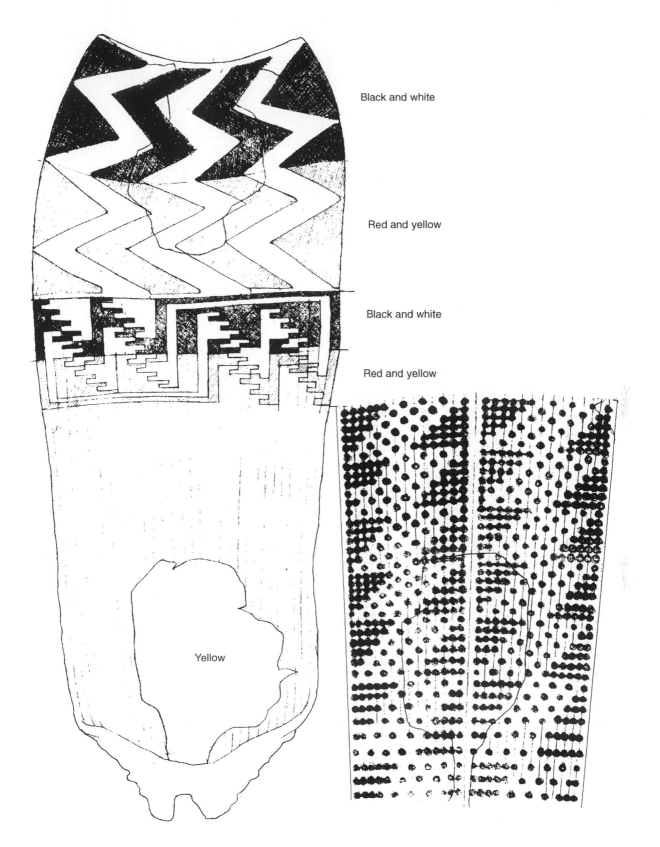

Black and white

Red and yellow

Black and white

Red and yellow

Yellow

Figure 6.25. Scalloped toe–puckered heel sandal (top view) with two one-dimensional bands of bifold rotational design on sole (*right*). (Sandal 280–J, length is 25.5 cm; Morris team sketch.)

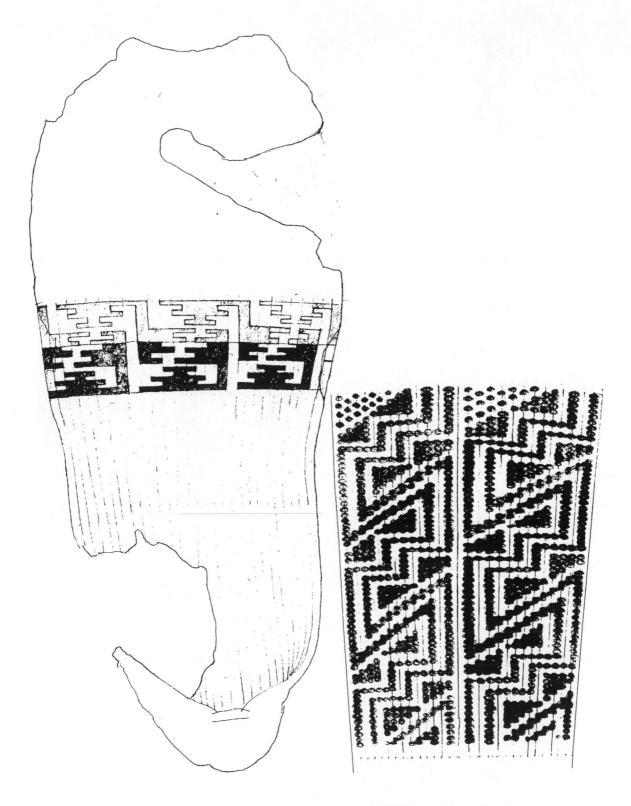

Figure 6.26. Scalloped toe–puckered heel sandal (top view) with bifold sole design (*right*). (Sandal 455–A, length is 25 cm; Morris team sketch.)

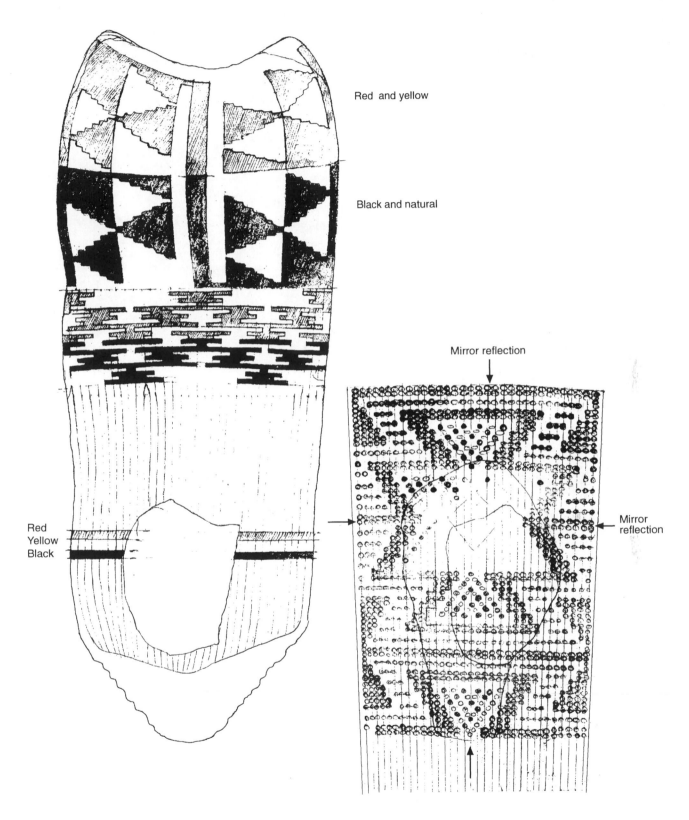

Red and yellow

Black and natural

Mirror reflection

Red
Yellow
Black

Mirror
reflection

Figure 6.27. Scalloped toe–puckered heel sandal (top view) with finite sole design (*right*) structured by horizontal and vertical axes of mirror reflection. (Sandal 280–E, length is 25 cm; Morris team sketch.)

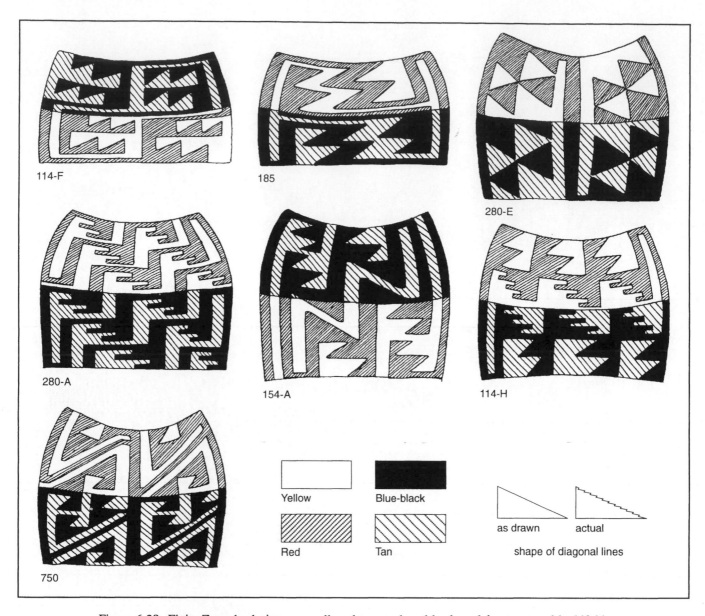

Figure 6.28. Finite Zone 1a designs on scalloped toe–puckered heel sandals, structured by bifold rotation, with color change. Lower left has imperfect symmetry: black triangles are double and red counterparts are single. Color and diagonal line keys also apply to Figures 6.29–6.32.

An Extended Zone 1a occurs in almost half the sandals with Zone 2 designs (Figs. 6.28–6.33). Thirty-three scalloped-puckered sandals have colored designs in this doubled-warp toe zone. Wefts are always the same four colors. Red and yellow are associated to make half the design; black and tan make up the other half, repeating the same design as a rotation or reflection of the red and yellow band.

Design elements are stepped triangles, fringed stepped triangles, straight, stepped, and rectilinear U-shaped lines and hooks (Figs. 6.34–6.43). The most frequent category for toe designs is biaxial (30%), that is, structured by two perpendicular axes of reflection (see Fig. 6.32, key in Fig. 6.2). Because of the 2/2 twill-twining technique, triangles and diagonal lines are toothed instead of stepped in the Extended Zone 1a (see Fig. 6.28).

Seventy scalloped-puckered sandals (including some fragments not considered in Chapter 5), have a Zone 2 consisting of complex twining (one has tapestry weave; see Table 5.3 for construction techniques). The same four colors appear here, paired in the same way, yellow

Figure 6.29. Finite Zone 1a designs on scalloped toe–puckered heel sandals, structured by bifold rotation, with a color change. Top row shows true finite designs with one center point of rotation. Bottom row designs have multiple point axes of bifold rotation.

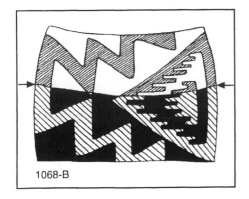

Figure 6.30. Finite Zone 1a design on scalloped toe–puckered heel sandal, structured by a horizontal axis of mirror reflection, with a color change.

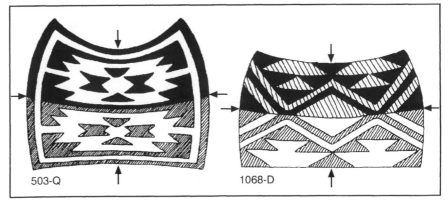

Figure 6.31. Finite Zone 1a designs on scalloped toe–puckered heel sandals, structured by vertical and horizontal axes of mirror reflection, with a color change along the horizontal axis.

Figure 6.32. Finite Zone 1a designs on scalloped toe–puckered heel sandals, structured by vertical and horizontal axes of mirror reflection, with a color change along the horizontal axis.

and red, black and tan. Design elements are much the same as in Zone 1a, but not as large or bold. The most frequent symmetry category for Zone 2 is a one-dimensional band with units repeated by bifold rotation (Figs. 6.34–6.36, 6.39), but many designs have axes of mirror reflection (Figs. 6.37, 6.38, 6.40, 6.41).

Color-coded drawings of Extended Zone 1a and Zone 2 designs appear in the Morris archives. One set of drawings consists of sketches of whole sandals (for example, Figs. 6.21–6.27). The other set, included here in its entirety, consists of ink drawings that separate toe designs (Extended Zone 1a) from band designs (Zone 2;

Figure 6.33. Two-dimensional Zone 1a designs on scalloped toe–puckered heel sandals; color reverses across a central horizontal axis.

Figs. 6.28–6.43). These drawings fill in missing areas, such as holes worn by big toes and raveling where ties have pulled out. The smooth diagonal lines in the drawings are actually stepped lines on the ribbed sandal midsole bands (Zone 2; Fig. 6.34 *bottom right*), and serrated or toothed lines on the 2/2 twill-twined toes (Extended Zone 1a; Fig. 6.28 *bottom right*). All three decorated zones (Extended Zone 1a, Zone 2, and Zone 3a) tend to have almost full design fields. Figure and ground do not separate visually because color pairs are symmetrical, that is, red figures are exactly the same size and shape as their interlocking counterparts, and recessed and raised areas have the same line weight. The whole sandal drawings do not suggest any regular relationships between toe and band designs in terms of color, structure, or content. Choice of a toe design did not seem to regularly influence the choice of a band design, or vice versa. A careful symmetry classification and statistical exploration of proportions of design categories, however, might yield some patterning.

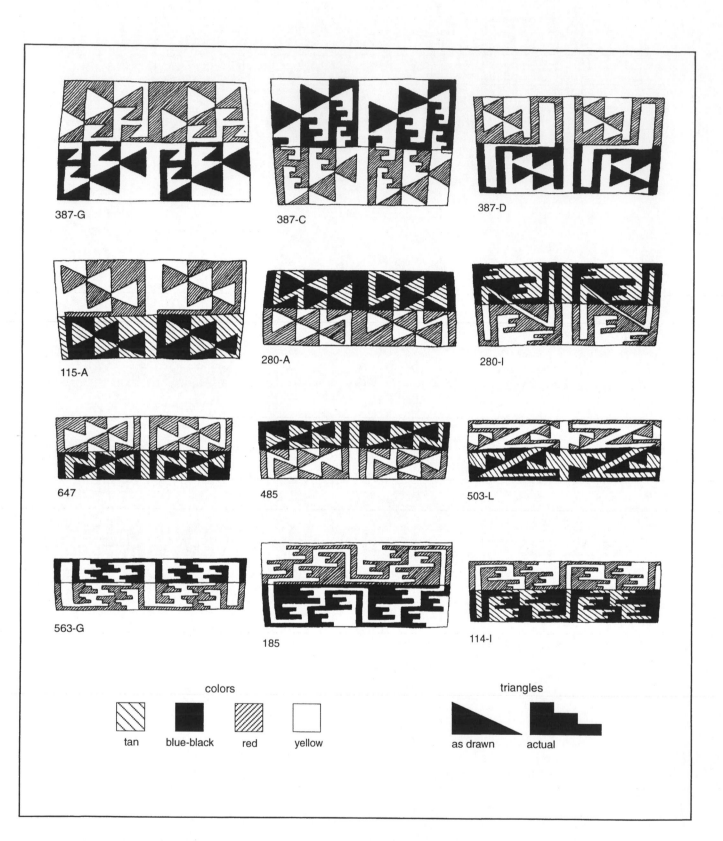

Figure 6.34. One-dimensional Zone 2 designs on scalloped toe–puckered heel sandals, structured by bifold rotation, with a color change. Color key and triangle diagram also appply to Figures 6.35–6.43.

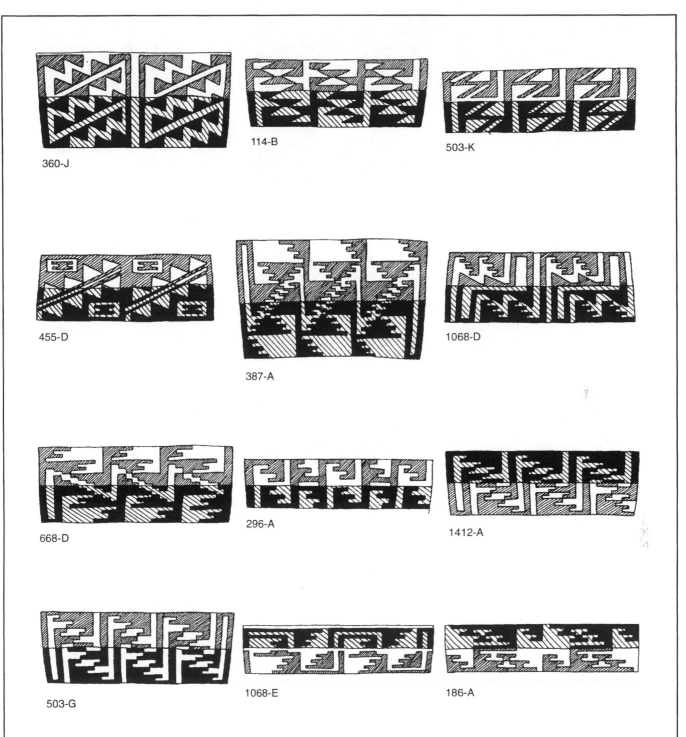

Figure 6.35. One-dimensional Zone 2 designs on scalloped toe–puckered heel sandals, structured by bifold rotation, with a color change.

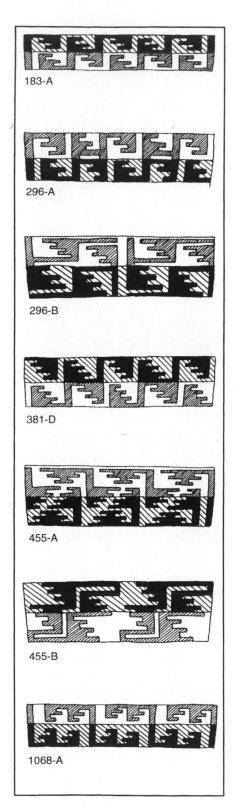

183-A

296-A

296-B

381-D

455-A

455-B

1068-A

Figure 6.36. One-dimensional Zone 2 designs on scalloped toe–puckered heel sandals, structured by bifold rotation, with a color change.

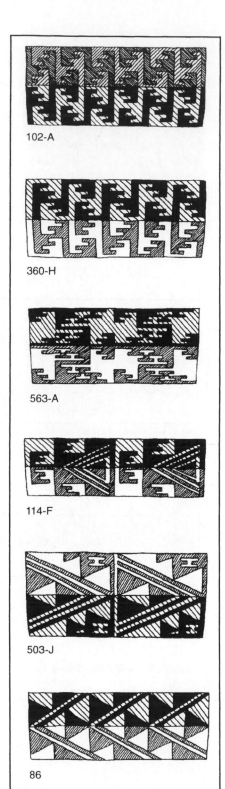

102-A

360-H

563-A

114-F

503-J

86

Figure 6.37. One-dimensional Zone 2 designs on scalloped toe–puckered heel sandals, structured by a horizontal axis of mirror reflection, with a color change.

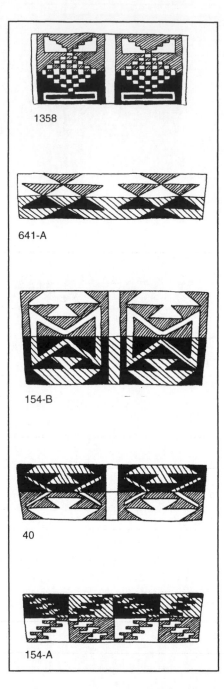

1358

641-A

154-B

40

154-A

Figure 6.38. One-dimensional Zone 2 designs on scalloped toe–puckered heel sandals, structured by vertical axes of mirror reflection (*top*, 1358), vertical and horizontal axes of mirror reflection with color change across the horizontal mirror axis (*middle*), and color changes across both the horizontal and vertical axes of reflection (*bottom*, 154–A).

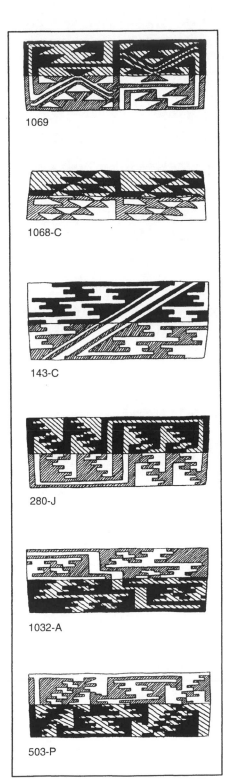

1069

1068-C

143-C

280-J

1032-A

503-P

Figure 6.39. Finite Zone 2 designs on scalloped toe–puckered heel sandals, structured by bifold rotation, with a color change.

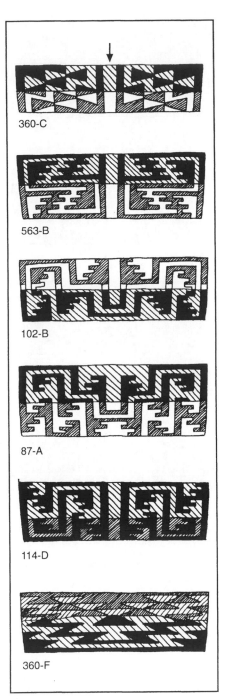

360-C

563-B

102-B

87-A

114-D

360-F

Figure 6.40. Finite Zone 2 designs on scalloped toe–puckered heel sandals, structured by a vertical axis of mirror reflection. Although the top half is colored differently from the lower half, there is no symmetrical color change across the vertical axis. The bottom two designs do not conform to the color pairs usually seen in this collection.

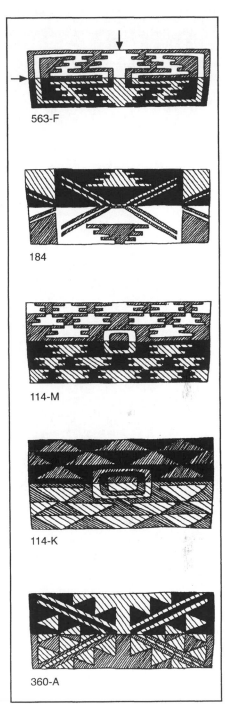

563-F

184

114-M

114-K

360-A

Figure 6.41. Finite Zone 2 designs on scalloped toe–puckered heel sandals, structured by horizontal and vertical axes of mirror reflection. Color changes across the horizontal axis only. The bottom two designs do not conform to the color pairs usually seen in this collection.

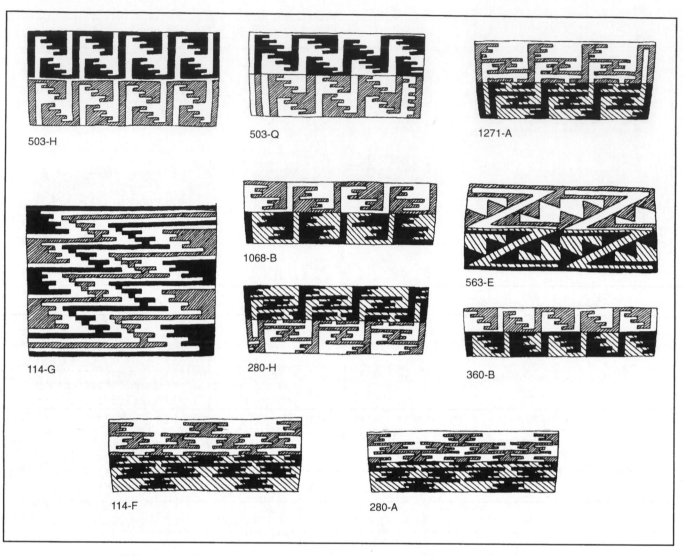

503-H   503-Q   1271-A

114-G   1068-B   563-E

280-H   360-B

114-F   280-A

Figure 6.42. Two-dimensional Zone 2 designs on scalloped toe–puckered heel sandals. Designs in top three rows are structured by bifold rotation. Designs in bottom row are structured by vertical axes of mirror reflection and bifold rotation.

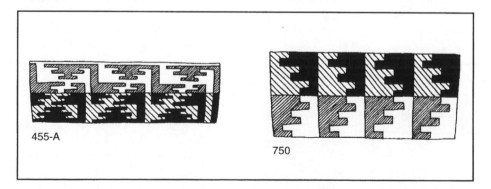

455-A   750

Figure 6.43. One-dimensional Zone 2 designs on scalloped toe–puckered heel sandals, structured by translation (*left*, 455–A), and a four-color one-dimensional design structured by rotation and mirror reflection (*right*, 750).

ROUND TOE–PUCKERED HEEL SANDALS

Round-puckered sandals were reported from Broken Flute Cave and Caves 2, 3, and 10. They occur in deposits with scalloped-puckered sandals, but always in the minority. Earl Morris (Chapter 2) thought that this type was later than the scalloped-toe sandal, based on his view of a technological evolution from square to scalloped to round toes. No depositional evidence in the excavation notes or artifact catalog supports the notion that round-puckered sandals actually replaced scalloped-puckered ones. Most likely the round-puckered sandal was another, less popular way of making footgear that was contemporaneous with the scalloped-puckered sandal.

I examined 48 round-toe, puckered-heel sandals. Of these, 12 are "winter" overshoes, a much greater proportion than among scalloped-puckered sandals. Zone 3a raised designs under the heel appear in 33 round-puckered sandals (Fig. 6.44), a smaller proportion than among scalloped-puckered sandals. This zone is usually more elongated than in scalloped-puckered sandals, because Zone 2 rarely truncates it. Most round-puckered sandals have only two zones, the undecorated Zone 1b in the toe area, which has natural-colored single warps and 2/2 twill twining, and Zone 3a, the raised patterned heel zone (Fig. 6.45).

Only ten round-toe sandals have colored designs on their top surfaces (Fig. 6.46), and one is limited to two simple stripes on the toe (not shown). Three-zone sandals have a Zone 2 with colored designs similar to those on scalloped-puckered sandals. Zone 2 may be adjacent to a plain Zone 1b (Fig. 6.47) or to a decorated Extended Zone 1b (Fig. 5.26). This toe zone sometimes splits into the usually undecorated Zone 1b, the actual round part of the toe, and a decorated Extended Zone 1b just behind it. In these sandals, Zone 2 is pushed back closer to the heel (Fig. 5.27). The raised patterned Zone 3a is greatly compressed. Sketches of seven raised pattern designs, three toe (Extended Zone 1b) designs, and eight Zone 2 designs are in the Morris archives.

One technological difference between round-puckered and scalloped-puckered sandals is in the construction of the toe zone. The greater proportion of winter sandals suggests a functional distinction as well. Decorative differences are subtle. First, there are far fewer toe designs on round-puckered sandals than on scalloped-puckered footwear. The three Extended Zone 1b designs that do occur consist of simple stripes, a speckled design, and a single solid triangle, rather than the elaborate four color counterchange designs on scalloped toes. Second, round-puckered raised sandal sole designs are apt to have a longitudinal axis of reflection, and scalloped-puckered raised sole designs are more likely to have a design that is repeated once by rotation, translation, or both.

TEMPORAL TRENDS IN DESIGN STRUCTURE AND CONTENT

Although each Basketmaker III sandal design is unique, the collection displays regular patterning in design placement and in element and color combinations. Regularity in these aspects of sandal decoration increased between the A.D. 400s, the time of the scalloped-square sandal, and the A.D. 600s, the time of scalloped-puckered and round-puckered sandals.

The early Basketmaker III scalloped-square sandals tend to have allover raised pattern soles, sometimes with simple colored decoration on their top surfaces. Elaborate designs appear only occasionally (colored Zone 3b), perhaps mainly (but not exclusively) in sandals made for mortuary contexts. The use of elaborate colored designs on the top surface precluded making a raised pattern design on the sole. If the textured design was deemed most important, the colored design had to be simple, thin stripes or a band of more complicated elements confined to its own zone. In the rare cases when allover colored design (Zone 3b in scalloped-square sandals) was used, sole texture was largely nonpatterned, with patterned raised designs appearing only as a band about a centimeter wide at the heel. The range of design elements was narrow, but at this time artisans positioned the designs in a variety of places on the sandal tops: colored bands on toes, midsoles, heels, or any combination of these.

Shape and placement of designs on the later Basketmaker III sandals, the scalloped-puckered and round-puckered types, are far more regular. The narrow zone at the tip of the toe (simple Zone 1a) is never decorated. If there is an Extended Zone 1a with colored decoration, it is a roughly square field at the toe. Round toes (Zone 1b) are rarely decorated (but see Fig. 5.26). Zone 2 is always a rectangular design across the middle of the sandal. The shape of Zone 3a depends on the presence or absence of colored decoration. Sandals without colored decoration have a textured sole that extends from the heel to the ball of the foot, and so the zone of textured sole decoration has a rectangular shape. Sandals with colored bands (Zone 2) have a shorter area of textured sole decoration that is square and extends from the heel to the instep. Expanding the zone of colored decoration on top meant that less sole area could bear textured design.

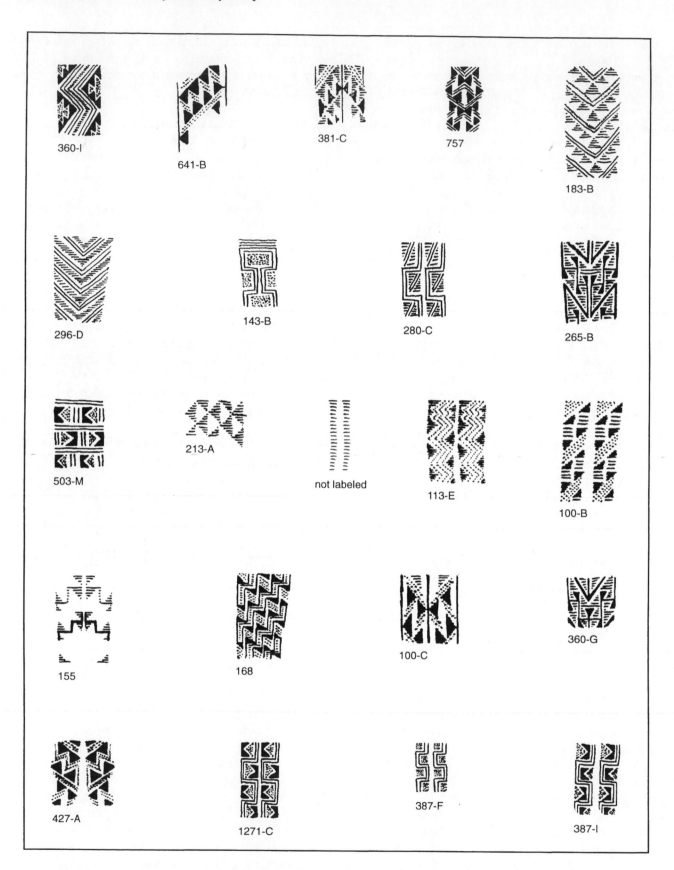

Figure 6.44. Zone 3a raised designs on the soles of round toe–puckered heel sandals.

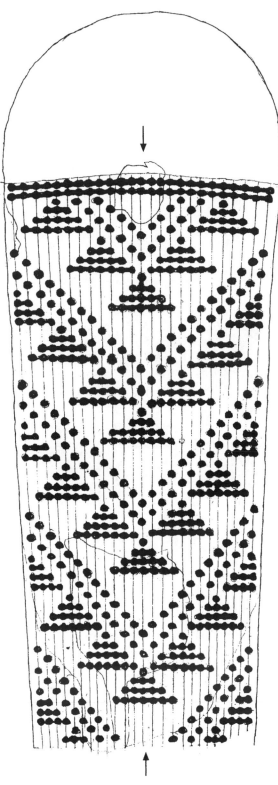

Figure 6.45. Round toe–puckered heel two-zone sandal with one-dimensional sole design structured by a vertical axis of mirror reflection in Zone 3a; undecorated Zone 1b. (Sandal 183–B, length is 23.5 cm; Morris team sketch.)

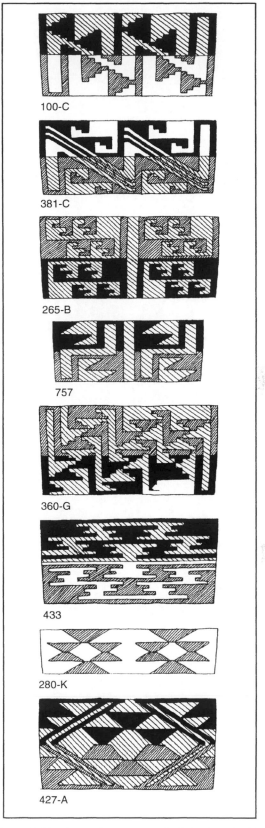

100-C

381-C

265-B

757

360-G

433

280-K

427-A

Figure 6.46. Two-color symmetrical designs in Zone 2 of round toe–puckered heel sandals, top views.

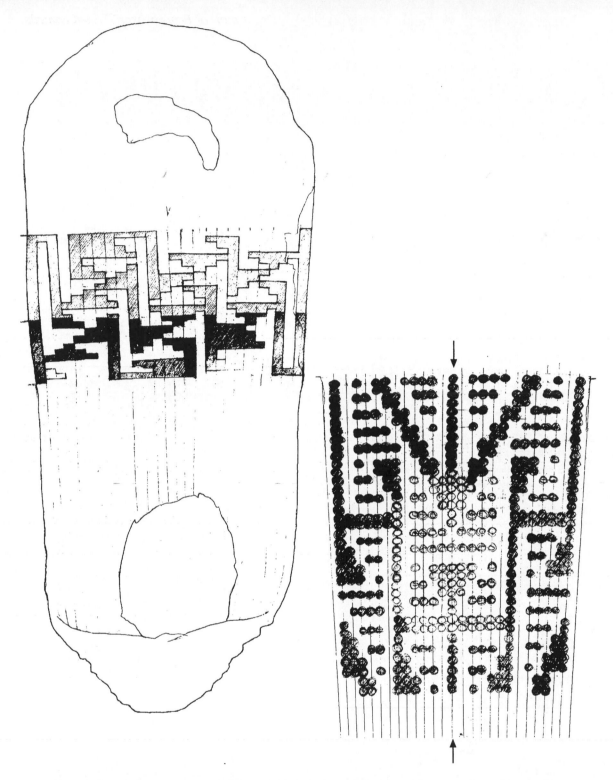

Figure 6.47. Round toe–puckered heel sandal (top view) with bilateral sole design (*right*) in Zone 3a, bifold Zone 2 design, and undecorated Zone 1b. (Sandal 360–G, length is 24 cm; Morris team sketch.)

Designs in the toe, instep, and sole positions (corresponding to technologically defined Zones 1, 2, and 3) in all three kinds of sandal are rectilinear, symmetrical, and composed of small, closely spaced elements. Design elements include straight, zigzag, and fringed lines; serrated, fringed, and stepped triangles; squares; and diamonds. All the elements appearing on earlier scalloped-square sandals occur later in the scalloped- and round-puckered sandals, but the later design repertoire is much more elaborate in content and complexity of symmetry.

Although designs on Basketmaker III sandals are varied and change between the A.D. 400s and 600s, they share numerous attributes. Not all possible designs that could have been used actually occur. Instead, the repertoire of sandal designs is bounded by conventions of color pairing, rectilinear line treatment, and a certain range of design elements that are repeated symmetrically into crowded square or rectangular fields. Part of the restriction of design variety is caused by the constraints of the materials and techniques used to make sandals.

TEXTILE TECHNIQUES AND DECORATIVE CONSTRAINTS

Textile artisans manipulate color, texture, and structure to express desired functional, symbolic, and aesthetic qualities (Teague 1991: 176). A large number of technical options are available to each artisan, but only a few combinations appear in any given culture area and time period. This uniformity is variously due to learning patterns, available materials, and social and aesthetic conventions.

Color

Color may be added to textiles by painting on the finished surface or by working colored elements into the textile structure. Throughout the world, most textiles are decorated by creating color and texture variations in the structure of the fabric itself. In contrast, painted textiles are common in the northern Southwest, especially in the Basketmaker period. Almost all tump bands (forehead straps used to carry burden baskets, see Fig. 6.50) are painted, but only two Prayer Rock District sandals carry painted designs. Amid hundreds of undecorated women's twined string aprons (see Fig. 6.49), one of the nine decorated aprons is painted. Most aprons and sandals with colored decoration have dyed yarns.

The natural colors of most plant fibers are green, yellowish, or brown. These can be lightened by bleaching. Fibers are bleached through exposure to moisture, to light and air, or to alkaline solutions (Teague 1991: 155–156). Sandals and many other Prayer Rock textiles, such as women's aprons, bags, and tump bands are made of light brown and yellowish yucca fibers. The fibers are soft, silky, and light enough in color to suggest at least some may have been bleached. The light tan fibers that are opposed to black areas in colored sandal designs may have been bleached.

A greater variety of natural colors can be obtained from animal fibers. Prayer Rock artisans used white and brown dog hair and brown and black human hair in women's aprons. In Prayer Rock footwear, however, human hair only appears in sandal ties, not in the sandal body.

To obtain other colors, Southwest textile artisans used pigments and dyes. Minerals, soot, and coal could be powdered and rubbed on the surface of the yarn or fabric or suspended in liquid. Mineral dyes include copper sulphate or azurite for blue and ferrous sulphate or other iron-bearing minerals for browns and reds. Dyes interact with the fiber so that color permeates it. Vegetal dyes made of barks, roots, leaves, and flowers can produce yellows, browns, and, rarely, blues and reds. Often mordants (metallic salts such as alum) are added, or an acid or base dye bath helps to make dyes adhere to fibers (Kent 1983a: 37; Teague 1991: 157–158).

Local materials and whatever could be obtained by trade limited the color selection of Prayer Rock artisans. The origins of the dyes and pigments used have not been identified conclusively. According to Earl Morris' notes (1931b: 2; see also Kent 1983a: 37), blue and faded blue-green pigments were probably produced with azurite (carbonate of copper). Red is ferruginous (iron oxide) and black is organic, possibly charcoal. Some browns contain iron and some contain carbonate with no iron. No information on what tests Morris used is given, and the yellows evidently were not identified. Kent notes that yellows are far more common on Prayer Rock District textiles than in any other part of the Southwest, including Canyon de Chelly. Indeed, yellow appears on almost every colored Late Basketmaker sandal and apron in the Prayer Rock collection. Yellows were probably obtained with vegetal dyes such as rabbit brush (*Chrysothamnus* sp.), which Hopi basket weavers use today (Colton 1965: 37).

Dyes vary in resistance to color change (fastness), but no dye is absolutely fast. Light, water, heat, and chemical substances affect color (Teague 1991: 158). The Prayer Rock textiles have all been exposed to one or more of these effects while in use, in the ground, and in museums. As a consequence, colors probably look somewhat different than when the sandals were constructed. The colors that we read today as being bluish-gray, black, and brown seem especially suspect. On the other hand, the sandals and aprons with dyed yarns seem much less altered than many of the painted tump bands and aprons.

Texture

The texture of fabrics depends on yarn diameter and structure and construction techniques. Weft wrapping and twining produce raised areas. There is no reason that color cannot be introduced into a weft wrapped structure, but the Prayer Rock sandal artisans usually left color out of their raised pattern sandal soles. Occasionally some simple stripes in raised structures were made with dyed yarns. When sandals were constructed with yarn of a single, natural color, the limited visibility of the design depended on the light reflection of raised areas and the shadows of recessed portions.

Luster varies with the fuzziness or smoothness of yarns and the tightness of the sandal body structure. The Prayer Rock sandals have smooth yarns and tight structures. As a result, colored areas are sharply delineated. Parallel columns appear in Zones 2 and 3 because each set of wefts twists around each warp in the same place in subsequent rows. Zones with 2/2 twill twining have especially smooth surfaces because the weft turns are diagonally offset.

Structure

In interlacing, the crossing of yarns produces a grid. Modifications like 2/2 twill twining produce variations in the grid, such as diagonal lines, zigzags, and diamonds. When two sets of elements, warp and weft, are interlaced, it is possible to make vertical, horizontal, and diagonal lines. In describing Basketmaker textiles, Teague (1991: 352) writes: "there is little in their techniques that inhibited textile design other than the necessity of following the lines of the basic twined or interlaced structures and designing within the often narrow widths of the design fields."

Twenty-one textile techniques were used by Prayer Rock artisans to interwork two sets of elements (see Table 5.8). Plain weave, a simple over–1/under–1 structure, and many of the weft-twining techniques produce a simple grid. When the weft is tightly packed and the warp does not show, a weft-faced textile results. Plain weave and simple weft-faced twining produce uniform surface textures and longitudinal parallel columns. By changing weft colors, any kind of rectilinear design can be produced. Curved lines can be approximated if the yarn is fine, if there is a high thread count, and if the design is large.

Since pattern is composed of "blocks" of intersecting elements, the curved line can only be roughly approximated in structurally-produced textile patterns. The greater the size of the design relative to the density of the fabric, the closer this approximation can be. However, it is generally not feasible to create small, convincingly curved motifs without an exceedingly fine and dense ground fabric. A rectilinear design is therefore far easier to produce in textiles (Teague 1991: 354).

In the Prayer Rock textiles, design elements are almost always small, and we do not find many curvilinear shapes. However, yarn is of sufficient fineness in aprons and sandals that if the size of design elements had been increased, it would have been possible to produce curved shapes and lines if the artisans had so chosen. Only three sandal designs of the 198 studied here show any attempt at curved lines (sandal numbers 455–B, 503–K, and 1271–A in Fig. 6.32). These examples do show, however, that it is possible to modify the rectilinear lines in sandals.

The correlation between textile techniques and shape and positioning of elements is also discussed by Kate Peck Kent (1983b: 120). Kent finds, for example, that with tapestry weaving, oblique lines must be stepped; twining has the same constraint. Therefore, it is not surprising that we find terrace and key elements on Prayer Rock textiles in aprons and in the ribbed center zones (Zone 2) of sandals and that we do not find true triangles there (see Figure 6.34).

The 2/2 twill twining of many sandal toe zones (Zone 1) produces a smooth surface. Oblique lines are much smoother in this structure than in plain weave or simple weft-twining because of offset but overlapping floats. Oblique lines on the sandal toes have a fine sawtooth edge (see Fig. 6.28) rather than the more obviously stepped edges of oblique lines in the adjacent Zone 2 bands of decoration.

The style of Prayer Rock textile designs was constrained by technology to favor rectilinear designs. It was not necessary to make small, repeated units. Single large units could have been made, but the textile technology used did encourage the repetition of small units. The actual shapes of units available to the artisan were to some degree a matter of choice, but were also constrained by the construction technique used in each zone. Oblique lines in Zone 2 had to be stepped, but in Zone 1 lines could be sawtoothed and finer, allowing the creation of triangles. The color palette was limited by available materials, but there is no technological reason for the regular pairing of certain colors. Such choice was a cultural convention, as was the range of symmetry categories used. As Kent (1983b: 120) notes, technique constrains texture and the size, spacing, and shape of elements, but "does not determine the symmetry processes by which a design is structured." To

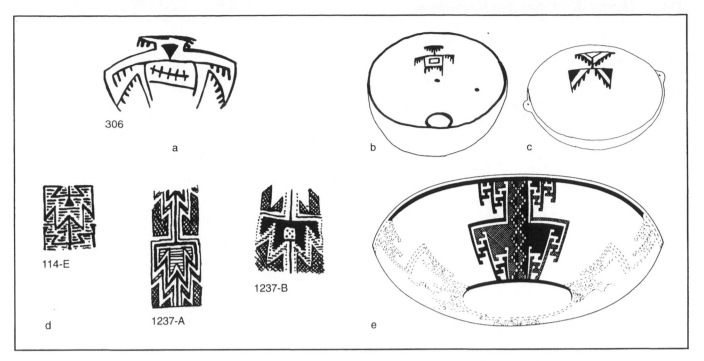

Figure 6.48. Bird designs on pottery bowls (*a*, Broken Flute Cave; *b*, Mesa Verde area; *c*, Las Vegas, Nevada area), sandal soles (*d*, Prayer Rock District), and a basket (*e*, Canyon del Muerto, after Morris and Burgh 1941).

understand the role of cultural convention in sandal decoration, it is necessary to explore how sandals were used and how the designs on them compare with designs on other objects.

CROSS-MEDIA AND CONTEXTUAL COMPARISONS

Insights into the meaning of sandal designs are gained by comparing design content and different aspects of design structure between sandals, on the one hand, and other kinds of artifacts, on the other. Archaeologists tend to assign artifact analyses to experts who specialize in stone tools, pottery, or textiles, for example. Earl Morris was unusual, even for his time, in that he studied many media, but for the most part he undertook and published his studies one medium at a time: pottery (E. H. Morris 1927), baskets (E. H. Morris and Burgh 1941), figurines (E. H. Morris 1951), and the sandal study presented here was intended to be a single volume describing one kind of artifact. Cross-media studies, however, expand the context for each kind of artifact by relating it to other kinds of artifacts used at the same time and place. Cross-media studies of decoration reveal that some cultures have *pervasive* design systems, a single design style is used to decorate all kinds of things, whereas others have *partitive* design systems, different styles for different kinds of artifacts, and many fall in between, on a continuum (DeBoer 1991).

Basketmaker people had a somewhat partitive design system, with one style for rock art and another for containers and clothing. Designs on Basketmaker III pottery, sandals, other textiles, and baskets are similar (Hays 1992). All have rectilinear designs. Points of rotation dominate design structures and design content is similar: small, repeated geometric elements such as parallel lines, dots, triangles, stepped elements (keys, stepped triangles), and fringed elements (lines, triangles, stepped triangles, and keys). Where life-forms appear in pottery and baskets, they are built up of straight lines and rectilinear fringed and stepped elements. No recognizable life-forms appear on sandals, but several sole designs closely resemble a spread-winged bird appearing on painted bowls from Broken Flute Cave, the Mesa Verde area, and even Las Vegas, Nevada (Fig. 6.48). A red and black Basketmaker III period basket from Canyon del Muerto bears a more elaborate version of the same icon (Fig. 6.48*e*).

Sandal designs most closely resemble decorated twined aprons worn by women (Fig. 6.49) and tump bands (Fig. 6.50) used to carry burden baskets. Designs on these three textile types have full design fields, a wide range of symmetry patterns, three or more colors, and a lack of separation between figure and ground. The same elements, especially the fringed triangles, occur on baskets (Fig. 6.51) and pottery bowls (Fig. 6.52).

Bags (Fig. 6.53) exhibit checkerboards, plain stripes, and fringed lines, elements also twined into sandals. In

Figure 6.49. Twined aprons from Broken Flute Cave and from Pocket
Cave (*lower right*, 1012); apron 127 is painted, the rest have dyed yarns.

668

654

USNM 350501

Figure 6.50. Painted twined tump bands, used with carrying baskets, from Broken Flute Cave.

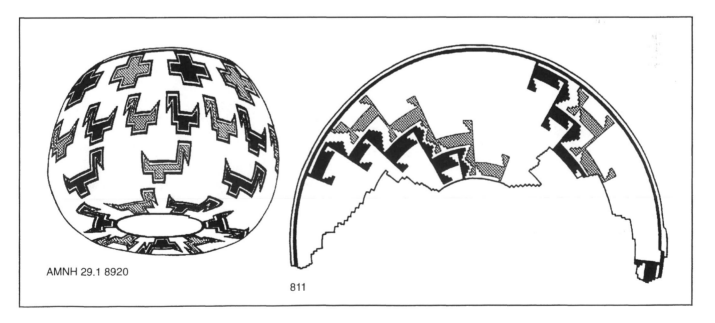

AMNH 29.1 8920

811

Figure 6.51. Baskets from Obelisk Cave (*left*) and Broken Flute Cave (*right*). (After Morris and Burgh 1941.)

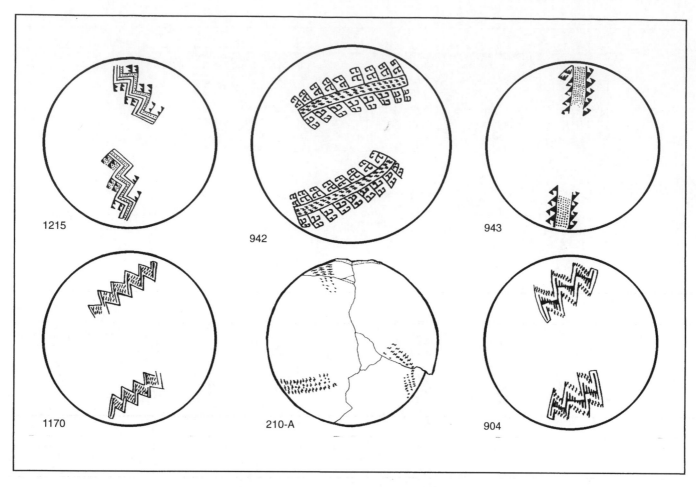

Figure 6.52. Painted pottery bowls from Prayer Rock caves tree-ring dated to the A.D. 600s. (Drawings by Kelley Ann Hays-Gilpin.)

other respects, however, baskets, bags, and pots are different. The potential design field is not filled, the range of symmetries is narrower, and colored figures stand out from the tan or gray colored ground. The number of colors ranges from two (black figures and tan ground) to three (red, black, and ground). Textiles meant to be worn, then, are stylistically different from decorated containers, even though designs on clothing and containers do share many attributes.

In contrast to the symmetrical, geometric, rectilinear style shared by clothing and containers, rock art has a predominance of unbounded, "free-floating" elements that are rarely repeated (Fig. 6.54). Rock art occurs in two forms. By definition, petroglyphs are pecked and incised into the rock surface, and pictographs are painted. No instances of painted petroglyphs were identified in the Prayer Rock caves, as occasionally occur elsewhere. Both petroglyphs and pictographs have an abundance of curvilinear forms and lines of reflection,

a few purely rectilinear forms, and a few points of rotation. Rock art content emphasizes life-forms, although a few triangles, zigzags, fringed elements, and lines of dots appear.

The differences between rock art designs on the one hand and designs on sandals, other textiles, baskets, and pottery on the other are not due to technological constraints. Designs like those in rock art could have been painted on textiles or pottery, and textilelike designs could have been painted or chipped onto rock surfaces. Our explanations of these differences must rest on the contexts of the artifacts and rock art, which differ in a multitude of ways.

SPATIAL AND FUNCTIONAL CONTEXTS

Although a few petroglyphs were made on loose rocks measuring a foot or two across, most rock art is non-

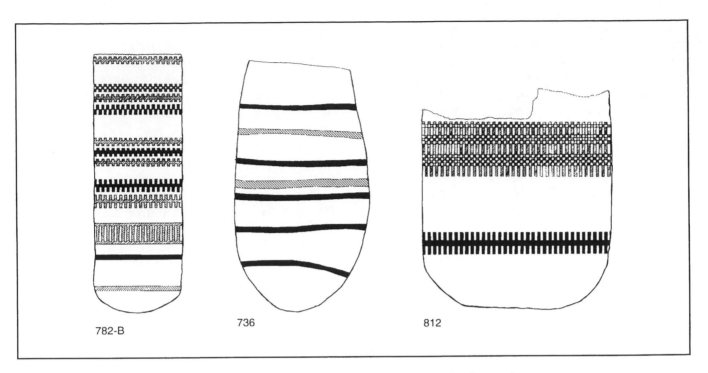

Figure 6.53. Decorated bags, with black and red stripes and designs (after Elizabeth Ann Morris 1959a.) Not to scale.

Figure 6.54. Rock art designs: petroglyphs (pecked into rock surface) and pictographs (painted) in Broken Flute Cave (after Hays 1991). Not to scale.

portable. Rock art would be a good medium for marking territory (Hyder 1994; Robins 1997). The large, highly visible paintings near the ends of the cave where access is easiest might signal the identity of the cave's inhabitants to outsiders. We can speculate that the smaller birds, animals, and geometrics near the storage cists and houses might mark ownership by kin groups or individuals. Ritual space in the east side of Broken Flute Cave was probably marked with special rock art motifs such as the processions, masks, and lobed circles that only occur near the great kiva. A tall white water bird appears on the cave wall over one of the graves, perhaps marking it.

In contrast, portable items are worn on the body or used in particular activities. Designs on portable items might identify the owner or maker of an object, but could also indicate the social identity of an individual using an item or refer to the social context of the activity in which the decorated object was meant to be used. Another distinction, then, can be made on the basis of

function. Rock art was placed on the sheltering walls of the cave itself, which were not further manipulated.

Other kinds of designs are put on objects that are worn on the body or used as containers. Tray baskets and pottery bowls must have had similar functions in that they likely held food, whether being stored or served. Large conical baskets were used to carry food, raw materials, and perhaps firewood, and these were outfitted with textile tump bands, many of which had painted decorations as described above.

Clothing, and certain activities, had important special roles in the process of coping with an increasingly complicated social world by facilitating the identification and differentiation of individuals. Interestingly, only the sandals leave behind evidence of each individual's presence and movements, in the form of unique tracks. For us, over a millennium later, it is these sandals, the hand prints on cave walls, and the occasional fingerprint in pottery or plaster that give us glimpses of ancient artists as individuals.

Epilogue: "...this sandal business"

Kelley Ann Hays-Gilpin

On February 28th, 1944, Alfred Vincent Kidder, the "father of South-western archaeology," wrote to Earl Morris, "Golly! Don't I wish I could work with you and Miss Zeigler on this stuff." A few weeks later (March 12, 1944), Morris replied, "I wish you could be in with us on this sandal business. It is the most fascinating study I have ever gotten into." Morris and Kidder appreciated the artistry of Anasazi twined san-dals, but also realized that these beautiful objects could provide archaeologists with significant clues about lifeways of the distant past.

The primary function of sandals is to protect the feet when walking outdoors. Intricately decorated Bas-ketmaker sandals were worn until large holes in the heel and toe areas rendered them ineffective. Decoration is irrelevant to foot protection, so the investment of time and skill in elaborate decoration suggests that Basket-maker III sandals also had other functions, social, ideo-logical, aesthetic, or all three. Of all the decorated artifacts made and used by the Prayer Rock Basketmak-ers, sandals have the most complicated technology and designs and are among the most frequently decorated items. For example, nearly half of the scalloped-puck-ered sandals have colored decoration and almost all have textured designs, but only nine of hundreds of women's aprons recovered from the same sites are decorated (see Fig. 6.49).

Colored designs would not have been visible while the sandals were being worn, suggesting that the de-signs were meant to be seen in some other context. Although each decorated sandal was undoubtedly a beautiful object to contemplate, what the social con-texts of sandals were remain a mystery. We cannot ask their makers and wearers what decorated sandals meant to them, but we can ponder their significance.

One possibility is that decorated sandals might have played important roles in gift-giving and trade, both ways of negotiating social and economic relationships among individuals, families, or even communities. In most social transactions, whether given in gift or trade, an object that was obviously invested with a great deal of skill, material, and labor (such as a twined sandal) usually had a higher value than one made more quickly and crudely (such as a braided leaf sandal). In this sense, decorated sandals embodied labor and skill in addition to their obvious aesthetic qualities. In a general survey of Native American clothing in North America, Evan Maurer (1979: 120) concludes:

> Often the act of making a garment was believed to be under the guidance and protection of sacred powers who taught people techniques such as weaving, or sent them inspiration for the concep-tions of decorative forms and the perfection of their execution. In this system, the maker as well as the wearer of a garment might share in the spiritual power and blessings that it represented.

In the Southwest, oral traditions credit Spider Grand-mother with teaching the arts of spinning, weaving, and other textile techniques. For the Hopi, then, the act of spinning takes one back to primordial times when the world was created, and all the textile patterns that can be created now were originally part of Spider Grand-mother's repertoire (Loftin 1991: 3–4).

In another possible social context, designs would have been visible if sandals were left in or near a doorway, such as next to the roof hatch entry of pit houses, when the owner entered a structure. In some of the burned houses in Broken Flute Cave, sandals were found piled near the ladder as if left there deliberately or as if they had fallen from the roof. In a small community like this one, the inhabitants would have known who wore sandals with which designs on them. If sandals were left by the ladder's top, an observant and knowledgeable passerby could "read" their designs to find out who was inside each house.

Raised patterned soles probably functioned for traction, but simple ridged soles would have worked almost as well to grip slippery surfaces. Raised patterned soles produced tracks that marked the wearer's movements. Tracking continues to be an important skill in the arts of hunting, war, and law enforcement. The heels of some Plains moccasins had distinctive "tags, strings, or tassels" called "trailers." Otis Mason (1896: 351) reported that "Each [Plains] tribe had a different number and order of this part, so that a good scout is said to have been able to tell the tribe to which an Indian belonged by the mark of his trailer in the snow." United States Border Patrol agents working along the Arizona–Mexico border often cut individual marks into the heels of their boots. They know each agent's mark and can silently keep track of each other's movements. Leon Lorentzen, a former agent, told me that the heel makes the deepest and clearest track, and agents only need a heel print to know the type and brand of shoe that made each track. Today, the light, fine sediment and the oblique light of Broken Flute Cave make the tracks of archaeologists' athletic shoes and hiking boots stand out so sharply one can read the words "Nike" and "Reebok" without bending over for a closer look. Indeed, sandy loam or silty soil is the most likely kind of surface to show a detailed impression, according to law enforcement specialists (Abbot 1964: 59), and officers favor oblique lighting of shoe impressions when photographing crime scene evidence (Bodziak 1990: 44).

Basketmakers, too, must have been aware of tracks made by textured soles in the rockshelters' silty soils, in the moist fine sand of the canyon bottom where they tended their crops, and where trails crossed moist sand or fine sandy loam. One would learn to identify and track individuals by observing the designs on their sandal soles. Even if tracks changed as sandals wore out and were replaced, the small size of Basketmaker communities meant that a motivated observer could have kept abreast of sandal inventories.

Tracks and tracking may also have had symbolic roles as signs of an individual's prayer or presence, not only to other humans but also to denizens of the spirit world. Handprints and, less frequently, footprints and sandal treads appear on the walls of Basketmaker period rockshelters, including those of the Prayer Rock District (Hays 1991). Sandal treads are a frequent motif in Pueblo III period rock art. We know, then, that tracks and prints were important in prehistory, but we cannot decipher their exact meanings. We can do better than merely guess at symbolic meanings, however, if we base our conjectures on the historic Puebloan world view rather than on European models.

A particularly striking petroglyph panel (see top of p. 121) at the mouth of Cha Canyon, now below the waters of Lake Powell, showed a trail of patterned sandal prints terminating in a "standing still" position, facing two plain sandal prints over a solid circle, perhaps representing a spring or the sipapu, a place of emergence (Turner 1963: 58). If this image represented a meeting between individuals of two different social groups, it resonated with Hopi migration stories in which members of each clan wandered until they came to the present location of the Hopi villages, where they petitioned for permission to settle.

A Pueblo III petroglyph panel in the Petrified Forest area shows footprints with phallic middle toes flanking what can only be described as penis prints next to a fluteplayer and an anatomically elaborate female figure identified as the Mother of Game Animals (McCreery and Malotki 1994, Fig. 9.1). The phallic feet may represent the presence of male hunters who made offerings to this provocative and occasionally dangerous female deity (see also McCreery and McCreery 1986). If sandal treads and footprints were viewed as the way spirit beings of the underworld perceive our movements on the earth's surface, an elaborate and highly individual footprint might be a form of prayer. Impressing one's unique sandal pattern in the soil of a cornfield, for example, might inform the god of germination which farmer is asking for an abundant harvest.

DECORATIVE STYLES AND GENDER DIFFERENCES

Distinguishing decoration on the basis of object function leads to consideration of whether certain objects are associated with different genders (the cultural values inscribed on male and female sex categories). In most cultures, women are responsible for processing and serving food. Where people reside in small groups and live by hunting and gathering, it is usually women who gather most plant foods (Watson and Kennedy 1991). In small-scale horticultural societies, women do much of the planting, tending, and harvesting, and make hand-built pottery (Rice 1991; Wright 1991), backstrap loom items, and nonloom textiles (Barber 1994). As craft specialization appears in more complicated economies, loom-woven textiles may be the purview of women, as in Europe, or of men, as in the historic Pueblos.

The most we can say based on ethnographic analogy is that the portable items, baskets, bowls, and textiles, all decorated with small, repeated geometric units, are *likely* to have been made by women. We do not really *know*, however, that women made sandals. Costin (1996: 116) argues that, "Perhaps our most relevant lesson from the ethnographic data is that craft production is gendered in largely idiosyncratic, historically contingent ways, making sweeping generalizations and general analogies problematic in many cases." The argument here, then, is not that sandals were made by women, but that they were to some degree assigned a feminine gender on the basis of decorations that resembled items made by women (raw materials and tools for making coiled baskets appeared with female burials in Canyon de Chelly) and items used by women. Aprons, in particular, were clearly worn only by women. Each has a stain of menstrual blood on the fringe where it would have passed between the legs. Aprons are found only on the bodies of women in Basketmaker burials. Fiber aprons are often preserved on clay figurines that are clearly identifiable as women by their body shape (Hays 1992; E. H. Morris 1951).

All geometrically decorated, portable items, except sandals, are likely to have been used primarily by women. Sandals, however, were used by everyone, and they appeared in male, female, and child burials and in the grave of two disembodied human arms (Morris 1923, 1925). A few tiny baby and child-sized sandals are in the Morris collections (see Fig. P.1, p. 6). Our efforts to examine sandal length as a possible indication of foot size resulted in a normal distribution, but not the bimodal distribution we would expect if most sandals were made for a sexually dimorphic adult population. That is, there was no evidence for big and small size categories that might correlate to big male feet and smaller female feet. There are so many variables affecting such a distribution, overlapping foot sizes among men, women, and growing children, inattention to whether sandals fit well or poorly, that it would have been surprising if this test had separated men's and women's footwear. Mimbres pottery, dating A.D. 1000 to 1150, depicts both men and women wearing sandals (Figs. E.1, E.2).

Rock art is different from the artistic expression on portable items, including sandals, and some of the differences may be partly explained by gender categories. Human figures depicted in the Basketmaker III period rock art in the Prayer Rock District are usually either male sexed or sex is not indicated. Female figures, identified by the hair whorls traditionally worn by unmarried Hopi women or by two or three short lines in the genital area, are rare in Basketmaker III rock art. Processions of males appear near Broken Flute Cave's great kiva, an unroofed circular structure probably used for ritual performances. Depictions of masks with lobed circles as earrings appear near this kiva and nowhere else in the Prayer Rock area. In the Basketmaker rock art of the greater Four Corners area, lobed circles are an important ritual icon (Manning 1992). Wooden pendants in the form of lobed circles were recovered in Broken Flute Cave (E. A. Morris 1980) and Canyon del Muerto (E. H. Morris 1925). This shape never appears in pottery or textile decoration.

Positing that different artifacts are used by the two sexes leads to questions about gender roles and gender identities. Anthropologists distinguish between the concept of sex as a biological distinction, and gender, which is culturally constructed. We can discuss a sexual division of labor if we mean people of male and female sex can be observed doing different kinds of work. If we want to discuss an abstract concept, such as attributing the ideas of masculine and feminine to two different art styles, we are discussing objects and ideas that do not have sex, but can have gender attributed to them. Understanding gender in the archaeological record goes beyond simply identifying men's and women's items and activities (Claassen 1992; Gero and Conkey 1991; Hodder 1986; Wright 1996). We also have to understand the role of gender in a wider array of differences that structure not only labor, but other social processes, even cosmology (McCafferty and McCafferty 1991; Weigle 1989; Young 1987).

Decoration of women's items intensified at the same time that we see architectural expression of a suprahousehold level of organization, the great kiva that emphasizes men in its associated art, and the depictions of males in processions and as isolated icons in the east half of Broken Flute Cave. At the same time, sandal decoration becomes more elaborate than at any time before or after, basket designs become more colorful and complicated, and pottery is decorated for the first time.

There is, then, an association between community aggregation (more households living together), new levels of organization (represented by the great kiva), intensi-

Figure E.1. Mimbres pottery bowl showing a woman, wearing sandals, and a man with macaws (after Brody 1983, Plate 22). Drawing by Karen M. Gardner, in Shaffer, Gardner, and Powell 1997.

fication of artifact decoration, and the visual expression of gender differentiation. Margaret Conkey (1991) has noted similar associations in the European Upper Paleolithic. One explanation, at least a partial one, of this apparent link rests in the increasing social differentiation taking place as a result of social stresses brought on by the expanding community. In small communities, even though there may be an idea of what tasks are appropriate for men and women, there is of necessity a great deal of flexibility. But as communities grow, male and female work becomes more differentially defined, leading to a more rigid division of labor. Perhaps individuals disagreed about the proper roles for men and women and marked out what they saw as their tools and their spaces using these elaborate decorative styles (see Hodder 1985, 1986: 105–116).

Comparison of Prayer Rock Basketmaker art with that of one other region, Canyon del Muerto, at about the same time, revealed no obvious differences between the two areas in designs or technology of artifacts or in rock art. This observation and the obviously low visibility of most decorated items suggest that signaling ethnicity or territory with portable decorated objects and rock art is not a plausible explanation for patterning in Basketmaker art. The regional pattern is one of similarity, indi-

cating that designs signal commonalities and connections and may symbolize or facilitate interaction, cooperation, and sharing in a highly mobile population engaged in high-risk subsistence activities across a wide area.

It may be possible to define the boundaries of regional patterns by studying sandal variation. Regional variation may occur in Basketmaker III sandal construction, because only people who lived in close enough contact with each other to take part in sandal production would likely have the same set of patterns and techniques.

How large were Basketmaker social networks? Most of the Broken Flute Cave scalloped-puckered sandals are remarkably similar to each other and to the Canyon del Muerto collections. One sandal stands out, however, in terms of both its technology and the size, placement, and symmetry of its colored design (Sandal 114–G, Fig. 5.19). Zone 2 decoration of this sandal is wider than the other Prayer Rock examples, and it lacks the usual structure of two parallel stripes of paired, counterchanged colors. Instead, it has diagonal stepped elements more similar to some twined aprons than to other sandals from Prayer Rock. Oddly enough, its top surface decoration closely resembles a photograph of a scalloped-puckered sandal from the Mesa Verde area, Site 519 in Fewkes Canyon (Rohn 1977: 229), which

Figure E.2. Mimbres pottery bowl showing a man, who has left his sandals and arrows on the ground (to the right), climbing a tree, aided by his sandal-clad companion (from Snodgrass 1977). Drawing by Karen M. Gardner, in Shaffer, Gardner, and Powell 1997.

also has a wide, diagonally structured Zone 2 band of decoration. Both sandals have 28 warps; the average number for Prayer Rock District scalloped-puckered sandals is 29 warps. Was sandal 114–G made at Mesa Verde and worn or carried to Broken Flute Cave? Not enough Mesa Verde sandals have been reported to know if the Fewkes Canyon sandal is typical of that area, but close attention to variations like these might help us understand ancient routes of trade and migration and the sizes and boundaries of interacting social groups.

At least some members of the seventh-century Broken Flute Cave community used decoration in an intensive and patterned way. Basketmaker society was not as "complex" as later Puebloan communities like those in and around Chaco Canyon. Archaeologists do not see evidence in the Prayer Rock District for wealth differ-

ences that mark elite and commoner classes. Yet we do see some indications of internal differentiation. This differentiation is expressed in the organization of gender, ritual, and perhaps craft specialization. The patterns we see here, and the exceptions to these patterns, may confirm some things we know but rarely discuss.

First, gender is not a simple matter of people of two sexes living together or people of two sexes engaging in different activities. People do not limit gender to animals or people that can be assigned to one sex or the other. Rather, people all over the world tend to attribute gender to things or ideas that do not have sex, from deities and natural phenomena such as the sun, moon, sky, earth, and colors, to mundane objects such as clothing styles or pottery designs. Calling the sun a male being or a geometric design style "feminine" is an intentional, historic, cultural act, not something determined by "nature."

It appears that the Prayer Rock Basketmakers extended gender attribution to many items and perhaps activities through the medium of design: sandal designs are more elaborate versions of the designs on women's twined aprons, tump bands, coiled baskets, and pottery. This decorative elaboration happened at a time when more people were living together than previously and life was becoming socially more complicated. Is it a coincidence that textile and pottery making, probably done by women, became more elaborate at the same time that ritual iconography and communal architecture, probably primarily the domain of men, is also elaborated? Such questions direct us toward what additional research on these sandals might reveal about the Basketmaker past.

THE FUTURE OF ANASAZI TWINED SANDALS

This volume has introduced the research and aesthetic values of Anasazi twined sandals to anthropologists, textile artists, scholars of handcrafts and of Native American fine arts, and many others. Although we have summarized and expanded on work started by Earl and Ann Morris more than half a century ago, it would have taken us at least another decade to explore the questions we would still like to ask of these fascinating objects. We hope others will take on these projects, any one of which would make a significant contribution to understanding past lifeways in the Southwest.

Distribution of Technological Features

The variety of complex construction techniques selected to make twined sandals, together with the intricate stylistic features documented here, are unlikely to have been independently invented by geographically separated peoples. What, then, can a large, regional, systematic study of textiles tell us about prehistoric population interaction and movements? Detailed study of construction and decorative characteristics may identify recurring features that one or a few individuals used; sandals might then contribute evidence for organization of production and even of individual or population movements. Although plant materials cannot be sourced, minerals used to make stone and pottery items sometimes can be matched to their geological sources. Identification of mineral pigments used in textiles, together

with chemical "fingerprinting" of pigments and minerals from potential source areas, might provide evidence for exchange of textiles, or at least of pigments.

Design Analyses

The colored designs themselves may encode a wealth of information about Basketmaker social interaction and iconography. In this book we did little more than follow Morris' lead in classifying designs by the kind of symmetry used to generate them. As numerous researchers have already demonstrated (see especially Washburn 1977, 1978; Washburn and Crowe 1988), artisans of any given culture and era tend to choose only a few of the mathematically possible symmetries. Detailed analysis of symmetries and of particular design units and colors should prove to be a rich avenue of inquiry about Basketmaker thought.

Building Regional Chronologies

Finally, it may be possible to refine the chronological sequence of sandal style and technology in each area where sandals are preserved, thereby teaching us much about the development of a kind of technology at least as complex and interesting as the technologies of stone tool and ceramic manufacture. Through direct radiocarbon dating or through analysis of dated construction and stylistic details, sandals may provide dates for architectural structures or perhaps sites, particularly in the Basketmaker era when pottery seems to have been adopted at different times in different places and remained uniform for several centuries.

In the way that ceramic styles and techniques are hypothesized to reflect communication spheres, so might textile technology. The time and places of origin of various techniques and the reasons for and rate of diffusion of textile technology complexes are of great interest. Why did this artistic form fall into disuse? Do the reasons reflect decline of the textile arts; more demands on the artisans' time; or placement of such creativity on another medium such as ceramic decoration, bodily adornment, or other insignia of identity and status?

Other lines of inquiry not considered here will emerge and flourish. We hope that anthropologists will find much to explore and that contemporary artists will discover designs that challenge their technical skills and pique their sense of beauty in these ancient artifacts.

Prayer Rock District Site Names and Numbers

Kelley Ann Hays-Gilpin

Name	Arizona State Museum Number	Museum of Northern Arizona Number
Atahonez Canyon		
Broken Flute Cave	AZ E:8:1	NA 10,602
Ram's Horn Cave	AZ E:8:3	NA 11,387
Morris Cave 1	AZ E:8:4	NA 11,388
Morris Cave 2	AZ E:8:5	NA 11,389
Morris Cave 3	AZ E:8:6	NA 11,392
Pocket Cave	AZ E:7:11	
Morris Cave 4	AZ E:7:12	
Morris Cave 5	AZ E:7:13	
Morris Cave 6	AZ E:7:14	
Morris Cave 10	AZ E:8:12	
Deception Cave	AZ E:7:15	
Obelisk Canyon		
Obelisk Cave	AZ E:7:10	NA 11,398
Bill Robinson Cave		NA 11,397
Morris Cave "?"		NA 11,395
Black Horse Canyon		
Morris Cave 7	AZ E:8:9	
Morris Cave 8	AZ E:8:10	

The Morris Twined Sandal Collection at the Arizona State Museum, with Sandal Lengths

Ann Cordy Deegan and Kelley Ann Hays-Gilpin

Sandal Type	Zones (E = Extended zone)	Length (cm)	Provenience	Morris No.	Arizona State Museum No.	Notes
Round toe–puckered heel						
	1b/2/3a	25.5	Broken Flute Cave C6	100–C	A–13870	
	1b/2/3a	25.0	Broken Flute Cave 8B	265–B	A–13869	
	1b/2/3a	26.0	Broken Flute Cave 8 +	280–K	A–13872	
	1b/2/3a	24.0	Broken Flute Cave 9	360–G	A–13911	
	1b/2/3a	24.0	Broken Flute Cave 9 +	381–C	A–13910	
	1b/2/3a	23.0	Broken Flute Cave 9	427–A	A–13900	
	1b/2/3a	24.0	Broken Flute Cave ??	433	A–13875	
	1b/2/3a	21.5	Broken Flute Cave 7U	757	A–13903	
	1b/3a	24.0	Broken Flute Cave C6	100–B	A–13891	Winter
	1b/3a	26.0	Broken Flute Cave 5 +	113–C	A–13868	
	1b/3a	26.0	Broken Flute Cave 5 +	113–E	A–13894	Winter
	1b/3a	24.0	Broken Flute Cave 5 +	115–B	A–13892	Winter
	1b/3a	22.0	Morris Cave 10	1271–C	A–13899	
	1b/3a	24.0	Broken Flute Cave C9	143–B	A–13896	
	1b/3a	27.5	Broken Flute Cave C20	183–B	A–13893	Winter
	1b/3a	13.0	Broken Flute Cave 7 +	213–B	A–13913	Child's
	1b/3a	26.0	Broken Flute Cave 8 +	280–C	A–13874	
	1b/3a	24.5	Broken Flute Cave 8NB	296–D	A–13879	
	1b/3a	25.0	Broken Flute Cave 9	360–I	A–13877	Winter
	1b/3a	24.0	Broken Flute Cave 10	387–B	A–13898	
	1b/3a	25.5	Broken Flute Cave 10	387–F	A–13881	
	1b/3a	21.0	Broken Flute Cave 10	387–I	A–13904	
	1b/3a	22.5	Broken Flute Cave 11 +	503–C	A–13897	
	1b/3a	26.0	Broken Flute Cave 11 +	503–M	A–13908	Winter
	1b/3a	24.0	Broken Flute Cave 12E	641–B	A–13902	Winter
	1b/3a	27.0	Broken Flute Cave C16	155	A–13884	Winter
	1b/3a	27.0	Broken Flute Cave 6–7R	168	A–13901	
	1b/3b		Broken Flute Cave 7 +	213–A		Dissected
	1b/3b	26.0	Broken Flute Cave C6	100–A	A–13890	Winter
	1b/3b	27.0	Broken Flute Cave 5 +	113–B	A–13889	
	1b/3b	26.0	Broken Flute Cave 5 +	113–D	A–13895	
	1b/3b	24.0	Morris Cave 3	1237–G	A–13883	
	1b/3b	29.0	Broken Flute Cave 7–8B	167–A	A–13882A	Winter

NOTE: Provenience is followed by pit house number or cist (C) number; + indicates pit house fill. Letters are directions in which sandal was found outside the pit house. G means "general" or unknown provenience; U means "under" the pit house; GE means generally in the east half of the cave; ES means east of the pit house on surface; NB means north and behind pit house; GKS means the Great Kiva structure.

Sandal Type	Zones (E = Extended zone)	Length (cm)	Provenience	Morris No.	Arizona State Museum No.	Notes
Round toe–puckered heel (continued)						
1b/3b	29.0	Broken Flute Cave 7–8B	167–B	A–13882B	Winter
1b/3b	23.5	Broken Flute Cave C20	186–B	A–13871	
1b/3b	26.0	Broken Flute Cave 8N	265–A	A–13876	
1b/3b	25.0	Broken Flute Cave 8NB	296–C	A–13878	
1b/3b	25.0	Broken Flute Cave C57	485–A	A–13909	
1b/3b	22.0	Broken Flute Cave 12NO	668–C	A–13880	
1b/3b	26.0	Broken Flute Cave G	74	A–13887	Winter
1b/E1b/2/3a	24.5	Broken Flute Cave C52	455–F	A–13905	
1b/E1b/2/3a		Broken Flute Cave 11	652–B	A–13912	Fragment
	26.0	Broken Flute Cave 5 +	113–A	A–13888	Winter
		Broken Flute Cave 7 +	218–B	A–13913	Fragment
	24.5	Broken Flute Cave 8 +	280–D	A–14002	
		Broken Flute Cave 9	360–D	A–14128–X	Burned?
	26.0	Broken Flute Cave 11E	563–C	A–13907	Winter
	24.5	Broken Flute Cave GE	73–A	A–13886	Winter
	24.0	Broken Flute Cave GE	73–B	A–13885	Winter
	28.0	Broken Flute Cave 11	653	A–14137	Winter
	22.0	Broken Flute Cave ECS	780	A–13906	Winter
Round toe–puckered heel?						
	21.5	Broken Flute Cave 11ES	563–H	A–13934	
		Broken Flute Cave C6	101	A–13914	Fragment
	25.0			A–14142	
Scalloped toe–puckered heel						
1a/2/3a	25.5	Broken Flute Cave C6	102–A	A–14051	
1a/2/3a	24.5	Broken Flute Cave 3–4	1032–A	A–14047	
1a/2/3a	26.0	Pocket Cave 4	1068–C	A–14096	
1a/2/3a	23.5	Broken Flute Cave 5 +	114–E	A–14122	
1a/2/3a	24.0	Broken Flute Cave 5 +	114–G	A–14124	
1a/2/3a	22.0	Broken Flute Cave 5 +	114–K	A–14093	
1a/2/3a	23.0	Broken Flute Cave 5 +	114–M	A–14037	
1a/2/3a		Broken Flute Cave 5 +	115–A	A–14091	Fragment
1a/2/3a	25.0	Morris Cave 8	1176–B	A–14077	
1a/2/3a	24.0	Broken Flute Cave G	1412–A	A–14035	
1a/2/3a	22.0	Broken Flute Cave C16	154–B	A–14063	
1a/2/3a	24.0	Broken Flute Cave C20	183–A	A–14010	
1a/2/3a		Broken Flute Cave C20	186–C	A–14086	Fragment
1a/2/3a	24.0	Broken Flute Cave 8 +	280–L	A–14075	
1a/2/3a		Broken Flute Cave 8B	296–B	A–14026	Fragment
1a/2/3a	20.0	Broken Flute Cave 9	360–A	A–14072	
1a/2/3a		Broken Flute Cave 9	360–C	A–14089	Fragment
1a/2/3a		Broken Flute Cave 9	360–F	A–14097	Fragment
1a/2/3a		Broken Flute Cave 9	360–H	A–14083	Fragment
1a/2/3a		Broken Flute Cave 9 +	381–E	A–14024	Fragment
1a/2/3a	24.5	Broken Flute Cave 10	387–C	A–14100	
1a/2/3a	24.5	Broken Flute Cave 10	387–D	A–14090	
1a/2/3a	26.5	Broken Flute Cave 10	387–G	A–14103	
1a/2/3a	25.0	Broken Flute Cave C50	455–A	A–14125	
1a/2/3a	24.0	Broken Flute Cave 11 +	503–H	A–14054	
1a/2/3a	24.0	Broken Flute Cave 11 +	503–J	A–14071	
1a/2/3a	24.0	Broken Flute Cave 11 +	503–L	A–14095	
1a/2/3a		Broken Flute Cave 11E	563–F	A–14105	
1a/2/3a		Broken Flute Cave 11	652–A	A–14112	Fragment
1a/2/3a	24.0	Broken Flute Cave 4	87–A	A–14041	

Sandal Type	Zones (E = Extended zone)	Length (cm)	Provenience	Morris No.	Arizona State Museum No.	Notes
Scalloped toe–puckered heel (continued)						
1a/2/3a			Broken Flute Cave 4	87–C	A–14111	Fragment
1a/2/3a	24.0		Broken Flute Cave 7–8	40	A–14015	
1a/2/3a	23.0		Broken Flute Cave 4	86	A–14039	
1a/2/3a			Broken Flute Cave 6–7	169	A–14060	Fragment
1a/2/3a	24.5		Broken Flute Cave C57	485	A–14066	
1a/2/3a			Broken Flute Cave 11ES	564	A–14085	Fragment?
1a/2/3a	24.0		Broken Flute Cave 9B	647	A–14068	
1a/2/3a	16.0		Broken Flute Cave 7	759	A–14101	Child's
1a/2/3a			Pocket Cave 4	1069	A–14117	Fragment
1a/3a	24.0		Broken Flute Cave 5 +	114–A	A–14056	
1a/3a	27.0		Broken Flute Cave 5 +	114–B	A–14107	
1a/3a	27.0		Broken Flute Cave 5 +	114–J	A–14099	
1a/3a	22.5		Broken Flute Cave 5 +	114–L	A–14044	
1a/3a	26.0		Broken Flute Cave 5 +	114–N	A–14028	
1a/3a	28.0		Morris Cave 10	1271–B	A–14079	
1a/3a			Morris Cave 10	1271–D	A–14049	Fragment
1a/3a	24.0		Broken Flute Cave 7–8	243–A	A–14016	
1a/3a			Broken Flute Cave 7–8	243–B	A–14073	Fragment
1a/3a	25.0		Broken Flute Cave 8 +	280–B	A–14050	
1a/3a			Broken Flute Cave 8 +	280–F	A–14043	Fragment
1a/3a			Broken Flute Cave 8 +	280–G	A–14022	Fragment
1a/3a	26.0		Broken Flute Cave 9 +	381–A	A–14121	Winter
1a/3a	25.0		Broken Flute Cave 9 +	381–B	A–14118	
1a/3a	24.5		Broken Flute Cave 10	387–E	A–14034	
1a/3a	28.0		Broken Flute Cave 8	427–B	A–14120	
	25.5		Broken Flute Cave C52	455–C	A–14084	
1a/3a	26.0		Broken Flute Cave C52	455–E	A–14055	
1a/3a	25.0		Broken Flute Cave C57	485–B	A–14059	
1a/3a	25.0		Broken Flute Cave 11 +	503–A	A–14009	
1a/3a	24.5		Broken Flute Cave 11 +	503–D	A–14011	
1a/3a	25.0		Broken Flute Cave 11 +	503–E	A–14115	Winter
1a/3a	23.0		Broken Flute Cave 11 +	503–F	A–14012	
1a/3a	26.0		Broken Flute Cave 11 +	503–I	A–14045	
1a/3a	19.0		Broken Flute Cave 11 +	503–N	A–14017	
1a/3a	27.0		Broken Flute Cave 11 +	503–R	A–14108	Winter
1a/3a	19.5		Broken Flute Cave 11 +	504–B	A–14064	
1a/3a			Broken Flute Cave 11 +	504–D	A–14127	Fragment
1a/3a	24.5		Broken Flute Cave 11ES	563–D	A–14126	
1a/3a	24.0		Broken Flute Cave 12N	668–E	A–14020	
1a/3a			Broken Flute Cave 4	87–B	A–14048	Fragment
1a/3a	25.0		Broken Flute Cave C55	481	A–14087	
1a/3a			Morris Cave 3 4 +	964	A–14109	Fragment
1a/3a	22.0		Pocket Cave 3	1058	A–14076	
1a/3a	21.0		Ram's Horn Cave	1366	A–14032	
1a/E1a/2/3a	25.0		Broken Flute Cave C6	102–B	A–14069	
1a/E1a/2/3a	25.5		Pocket Cave 4	1068–A	A–14082	
1a/E1a/2/3a	25.0		Pocket Cave 4	1068–B	A–14053	
1a/E1a/2/3a	23.5		Pocket Cave 4	1068–D	A–14013	
1a/E1a/2/3a			Pocket Cave 4	1068–E	[not at ASM]	
1a/E1a/2/3a	26.0		Broken Flute Cave 5 +	114–D	A–14074	
1a/E1a/2/3a	25.0		Broken Flute Cave 5 +	114–F	A–14023	
1a/E1a/2/3a	25.5		Broken Flute Cave 5 +	114–H	A–14038	
1a/E1a/2/3a	25.0		Broken Flute Cave 5 +	114–I	A–14062	
1a/E1a/2/3a	26.0		Morris Cave 10	1271–A	A–14092	

Sandal Type	Zones (E = Extended zone)	Length (cm)	Provenience	Morris No.	Arizona State Museum No.	Notes
Scalloped toe–puckered heel (continued)						
1a/E1a/2/3a			Broken Flute Cave C9	143–C	A–14061	Fragment
1a/E1a/2/3a	23.0		Broken Flute Cave C16	154–A	A–14019	
1a/E1a/2/3a			Broken Flute Cave C20	186–A	A–14113	Fragment
1a/E1a/2/3a	24.0		Broken Flute Cave 8+	280–A	A–14067	
1a/E1a/2/3a	25.0		Broken Flute Cave 8+	280–E	A–14030	
1a/E1a/2/3a	23.0		Broken Flute Cave 8+	280–H	A–14018	
1a/E1a/2/3a	27.0		Broken Flute Cave 8+	280–I	A–14078	
1a/E1a/2/3a	25.5		Broken Flute Cave 8+	280–J	A–14104	
1a/E1a/2/3a	24.5		Broken Flute Cave 8B	296–A	A–14070	
1a/E1a/2/3a	26.0		Broken Flute Cave 9	360–J	A–14040	
1a/E1a/2/3a			Broken Flute Cave 9+	381–D	A–14052	Fragment
1a/E1a/2/3a	26.0		Broken Flute Cave9+	387–A	A–13942	
1a/E1a/2/3a	25.0		Broken Flute Cave C52	455–B	A–14036	
1a/E1a/2/3a	25.0		Broken Flute Cave C52	455–D	A–14106	
1a/E1a/2/3a	24.0		Broken Flute Cave 11+	503–G	A–14031	
1a/E1a/2/3a	24.0		Broken Flute Cave 11+	503–K	A–14014	
1a/E1a/2/3a	25.0		Broken Flute Cave 11+	503–P	A–14027	
1a/E1a/2/3a	25.0		Broken Flute Cave 11+	503–Q	A–14042	
1a/E1a/2/3a	24.5		Broken Flute Cave 11ES	563–A	A–14080	
1a/E1a/2/3a	24.5		Broken Flute Cave 11ES	563–B	A–14081	
1a/E1a/2/3a	27.0		Broken Flute Cave 11ES	563–E	A–14057	
1a/E1a/2/3a			Broken Flute Cave	563–G	A–14110	Fragment
1a/E1a/2/3a			Broken Flute Cave 12E	641–A	A–14025	Fragment
1a/E1a/2/3a	22.0		Broken Flute Cave 21N	668–D	A–14021	
1a/E1a/2/3a	26.5		Broken Flute Cave C20	184	A–14098	
1a/E1a/2/3a	24.5		Broken Flute Cave C20	185	A–14116	
1a/E1a/2/3a			Broken Flute Cave 12E	750	A–14102	Fragment
1a/E1a/2/3a	24.0		Unknown	1358	A–14029	
			Pocket Cave S	1009–M	A–14114	Fragment
	23.5		Broken Flute Cave 5+	114–C	A–14046	
	25.0		Broken Flute Cave 8B	265–C	A–14088	Winter?
			Broken Flute Cave 9	360–A	A–14072	Fragment?
			Broken Flute Cave 9	360–D	A–14128	Fragment
			Broken Flute Cave 9+	381–F	A–14123	Fragment
	20.0		Broken Flute Cave 10	387–H	A–14033	
	24.5		Broken Flute Cave 11ES	463–D	A–14126	
	24.0		Broken Flute Cave 11+	503–G	A–14042	
			Broken Flute Cave 11+	504–C	A–14065	Fragment
	27.5		Broken Flute Cave 12S	688–A	A–14058	Winter
			Unknown	207	A–14152	Fragment
			Broken Flute Cave 7+	212	A–14094	Winter
			Unknown		A–14130	Fragment
Scalloped toe–puckered heel?						
1a/E1a/2/3a			Broken Flute Cave 9	360–B	A–14129	Fragment
			Broken Flute Cave 12NS	668–A		
Scalloped toe–square heel						
1a/2/3a	22.5		Pocket Cave S	1009–B	A–13844	
1a/2/3a			Pocket Cave S	1009–C	[not at ASM]	Dissected
1a/2/3a	22.5		Pocket Cave S	1009–G	A–13832	
1a/2/3a	24.0		Pocket Cave S	1009–H	A–13862	
1a/2/3a	22.0		Pocket Cave E	1009–I	A–13826	
1a/2/3a	23.5		Morris Cave 3	1237–A	A–14147	
1a/2/3a	23.5		Morris Cave 3	1237–F	A–13831	

Sandal Type	Zones (E = Extended zone)	Length (cm)	Provenience	Morris No.	Arizona State Museum No.	Notes
Scalloped toe–square heel (continued)						
1a/2/3a		22.5	Morris Cave 3	1237–J	A–14132	
1a/2/3a		18.0	Morris Cave 3	1237–K	A–13827	Painted
1a/2/3a		21.3	Broken Flute Cave C9	143–A	A–13828	
1a/2/3a			Broken Flute Cave GE	27–A	A–13835	Fragment
1a/2/3a			Broken Flute Cave GE	27–C	A–14133	Fragment?
1a/2/3a		24.0	Broken Flute Cave GKS	49–D	A–13840	
1a/2/3a		24.0	Broken Flute Cave 11+	503–O	A–13822	
1a/2/3a		22.5	Broken Flute Cave 3+	63–A	A–13850	
1a/2/3a			Broken Flute Cave 3+	63–D	A–13854	Painted
1a/2/3a		22.5	Broken Flute Cave 3+	63–F	A–13829	
1a/2/3a		22.0	Broken Flute Cave 16+	683–D	A–13873	
1a/2/3a			Broken Flute Cave 16+S	684–A	A–13858	Fragment
1a/2/3a		22.0	Broken Flute Cave 7N	761	A–13845	
1a/2/3a		25.0	Obelisk Cave	1322	A–13863	
1a/3a		22.5	Pocket Cave S	1009–A	A–13837	
1a/3a			Pocket Cave S	1009–J	A–14119	Fragment
1a/3a		22.0	Pocket Cave S	1009–K	A–13866	
1a/3a		23.0	Pocket Cave S	1009–L	A–13830	
1a/3a		23.0	Pocket Cave 3–4	1032–B	A–13842	
1a/3a		27.5	Morris Cave 3	1237–B	A–13864	
1a/3a			Broken Flute Cave 7–8B	244–A	A–13851	Fragment
1a/3a		23.5	Broken Flute Cave GE	26–A	A–13823	
1a/3a		25.0	Broken Flute Cave GE	26–B	A–13931	
1a/3a		23.5	Broken Flute Cave GE	26–C	A–13861	
1a/3a		23.0	Broken Flute Cave GE	26–D	A–13860	
1a/3a		22.0	Broken Flute Cave GE	26–E	A–13836	
1a/3a		21.5	Broken Flute Cave GKS	49–A	A–13852	
1a/3a		22.5	Broken Flute Cave GKS	49–B	A–13853	
1a/3a		23.5	Broken Flute Cave 3+	63–B	A–13848	
1a/3a			Broken Flute Cave 3+	63–E	A–13825	
1a/3a		22.5	Broken Flute Cave 3+	63–G	A–13821	
1a/3a		24.0	Broken Flute Cave + S	683–A	A–13824	
1a/3a		23.5	Broken Flute Cave + S	683–B	A–13865	
1a/3a		24.0	Broken Flute Cave 16+	683–E	A–13833	
1a/3a		22.0	Obelisk Cave	803–B	A–13838	
1a/3a		22.5	Obelisk Cave	848–B	A–13834	
1a/3a		22.5	Broken Flute Cave 2+	41	A–13843	
1a/3a		22.0	Broken Flute Cave 17+	772	A–13846	
1a/3a		17.0	Obelisk Cave	899	A–13841	
1a/3a		23.0	Broken Flute Cave 7N	760	A–13847	
1a/3b/3a		23.5	Pocket Cave 5	1009–F	A–13849	
1a/3b/3a		21.0	Broken Flute Cave G	1412–B	A–13867	
			Pocket Cave E	1059–E	A–13855	Fragment
			Pocket Cave E	1059–F	A–13856	Fragment
			Broken Flute Cave GE	27–D	A–13839	Fragment?
		19.5	Broken Flute Cave 3+	63–C	A–13941	
		17.0	Broken Flute Cave 3+	63–R	A–13825	Fragment?
			Broken Flute Cave GKS	50	A–13859	Fragment
			Obelisk Cave	831	A–13919	Fragment
			Obelisk Cave	836	A–13857	Fragment
		24.0	Broken Flute Cave 11+	503	A–13822	
Scalloped toe–square heel?						
		22.0	Pocket Cave S	1009–D	A–13922	
		22.5	Pocket Cave S	1009–E	A–13924	

Sandal Type	Zones (E = Extended zone)	Length (cm)	Provenience	Morris No.	Arizona State Museum No.	Notes
Scalloped toe–square heel? (continued)						
		22.5	Pocket Cave E	1059–C	A–13915	
			Pocket Cave E	1059–D	A–13917	Fragment
		20.5	Morris Cave 8	1176–A	A–13927	
		24.0	Morris Cave 4	1218–A	A–13928	
		23.5	Morris Cave 3	1237–C	A–13920	
		22.5	Morris Cave 3	1237–D	A–13925	
		27.0	Morris Cave 3	1237–E	A–13916	
		22.5	Morris Cave 3	1237–I	A–13926	
		24.0	Broken Flute Cave 11+	503–B	A–13921	
		25.0	Broken Flute Cave 12N	668–B	A–13933	Winter
		21.5	Obelisk Cave	803–D	A–13923	
		17.0	Obelisk Cave	848–A	A–13930	Winter
		20.0	Obelisk Cave	848–C	A–13932	
		15.5	Unknown		A–14131	Child's
			Pocket Cave	1009–N	A–13936	Fragment
			Pocket Cave	1032–C	A–14006	Fragment
		24.0	Pocket Cave E	1059–A	A–13938	
			Pocket Cave	1059–B	A–13939	Fragment
		17.3	Morris Cave 4	1218–B	A–14004	
			Morris Cave 11	1301–A	A–14150	Fragment
			Broken Flute Cave 7–8B	244–B	A–14008	Fragment
		20.0	Broken Flute Cave GE	27–B	A–14005	
			Broken Flute Cave 9	360–E	A–14136	Fragment
			Broken Flute Cave 9	360?	A–14134	Fragment
			Broken Flute Cave 9	360?	A–14135	Fragment
		20.5	Broken Flute Cave GKS	49–C	A–13937	
			Broken Flute Cave 11+	504–A	A–13935	Fragment
		22.0	Broken Flute Cave 16+	683–C	A–14003	
			Broken Flute Cave 16+S	684–C	A–14007	Fragment
		21.5	Obelisk Cave	803–A	A–13940	
		20.5	Obelisk Cave	803–C	A–14001	
			Broken Flute Cave 7–8B	75	A–14145	Fragment?
			Broken Flute Cave C16	156	A–14144	Fragment
			Broken Flute Cave 7+	211	A–13918	Fragment
			Broken Flute Cave G	245	A–14146	Fragment
			Broken Flute Cave 8+	281	A–14143	Fragment
			Broken Flute Cave	570	A–14139	Fragment
		25.0	Morris Cave 3	988	A–13943	
			Unknown		A–14087	
			Unknown		A–14138–X	Fragment
			Unknown		A–14140	Fragment
		22.0	Unknown		A–14148	

References

ABBOT, JOHN REGINALD
1964   *Footwear Evidence: The Examination, Identification, and Comparison of Footwear Impressions*. Springfield, Illinois: Charles C. Thomas.

ADAMS, E. CHARLES
1991   *The Origins and Development of the Pueblo Katsina Cult*. Tucson: University of Arizona Press.

AHLSTROM, RICHARD V. N.
1985   *The Interpretation of Archaeological Tree-Ring Dates*. Doctoral dissertation, University of Arizona, Tucson. Ann Arbor: University Microfilms.

AMBLER, J. RICHARD
1968   NA 7523–Sand Dune Cave, and NA 7613–Dust Devil Cave. In "Survey and Excavations North and East of Navajo Mountain, Utah, 1959–1962," edited by Alexander J. Lindsay, Jr., J. Richard Ambler, Mary Anne Stein, and Philip M. Hobler. *Museum of Northern Arizona Bulletin 45, Glen Canyon Series* 8: 30–102, 102–121. Flagstaff: Northern Arizona Society of Science and Art.

AMSDEN, CHARLES AVERY
1949   *Prehistoric Southwesterners from Basketmaker to Pueblo*. Los Angeles: Southwest Museum.

ANDERSON, KEITH M.
1969   Tsegi Phase Technology. MS, Doctoral dissertation, Department of Anthropology, University of Washington, Seattle.

BALDWIN, GORDON C.
1938   An Analysis of Basket Maker III Sandals from Northeastern Arizona. *American Anthropologist* 40(3): 465–485.
1939   An Analysis of Basket Maker III Sandals from Northeastern Arizona. *American Anthropologist* 41(2): 223–244.

BANNISTER, BRYANT, JEFFREY S. DEAN, AND ELIZABETH A. MORRIS GELL
1966   *Tree-Ring Dates from Arizona E: Chinle-De Chelly-Red Rock Area*. Tucson: Laboratory of Tree-Ring Research, University of Arizona.

BARBER, ELIZABETH WAYLAND
1994   *Women's Work: The First 20,000 Years: Women, Cloth, and Society in Early Times*. New York: W. W. Norton.

BEAN, SUSAN
1989   Gandhi and *Khadi*, the Fabric of Indian Independence. In *Cloth and Human Experience*, edited by Annette B. Weiner and Jane Schneider, pp. 355–376. Washington: Smithsonian Institution Press.

BERNHEIMER, CHARLES L.
1930   Charles L. Bernheimer Expedition 1930. In "Report of the Charles L. Bernheimer Expeditions, 1922-1930." MS on file, American Museum of Natural History, New York.

BODZIAK, WILLIAM J.
1990   *Footwear Impression Evidence*. New York: Elsevier.

BRAINERD, GEORGE W.
1942   Symmetry in Primitive Conventional Design. *American Antiquity* 8(2): 164–166.

BRODY, J. J.
1977   *Mimbres Painted Pottery*. Santa Fe: School of American Research.
1983   Mimbres Painting. In *Mimbres Pottery: Ancient Art of the American Southwest*, by J. J. Brody, Catherine J. Scott, and Steven A. LeBlanc, pp. 69–125. New York: Hudson Hill Press.

BRUNSON, JUDY L.
1985   Corrugated Ceramics as Indicators of Interaction Spheres. In *Decoding Prehistoric Ceramics*, edited by Ben A. Nelson, pp. 102–127. Carbondale: Southern Illinois University Press.

BUSH, GEORGE, AND PERRY LONDON
1960   On the Disappearance of Knickers: Hypotheses for the Functional Analysis of the Psychology of Clothing. *Journal of Social Psychology* 51: 359–366.

CHAPMAN, MALCOLM
1995   "Freezing the Frame": Dress and Ethnicity in Brittany and Gaelic Scotland. In *Dress and Ethnicity: Change Across Space and Time*, edited by Joanne B. Eicher, pp. 7–28. Oxford: Berg.

CLAASSEN, CHERYL, EDITOR
1992   *Exploring Gender Through Archaeology: Selected Papers from the 1991 Boone Conference*. Madison: Prehistory Press.

COHN, BERNARD S.
1989   Cloth, Clothes, and Colonialism: India in the Nineteenth Century. In *Cloth and Human Experi-*

COHN, BERNARD S. (*continued*)

ence, edited by Annette B. Weiner and Jane Schneider, pp. 303–353. Washington: Smithsonian Institution Press.

COLE, SALLY J.

1990   *Legacy on Stone: Rock Art of the Colorado Plateau and Four Corners Region.* Boulder: Johnson Books.

COLTON, MARY-RUSSELL FERRELL

1965   Hopi Dyes. *Museum of Northern Arizona Bulletin* 41. Flagstaff: Northern Arizona Society of Science and Art.

CONKEY, MARGARET W.

1991   Contexts of Action, Contexts for Power: Material Culture and Gender in the Magdalenian. In *Engendering Archaeology: Women and Prehistory*, edited by Joan M. Gero and Margaret W. Conkey, pp. 57–92. Oxford: Basil Blackwell.

COSGROVE, CORNELIUS BURTON

1947   Caves of the Upper Gila and Hueco Areas in New Mexico and Texas. *Papers of the Peabody Museum of American Archaeology and Ethnology* 24(2). Cambridge: Harvard University.

COSTIN, CATHY LYNNE

1996   Exploring the Relationship between Gender and Craft in Complex Societies: Methodological and Theoretical Issues of Gender Attribution. In *Gender and Archaeology*, edited by Rita P. Wright, pp. 111–140. Philadelphia: University of Pennsylvania Press.

CRESSMAN, LUTHER S.

1942   *Archaeological Researches in the Northern Great Basin.* Carnegie Institution of Washington Publication 538. Washington.

CROTTY, HELEN KOEFOED

1995   *Anasazi Mural Art of the Pueblo IV Period, A.D. 1300–1600: Influences, Selective Adaptation, and Cultural Diversity in the Prehistoric Southwest.* Doctoral dissertation, Department of Art History, University of California, Los Angeles. Ann Arbor: University Microfilms.

CUMMINGS, BYRON

1910   The Ancient Inhabitants of the San Juan Valley. *University of Utah Bulletin* 3(3, Part 2), 2nd Archaeological Number. Salt Lake City: University of Utah.

1953   *The First Inhabitants of Arizona and the Southwest.* Tucson: Cummings Publication Council.

DARISH, PATRICIA

1989   Dressing for the Next Life: Raffia Textile Production and Use among the Kuba of Zaire. In *Cloth and Human Experience*, edited by Annette B. Weiner and Jane Schneider, pp. 118–140. Washington: Smithsonian Institution Press.

DAVIS, CAROLINE O'BAGY

1995   *Treasured Earth: Hattie Cosgrove's Mimbres Archaeology in the American Southwest.* Tucson: Sanpete Publications and the Old Pueblo Archaeology Center.

DEBOER, WARREN

1991   The Decorative Burden. In *Ceramic Ethnoarchaeology*, edited by William A. Longacre, pp. 144–161. Tucson: University of Arizona Press.

DEEGAN, ANN CORDY

1992   Scalloped-Toe Anasazi Sandals: Fabric and Overall Construction. *Ars Textrina* 18: 171–192.

1993   Anasazi Fibrous Sandal Terminology. *Kiva* 59(1): 49–64.

1995   Anasazi Sandal Features: Their Research Value and Identification. *Kiva* 61(1): 57–69.

1996   Anasazi Square Toe–Square Heel Twined Sandals: Construction and Cultural Attributes. *Kiva* 62(1): 27–44.

1997   Anasazi Sandals of Tseyi-Hatsosi Canyon, Arizona: Attributes and Cultural Context. *Clothing and Textiles Research Journal* 15: 12–19.

DRIVER, HAROLD E., AND WILLIAM C. MASSEY

1957   *Comparative Studies of North American Indians.* Transactions of the American Philosophical Society, New Series 47(2): 165–456. Philadelphia.

EICHER, JOANNE B.

1995   Introduction: Dress Expression of Ethnic Identity. In *Dress and Ethnicity: Change Across Space and Time*, edited by Joanne B. Eicher, pp. 1–5. Oxford: Berg.

EICHER, JOANNE B., AND BARBARA SUMBERG

1995   World Fashion, Ethnic, and National Dress. In *Dress and Ethnicity: Change Across Space and Time*, edited by Joanne B. Eicher, pp. 295–306. Oxford: Berg.

EMERY, IRENE

1980   *The Primary Structures of Fabrics: An Illustrated Classification.* Washington: The Textile Museum. (Originally published 1966.)

FEWKES, JESSE W.

1909   Antiquities of Mesa Verde National Park. *Bureau of Ethnology Bulletin* 41. Washington: Smithsonian Institution.

FOOTE, SHELLY

1989   Challenging Gender Symbols. In *Men and Women: Dressing the Part*, edited by Claudia Brush Kidwell and Valerie Steele, pp. 144–157. Washington: Smithsonian Institution Press.

FULTON, WILLIAM SHIRLEY

1941   *A Ceremonial Cave in the Winchester Mountains, Arizona.* The Amerind Foundation 2. Dragoon, Arizona: The Amerind Foundation.

GEIB, PHIL R.

1995   Evidence for Middle Archaic Occupancy of the

Central Colorado Plateau: AMS Dating of Plain Weave Sandals. Unpublished MS on file at the Navajo Nation Archaeology Department.

GERO, JOAN M., AND MARGARET W. CONKEY, EDITORS
1991   *Engendering Archaeology: Women and Prehistory*. Oxford: Basil Blackwell.

GUERNSEY, SAMUEL J.
1931   Explorations in Northeastern Arizona. *Papers of the Peabody Museum of American Archaeology and Ethnology* 12(1). Cambridge: Harvard University.

GUERNSEY, SAMUEL J., AND ALFRED VINCENT KIDDER
1921   Basket-maker Caves of Northeastern Arizona. *Papers of the Peabody Museum of American Archaeology and Ethnology* 8(2). Cambridge: Harvard University.

HAMILTON, JEAN A., AND JAMES W. HAMILTON
1989   Dress as a Reflection and Sustainer of Social Reality: A Cross-Cultural Perspective. *Clothing and Textiles Research Journal* 7(2): 16–22.

HATT, GUDMUND
1916   Moccasins and Their Relation to Arctic Footwear. *American Anthropological Association Memoir* 3: 149–250.

HAURY, EMIL W.
1950   *The Stratigraphy and Archaeology of Ventana Cave, Arizona*. Albuquerque: University of New Mexico Press, and Tucson: University of Arizona Press.

HAYS, KELLEY ANN
1991   Rock Art of the Prayer Rock District, Apache County, Arizona: A Descriptive Report. MS, Report to the Navajo Nation Historic Preservation Department and Arizona State Museum.
1992   *Anasazi Ceramics as Text and Tool: Toward a Theory of Ceramic Design "Messaging."* Doctoral dissertation, University of Arizona, Tucson. Ann Arbor: University Microfilms.

HIBBEN, FRANK
1975   *Kiva Art of the Anasazi at Pottery Mound*. Las Vegas: KC Publications.

HILDEBRANT, BARBARA S.
1989   The Archaeology and Ethnohistory of Red Rock Valley: A Study of Prehistoric and Historic Land Use in Northeastern Arizona. *Zuni Archaeology Program Report* 262. Zuni, New Mexico.

HOCKINS, PAUL
1979   Bagada Apparel: Protection and Symbol. In *The Fabrics of Culture: The Anthropology of Clothing and Adornment*, edited by Justine M. Cordwell and Ronald A. Schwartz, pp. 143–174. The Hague: Mouton.

HODDER, IAN
1985   Boundaries as Social Strategies: An Ethnoarchaeological Study. In *The Archaeology of Frontiers*

and Borders, edited by S. W. Green and S. M. Perlman, pp. 141–159. New York: Academic Press.
1986   *Reading the Past: Current Approaches to Interpretation in Archeology*. Cambridge: Cambridge University Press.

HOPI DICTIONARY PROJECT
1997   *Hopi Dictionary/Hopìikwa Lavàytutuveni. A Hopi-English Dictionary of the Third Mesa Dialect*. Compiled by the Hopi Dictionary Project (Kenneth C. Hill, Emory Sekaquaptewa, and Mary E. Black). Tucson: University of Arizona Press.

HOSKINS, JANET
1989   Why Do Ladies Sing the Blues? Indigo Dyeing, Cloth Production, and Gender Symbolism in Kodi. In *Cloth and Human Experience*, edited by Annette B. Weiner and Jane Schneider, pp. 141–173. Washington: Smithsonian Institution Press.

HOWELL, TODD L.
1995   Tracking Zuni Gender and Leadership Roles across the Contact Period. *Journal of Anthropological Research* 51(2): 125–147.

HYDER, WILLIAM D.
1994   Basketmaker Social Identity: Rock Art as Culture and Praxis. Paper presented at the 1994 International Rock Art Conference, American Rock Art Research Association, Flagstaff, Arizona.

JOSHI, O. P.
1992   The Significance of Dress for the Orthodox Hindu Woman. In *Dress and Gender: Making and Meaning in Cultural Contexts*, edited by Ruth Barnes and Joanne B. Eicher, pp. 214–231. Oxford: Berg.

JUDD, NEIL M.
1954   The Material Culture of Pueblo Bonito. *Smithsonian Miscellaneous Collections* 124. Washington: Smithsonian Institution.

KAISER, SUSAN B.
1989   Clothing and the Social Organization of Gender Perception: A Developmental Approach. *Clothing and Textiles Research Journal* 7(2): 46–56.
1990   *The Social Psychology of Clothing: Symbolic Appearances in Context*. Second Edition. New York: Macmillan.

KANKAINEN, KATHY, EDITOR
1995   *Treading in the Past: Sandals of the Anasazi*. Salt Lake City: Utah Museum of Natural History and University of Utah Press.

KEALI'INOHOMOKU, JOANN W.
1979   You Dance What You Wear, and You Wear Your Cultural Values. In *The Fabrics of Culture: The Anthropology of Clothing and Adornment*, edited by Justine M. Cordwell and Ronald A. Schwartz, pp. 77–83. The Hague: Mouton.

KENT, KATE PECK

1983a   *Prehistoric Textiles of the Southwest*. Santa Fe: School of American Research.

1983b   Temporal Shifts in the Structure of Traditional Southwestern Textile Design. In *Structure and Cognition in Art*, edited by Dorothy K. Washburn, pp. 113–137. Cambridge: Cambridge University Press.

KIDDER, ALFRED V.

1926   A Sandal from Northeastern Arizona. *American Anthropologist* 28: 618–632.

1944a   Letter from Alfred V. Kidder to Earl H. Morris, February 28, 1944. Archives of the Arizona State Museum, File A–144: 250–251, University of Arizona, Tucson.

1944b   Letter from Alfred V. Kidder to Earl H. Morris, March 16, 1944. Earl Morris Papers, University of Colorado Museum, Boulder, Colorado.

KIDDER, ALFRED V., AND SAMUEL J. GUERNSEY

1919   Archaeological Explorations in Northeastern Arizona. *Bureau of American Ethnology Bulletin* 65. Washington: Smithsonian Institution.

KIDWELL, CLAUDIA BRUSH

1989   Gender Symbols or Fashionable Details? In *Men and Women: Dressing the Part*, edited by Claudia Brush Kidwell and Valerie Steele, pp. 124–143. Washington: Smithsonian Institution Press.

KROEBER, ALFRED L.

1919   On the Principle of Order in Civilization as Exemplified by Changes in Fashion. *American Anthropologist* 21(2): 235–263.

LEBLANC, STEVEN A.

1983   *The Mimbres People: Ancient Pueblo Painters of the American Southwest*. London: Thames and Hudson.

LOFTIN, JOHN D.

1991   *Religion and Hopi Life in the Twentieth Century*. Bloomington: Indiana University Press.

LONGACRE, WILLIAM A.

1970   Archaeology as Anthropology: A Case Study. *Anthropological Papers of the University of Arizona* 17. Tucson: University of Arizona Press.

LOUD, LLEWELLYN L., AND MARK R. HARRINGTON

1929   Lovelock Cave. *University of California Publications in American Archaeology and Ethnology* 25(1). Berkeley and Los Angeles: University of California.

MAGERS, PAMELA C.

1986   Chapter 18: Weaving at Antelope House. In *Archeological Investigations at Antelope House*, edited by Don P. Morris, Senior Author and Project Director, pp. 252–265. Washington: National Park Service.

MANNING, STEVEN JAMES

1992   The Lobed-Circle Image in the Basket Maker Petroglyphs of Southwestern Utah. *Utah Archaeology* 1992: 1–37.

MARTIN, PAUL S., JOHN B. RINALDO, ELAINE A. BLUHM, HUGH C. CUTLER, AND ROGER T. GRANGE, JR.

1952   Mogollon Cultural Continuity and Change: The Stratigraphic Analysis of Tularosa and Cordova Caves. *Fieldiana: Anthropology* 40. Chicago: Chicago Natural History Museum.

MASON, OTIS T.

1896   Primitive Travel and Transportation. Annual Report of the Board of Regents of the Smithsonian Institution for the Year Ending June 30, 1894.

MAURER, EVAN M.

1979   Symbol and Identification in North American Indian Clothing. In *The Fabrics of Culture: The Anthropology of Clothing and Adornment*, edited by Justine M. Cordwell and Ronald A. Schwartz, pp. 119–135. The Hague: Mouton.

MCCAFFERTY, SHARISSE D., AND GEOFFREY G. MCCAFFERTY

1991   Spinning and Weaving as Female Gender Identity in Post-Classic Mexico. In *Textile Traditions of Mesoamerica and the Andes: An Anthology*, edited by M. B. Schevill, J. C. Berlo, and E. B. Dwyer. New York: Garland Publishing.

MCCRACKEN, GRANT D.

1988   *Culture and Consumption: New Approaches to the Symbolic Character of Consumer Goods and Activities*. Bloomington: Indiana University Press.

MCCREERY, PATRICIA, AND EKKEHART MALOTKI

1994   *Tapamveni: The Rock Art Galleries of Petrified Forest and Beyond*. Petrified Forest, Arizona: Petrified Forest Museum Association.

MCCREERY, PATRICIA, AND JACK MCCREERY

1986   A Petroglyph Site with Possible Hopi Ceremonial Association. *American Indian Rock Art II*, edited by Ernesto Snyder, pp. 1–7. El Toro, California: American Rock Art Research Association.

MCDOWELL, COLIN

1989   *Shoes: Fashion and Fantasy*. London: Thames and Hudson.

MILLER, MARGARET THOMPSON

1979   Sexual Differentiation and Acculturation in Potawatomi Costume. In *The Fabrics of Culture: The Anthropology of Clothing and Adornment*, edited by Justine M. Cordwell and Ronald A. Schwartz, pp. 313–330. The Hague: Mouton.

MORRIS, EARL HALSTEAD

1919   The Aztec Ruin. *Anthropological Papers of the American Museum of Natural History* 26(1). New York: American Museum of Natural History.

1923   Field notes from Canyon del Muerto. MS, American Museum of Natural History, New York.

1925   Exploring in the Canyon of Death. *National Geographic Magazine* 48(3): 263–300.

1927   The Beginnings of Pottery Making in the San Juan Area: Unfired Proto-types and the Wares of the Earliest Ceramic Period. *Anthropological Papers of the American Museum of Natural History* 28(2): 125–198.

1931a   Report on Archaeological Reconnaissance in the Carriso-Lukachukai District of Northeastern Arizona and Northwestern New Mexico, made by the Eighth Bernheimer Expedition of the American Museum of Natural History in 1930 under permit from the Department of the Interior issued to the American Museum of Natural History May 5, 1930. MS on file, American Museum of Natural History, New York.

1931b   Field notes and catalog of artifacts collected by the 1931 Carnegie Expedition. Arizona State Museum Archives, File A–133, University of Arizona, Tucson.

1944a   Anasazi Sandals. *Clearing House for Southwestern Museums News-Letters* #68–69: 239–241.

1944b   Letter from Earl H. Morris to Alfred V. Kidder, March 12, 1944. Earl Morris Papers, University of Colorado Museum, Boulder.

1944c   Letter from Earl H. Morris to Alfred V. Kidder, June 12, 1944. Earl Morris Papers, University of Colorado Museum, Boulder. [Includes typed version of the report submitted to the Carnegie Institution Yearbook but not published in its entirety.]

1951   Basketmaker III Human Figurines from Northeastern Arizona. *American Antiquity* 17(1): 33–40.

MORRIS, EARL H., AND ROBERT F. BURGH

1941   Anasazi Basketry, Basket Maker II Through Pueblo III: A Study Based on Specimens from the San Juan River Country. *Carnegie Institution of Washington Publication* 533. Washington.

1954   Basket-Maker II Sites Near Durango, Colorado. *Carnegie Institution of Washington Publication* 604. Washington.

MORRIS, ELIZABETH ANN

1958   A Possible Early Projectile Point from the Prayer Rock District, Arizona. *Southwestern Lore* 24(1): 1–4.

1959a   *Basketmaker Caves in the Prayer Rock District, Northeastern Arizona.* Doctoral dissertation, University of Arizona, Tucson. Ann Arbor: University Microfilms.

1959b   Basketmaker Flutes from the Prayer Rock District, Arizona. *American Antiquity* 24(4): 406–411.

1975   Seventh Century Basketmaker Textiles from Northern Arizona. *Proceedings of the 1974 Irene Emery Roundtable on Museum Textiles: Archaeological Textiles*, pp. 125–132. Washington: The Textile Museum.

1980   Basketmaker Caves in the Prayer Rock District, Northeastern Arizona. *Anthropological Papers of the University of Arizona* 35. Tucson: University of Arizona Press.

MORSS, NOEL

1927   Archaeological Explorations on the Middle Chinlee, 1925. *Memoirs of the American Anthropological Association* 34.

MOULARD, BARBARA

1984   *Within the Underworld Sky.* Pasadena, California: Twelvetrees Press.

MURRA, JOHN

1989   Cloth and Its Functions in the Inka State, in *Cloth and Human Experience*, edited by Annette B. Weiner and Jane Schneider, pp. 275–302. Washington: Smithsonian Institution Press.

NASH, MANNING

1989   *The Cauldron of Ethnicity in the Modern World.* Chicago: University of Chicago Press.

NORDENSKIÖLD, GUSTAV

1979   *The Cliff Dwellers of the Mesa Verde, Southwestern Colorado.* Glorieta, New Mexico: The Rio Grande Press. (Originally published 1893, P. A. Norstedt and Söner, Stockholm.)

NUSBAUM, JESSE L., ALFRED V. KIDDER, AND SAMUEL J. GUERNSEY

1922   A Basket-Maker Cave in Kane County, Utah. *Indian Notes and Monographs* 29. New York: Museum of the American Indian, Heye Foundation.

OSBORNE, CAROLYN M.

1980   Objects of Perishable Materials. In *Long House: Mesa Verde National Park, Colorado*, by George S. Cattanach, Jr., pp. 317–367. Washington: National Park Service.

PAOLETTI, JO B., AND CAROL L. KREGLOH

1989   The Children's Department. In *Men and Women: Dressing the Part*, edited by Claudia Brush Kidwell and Valerie Steele, pp. 22–41. Washington: Smithsonian Institution Press.

PARSONS, ELSIE CLEWS

1936   *Pueblo Indian Religion.* Chicago: University of Chicago Press.

PEPPER, GEORGE H.

1920   Pueblo Bonito. *Anthropological Papers of the American Museum of Natural History* 27. New York: American Museum of Natural History.

PLOG, STEPHEN

1980   *Stylistic Variation in Prehistoric Ceramics: Design Analysis in the American Southwest.* Cambridge: Cambridge University Press.

REED, PAUL F., AND SCOTT WILCOX

1996   Early and Intensive: The Basketmaker III Occupation of Cove-Redrock Valley, Northeastern Arizona. Paper presented at the 61st Annual Meet-

REED, PAUL F., AND SCOTT WILCOX (*continued*)
    ing of the Society for American Archaeology, New Orleans, Louisiana, April 1996.

RICE, PRUDENCE M.
1991   Women and Prehistoric Pottery Production. In *Gender and Archaeology: Proceedings of the 22nd Chacmool Conference*, edited by Dale Walde and Noreen Willows. Calgary.

RICHARDSON, JANE, AND ALFRED L. KROEBER
1940   Three Centuries of Women's Dress Fashions: A Quantitative Analysis. *Anthropological Records* 5(2): 111–153. Berkeley and Los Angeles: University of California Press.

ROACH, MARY ELLEN
1979   The Social Symbolism of Women's Dress. In *The Fabrics of Culture: The Anthropology of Clothing and Adornment*, edited by Justine M. Cordwell and Ronald A. Schwartz, pp. 415–422. The Hague: Mouton.

ROACH, MARY ELLEN, AND JOANNE BUBOLZ EICHER
1979   The Language of Personal Adornment. In *The Fabrics of Culture: The Anthropology of Clothing and Adornment*, edited by Justine M. Cordwell and Ronald A. Schwartz, pp. 7–21. The Hague: Mouton.

ROBINS, MICHAEL R.
1997   Modeling Social and Economic Organization of the San Juan Basketmakers: A Preliminary Study in Rock Art and Social Dynamics. MS, Master's Thesis, Department of Anthropology, Northern Arizona University, Flagstaff.

ROHN, ARTHUR H.
1977   *Cultural Change and Continuity on Chapin Mesa.* Lawrence, Kansas: Regents Press of Kansas.

SALWEN, BERT
1960   The Introduction of Leather Footgear in the Pueblo Area. *Ethnohistory* 7(3): 206–238.

SCHAAFSMA, POLLY
1980   *Indian Rock Art of the Southwest.* Santa Fe: School of American Research, and Albuquerque: University of New Mexico Press.

SCHNEIDER, JANE
1987   The Anthropology of Cloth. *Annual Review of Anthropology* 16: 408–448.

SHAFFER, BRIAN S., KAREN M. GARDNER, AND JOSEPH F. POWELL
1997   Who's Who in Mimbres Pottery Motifs: Identifying the Sex of Portrayed Human Figures. Poster presented at the 62nd Annual Meeting of the Society for American Archaeology, Nashville.

SHEPARD, ANNA O.
1948   The Symmetry of Abstract Design with Special Reference to Ceramic Decoration. *Carnegie Institution of Washington Publication* 574. Washington.

1956   Ceramics for the Archaeologist. *Carnegie Institution of Washington Publication* 609. Washington.

SMILEY, FRANCIS E., AND MICHAEL R. ROBINS
1997   Chronometric Sampling in Disturbed Contexts. Paper presented at the 62nd Annual Meeting of the Society for American Archaeology, Nashville.

SMITH, WATSON
1952   Kiva Mural Decorations at Awatovi and Kawaika-a. *Papers of the Peabody Museum of American Archaeology and Ethnology* 37. Cambridge: Harvard University.

SNODGRASS, O. T.
1977   *Realistic Art and Times of the Mimbres Indians.* El Paso: Privately published, O. T. Snodgrass.

STEELE, VALERIE
1989a   Appearance and Identity. In *Men and Women: Dressing the Part*, edited by Claudia Brush Kidwell and Valerie Steele, pp. 6–21. Washington: Smithsonian Institution Press.

1989b   Dressing for Work. In *Men and Women: Dressing the Part*, edited by Claudia Brush Kidwell and Valerie Steele, pp. 64–91. Washington: Smithsonian Institution Press.

TALGE, JULIA
1995   Replication of Ancient Puebloan Sandal-Toe Constructions: Comparison of Complexity. MS, Masters Thesis, Department of Human Environments, Utah State University, Logan.

TEAGUE, LYNN S.
1991   The Materials and Technology of Textiles: An Archaeological Perspective. Manuscript on file, Arizona State Museum Library, University of Arizona, Tucson.

TOBERT, NATALIE, EDITOR
1993   *Feet of Ingenuity: A Catalog of Footwear from the Ethnographic Collections at the Horniman Museum.* Horniman World Heritage Series. London: The Horniman Museum and Gardens.

TURNER III, CHRISTY G.
1963   Petroglyphs of the Glen Canyon Region. *Museum of Northern Arizona Bulletin* 38. *Glen Canyon Series* 4. Flagstaff: Northern Arizona Society of Science and Art.

WASHBURN, DOROTHY KOSTER
1977   Symmetry Analysis of Upper Gila Area Ceramic Design. *Papers of the Peabody Museum of Archaeology and Ethnology* 68. Cambridge: Harvard University Press.

1978   A Symmetry Classification of Pueblo Ceramic Designs. In *Discovering Past Behavior: Experiments in the Archaeology of the Southwest*, edited by Paul Grebinger, pp. 101–121. New York: Gordon and Breach.

WASHBURN, DOROTHY K., AND DONALD W. CROWE
1988   *Symmetries of Culture: Theory and Practice of Plane Pattern Analysis*. Seattle: University of Washington Press.

WATSON, PATTY J., AND MARY C. KENNEDY
1991   The Development of Horticulture in the Eastern Woodlands of North America: Women's Role. In *Engendering Archaeology: Women and Prehistory*, edited by Joan M. Gero and Margaret W. Conkey, pp. 255–275. Oxford: Basil Blackwell.

WEBSTER, LAURIE D.
1995   Textiles and Basketry. Manuscript for Lone Pine Project, Southwestern Colorado. Tucson: SWCA Environmental Consultants.

1996a   Basketry and Textiles. In "Draft Technical Report for the N30–N31 Project: Investigations at 22 Sites between Mexican Springs and Navajo, McKinley County, NM," edited by Jonathan Damp and Elizabeth Skinner, pp. 185–222. *Zuni Cultural Resource Enterprise Report* 466, Vol. 3, Part 1. Zuni Cultural Resource Enterprise Research Series. Pueblo of Zuni: Zuni Cultural Resource Enterprise.

1996b   Textiles and Basketry from Basketmaker III and Pueblo II Sites in the Southern Chuska Valley. In "Supporting Studies: Nonceramic Artifacts, Subsistence and Environmental Studies, and Chronometric Studies," compiled by T. M. Kearns and J. L. McVickar, pp. 9–1 through 9–30. *Pipeline Archaeology 1990–1993: The El Paso Natural Gas North System Expansion Project, New Mexico and Arizona*. Draft Volume 12. Report No. WCRM(F)074. Farmington, New Mexico: Western Cultural Resource Management.

1997   *Effects of European Contact on Textile Production and Exchange in the North American Southwest: A Pueblo Case Study*. Doctoral dissertation, University of Arizona, Tucson. Ann Arbor: University Microfilms.

WEIGLE, MARTA
1989   *Creation and Procreation: Feminist Reflections on Mythologies of Cosmogony and Parturition*. Philadelphia: University of Pennsylvania Press.

WILSON, MIKE P.
1990   Development of SATRA Slip Test and Tread Pattern Design Guidelines. In *Slips, Stumbles, and Falls: Pedestrian Footwear and Surfaces*, edited by B. Everett Gray, pp. 113–123. Philadelphia: American Society for Testing and Materials.

WISSLER, CLARK
1950   *The American Indian: An Introduction to the Anthropology of the New World*. 3rd ed. New York: Oxford University Press. (Originally published 1938.)

WOBST, MARTIN
1977   Stylistic Behavior and Information Exchange. In "For the Director: Research Essays in Honor of James B. Griffin," Charles E. Cleland, editor, pp. 317–342. *Anthropological Papers of the Museum of Anthropology* 61. Ann Arbor: University of Michigan.

WRIGHT, RITA P.
1991   Women's Labor and Pottery Production in Prehistory. In *Engendering Archaeology: Women and Prehistory*, edited by Joan M. Gero and Margaret W. Conkey, pp. 194–223. Oxford: Basil Blackwell.

1996   [Editor] *Gender and Archaeology*. Philadelphia: University of Pennsylvania Press.

YOUNG, M. JANE
1987   Women, Reproduction, and Religion in Western Puebloan Society. *Journal of American Folklore* 100: 436–445.

ZASLOW, BERT
1981   Pattern Dissemination in the Prehistoric Southwest and Mesoamerica: A Comparison of Hohokam Decorative Patterns with Patterns from the Upper Gila Area and from the Valley of Oaxaca. *Arizona State University Anthropological Research Papers* 25. Tempe: Arizona State University.

ZASLOW, BERT, AND ALFRED E. DITTERT, JR.
1977   Pattern Technology of the Hohokam. *Arizona State University Anthropological Research Papers* 2. Tempe: Arizona State University.

Index

Abstract

Twined sandals of the Basketmaker III period (about A.D. 400–700) are one of the most technologically complicated and highly decorated kinds of prehistoric artifacts found in the U.S. Southwest. Such sandals caught the attention of Earl Halstead Morris and Ann Axtell Morris during their many years of fieldwork in northeastern Arizona. In the late 1920s, Ann Morris began a study of sandals from Canyon del Muerto and Grand Gulch, and later, Earl Morris began work on a book describing sandals from his 1931 excavations in the Prayer Rock District. Through the 1940s, his assistants at the University of Colorado illustrated hundreds of Basketmaker period sandals, dissecting a few of them to create detailed diagrams of their construction.

This volume presents most of these drawings, together with the annotated texts of Ann Morris' proposed article, a preliminary report by Earl Morris, and an updated discussion of the chronology of structures and deposits in the Prayer Rock caves. Results of recent research by Kelley Hays-Gilpin, Ann Cordy Deegan, and Elizabeth Ann Morris elucidate the history of the Morris sandal project, demonstrate how twined sandals were made, describe decorative techniques through symmetry analysis, and compare the complicated decorative system with contemporaneous pottery, baskets, and textiles. The many possible roles of sandals (functional, aesthetic, and symbolic) in Basketmaker lives are explored here from the points of view of three generations of researchers.

Simple twined sandals appear in the Archaic period as early as 8000 B.C. By 200 B.C., Basketmaker peoples made and wore complicated, densely twined sandals made of yucca yarn. Later Basketmaker sandals dating around A.D. 400 to 700 were decorated with colored and textured patterns. About 200 sandals of this period from the Prayer Rock District provide the core material for this study. Three major types and several variants of twined sandals were identified by the Morrises. The authors have preserved the original typology and they provide more detailed information about sandal chronology, technology, and style. Sandal types are classified according to heel and toe shapes: scalloped toe–square heel sandals are earlier than scalloped toe–puckered heel and round toe–puckered heel sandals, which appear to be roughly contemporaneous.

Resumen

Las sandalias trenzadas del período Basketmaker III (aproximadamente 400–700 años d.C.) son uno de los artefactos prehistóricos más complicados y altamente decorados encontrados en el Suroeste de los Estados Unidos. Estas sandalias atrajeron la atención de Earl Halstead Morris y Ann Axtell Morris durante muchos años de trabajo de campo en el noreste de Arizona. Hacia fines de los años 20, Ann Morris empezó su estudio de sandalias provenientes de Cañon del Muerto y Grand Gulch, y más tarde, Earl Morris empezó a escribir un libro describiendo las sandalias recuperadas en sus escavaciones en el distrito Prayer Rock en 1931. A través de los años 40, sus asistentes en la Universidad de Colorado ilustraron cientos de sandalias del período Basketmaker, analizando algunas de ellas para crear diagramas detallados de su construcción.

Este volumen presenta la mayoría de aquellos dibujos, junto con los textos y anotaciones del artículo propuesto por Ann Morris, un reporte preliminar por Earl Morris, y una discusión moderna de la cronología de las estructuras y depósitos en las cuevas de Prayer Rock. Los resultados de la reciente investigación conducida por Kelley Hays-Gilpin, Ann Cordy Deegan, y Elizabeth Ann Morris elucidan la historia del projecto de sandalias de los Morris, demuestran cómo se produjeron las sandalias trenzadas, describen las técnicas decorativas usando análisis de simetría, y comparan este complejo sistema decorativo con el de cerámica, canastas, y textiles contemporáneos. Se explora el número de posibles papeles (funcional, estético, y simbólico) que jugaron las sandalias en la vida de los groupos Basketmaker desde de los puntos de vista de tres generaciones de investigadores.

Las sandalias trenzadas simples aparecen en el período Arcaico a partir de los 8000 años a.C. Hacia los 200 años a.C., la gente Basketmaker construyó y usó sandalias de trenzado complejo y altamente denso, hechas con fibra de yuca. Las sandalias Basketmaker más tardías, que datan entre 400 y 700 años d.C., fueron decoradas con patrones de textura y color. Aproximadamente 200 sandalias de este período, provenientes del distrito Prayer Rock, constituyen la base de este estudio. Los arqueológos Morris identificaron tres tipos principales de sandalias trenzadas y algunas variantes. Los autores han preservado la tipología original, y pro-

Items of dress, including footwear, are not merely functional but carry social and symbolic information about their makers and users. Comparison of sandal decoration with other media demonstrates that sandals were the most elaborately decorated artifacts made by Basketmaker people, although they shared much of their stylistic repertoire with other textiles, coiled baskets, and, to a lesser degree, painted pottery. The authors speculate that all these items were made by women, who deliberately developed a decorative style that differed from the style in rock art.

veen además información detallada sobre la cronología, tecnología, y estilo de sandalias. Los tipos de sandalia son clasificados de acuerdo a la forma de la punta y el talón: las sandalias de punta ondulada con talóncuadrado son más tempranas que aquéllas de punta fruncida con talón quadrado, y punta fruncida con talón redondo, las cuales parecen ser más o menos contemporáneas.

Artículos de vestir, incluyendo sandalias, no son meramente funcionales sino que también contienen información social y simbólica acerca de los productores y usuarios. Una comparación de la decoración de sandalias con la de otros medios demuestra que las sandalias fueron los artículos más elaboradamente decorados hechos por los grupos Basketmaker, aún cuando aquéllas compartieron su repertorio estilístico con otros textiles, canastas acordonadas y, en menor grado, cerámica pintada. Los autores especulan que todos estos artículos fueron hechos por mujeres, quienes deliberadamente desarollaron un estilo decorativo que difirió del estilo presente en el arte rupestre.

ANTHROPOLOGICAL PAPERS OF THE UNIVERSITY OF ARIZONA

1. Excavations at Nantack Village, Point of Pines, Arizona. David A. Breternitz. 1959. (O.P.)

2. Yaqui Myths and Legends. Ruth W. Giddings. 1959. *Now in book form.*

3. Marobavi: A Study of an Assimilated Group in Northern Sonora. Roger C. Owen. 1959. (O.P.)

4. A Survey of Indian Assimilation in Eastern Sonora. Thomas B. Hinton. 1959. (O.P.)

5. The Phonology of Arizona Yaqui. Lynn S. Crumrine. 1961. (O.P., D)

6. The Maricopas: An Identification from Documentary Sources. Paul H. Ezell. 1963. (O.P.)

7. The San Carlos Indian Cattle Industry. Harry T. Getty. 1964. (O.P.)

8. The House Cross of the Mayo Indians of Sonora, Mexico. N. Ross Crumrine. 1964. (O.P.)

9. Salvage Archaeology in Painted Rocks Reservoir, Western Arizona. William W. Wasley and Alfred E. Johnson. 1956.

10. An Appraisal of Tree-Ring Dated Pottery in the Southwest. David A. Breternitz. 1966. (O.P.)

11. The Albuquerque Navajos. William H. Hodge. 1969. (O.P.)

12. Papago Indians at Work. Jack O. Waddell. 1969.

13. Culture Change and Shifting Populations in Central Northern Mexico. William B. Griffen. 1969.

14. Ceremonial Exchange as a Mechanism in Tribal Integration Among the Mayos of Northwest Mexico. Lynn S. Crumrine. 1969. (O.P.)

15. Western Apache Witchcraft. Keith H. Basso. 1969. (O.P., D)

16. Lithic Analysis and Cultural Inference: A Paleo-Indian Case. Edwin N. Wilmsen. 1970. (O.P.)

17. Archaeology as Anthropology: A Case Study. William A. Longacre. 1970.

18. Broken K Pueblo: Prehistoric Social Organization in the American Southwest. James N. Hill. 1970. (O.P., D)

19. White Mountain Redware: A Pottery Tradition of East-Central Arizona and Western New Mexico. Roy L. Carlson. 1970. (O.P., D)

20. Mexican Macaws: Comparative Osteology. Lyndon L. Hargrave. 1970.

21. Apachean Culture History and Ethnology. Keith H. Basso and Morris E. Opler, eds. 1971. (O.P., D)

22. Social Functions of Language in a Mexican-American Community. George C. Barker. 1972.

23. The Indians of Point of Pines, Arizona: A Comparative Study of Their Physical Characteristics. Kenneth A. Bennett. 1973. (O.P.)

24. Population, Contact, and Climate in the New Mexico Pueblos. Ezra B. W. Zubrow. 1974. (O.P.)

25. Irrigation's Impact on Society. Theodore E. Downing and McGuire Gibson, eds. 1974. (O.P.)

26. Excavations at Punta de Agua in the Santa Cruz River Basin, Southeastern Arizona. J. Cameron Greenleaf. 1975.

27. Seri Prehistory: The Archaeology of the Central Coast of Sonora, Mexico. Thomas Bowen. 1976. (O.P.)

28. Carib-Speaking Indians: Culture, Society, and Language. Ellen B. Basso, ed. 1977. (O.P.)

29. Cocopa Ethnography. William H. Kelly. 1977. (O.P.)

30. The Hodges Ruin: A Hohokam Community in the Tucson Basin. Isabel Kelly, James E. Officer, and Emil W. Haury, collaborators; Gayle H. Hartmann, ed. 1978. (O.P.)

31. Fort Bowie Material Culture. Robert M. Herskovitz. 1978. (O.P.)

32. Artifacts from Chaco Canyon, New Mexico: The Chetro Ketl Collection. R. Gwinn Vivian, Dulce N. Dodgen, and Gayle H. Hartmann. 1978. (O.P.)

33. Indian Assimilation in the Franciscan Area of Nueva Vizcaya. William B. Griffen. 1979.

34. The Durango South Project: Archaeological Salvage of Two Late Basketmaker III Sites in the Durango District. John D. Gooding. 1980.

35. Basketmaker Caves in the Prayer Rock District, Northeastern Arizona. Elizabeth Ann Morris. 1980.

36. Archaeological Explorations in Caves of the Point of Pines Region, Arizona. James C. Gifford. 1980.

37. Ceramic Sequences in Colima: Capacha, an Early Phase. Isabel Kelly. 1980.

38. Themes of Indigenous Acculturation in Northwest Mexico. Thomas B. Hinton and Phil C. Weigand, eds. 1981.

39. Sixteenth Century Maiolica Pottery in the Valley of Mexico. Florence C. Lister and Robert H. Lister. 1982.

40. Multidisciplinary Research at Grasshopper Pueblo, Arizona. William A. Longacre, Sally J. Holbrook, and Michael W. Graves, eds. 1982.

41. The Asturian of Cantabria: Early Holocene Hunter-Gatherers in Northern Spain. Geoffrey A. Clark. 1983.

42. The Cochise Cultural Sequence in Southeastern Arizona. E. B. Sayles. 1983.

43. Cultural and Environmental History of Cienega Valley, Southeastern Arizona. Frank W. Eddy and Maurice E. Cooley. 1983.